Data-Centric Systems and Applications

T0181203

Carlo Batini · Monica Scannapieca

Data Quality

Concepts, Methodologies and Techniques

With 134 Figures

 Springer

Carlo Batini

Università di Milano Bicocca
Dipartimento di Informatica
Sistemistica e Comunicazione
Piazza dell'Ateneo Nuovo
20126 Milano
Italy
batini@disco.unimib.it

Monica Scannapieca

Dipartimento di Informatica e Sistemistica "A. Ruberti"
Università di Roma "La Sapienza"
Via Salaria 113
00198 Roma
Italy
monscan@dis.uniroma1.it

ACM Computing Classification (1998): H.2, H.1

ISBN 978-3-642-06970-3   e-ISBN 978-3-540-33173-5

Springer is a part of Springer Science+Business Media
springer.com

© Springer-Verlag Berlin Heidelberg 2006
 Softcover reprint of the hardcover 1st edition 2006

Cover Design: KünkelLopka, Heidelberg

To my wonderful children, Chiara, Laura, and Giulio.
Carlo

To Massimo and to my "Ernania" world.
Monica

Preface

Motivation for the Book

Electronic data play a crucial role in the information and communication technology (ICT) society: they are managed by business and governmental applications, by all kinds of applications on the Web, and are fundamental in all relationships between governments, businesses, and citizens. Because electronic data is so widely diffused, the "quality" of such data and its related effects on every kind of activity of the ICT society are more and more critical.

The relevance of data quality in both decisional and operational processes is recognized by several international institutions and organizations. As an example, the importance of data quality in decisional processes is clearly stated in the quality declaration of the European Statistical System [72], in which its mission is identified as follows: "We provide the European Union and the world with high quality information on the economy and society at the European, national, and regional levels and make the information available to everyone for decision-making purposes, research, and debate."

Furthermore, quality of data is also a significant issue for operational processes of businesses and organizations. The Data Warehousing Institute in a 2002 report on data quality (see [52]) shows that there is a significant gap between perception and reality regarding the quality of data in many organizations, and that data quality problems cost U.S. businesses more than 600 billion dollars a year.

The "Year 2000 problem", which led to modify software applications and databases using a two-digit field to represent years, has been a data quality problem. The costs to modify such software applications and databases have been estimated to be around 1.5 trillion US dollars (see [68]).

Some disasters are due to the presence of data quality problems, among them the use of inaccurate, incomplete, out-of-date data. For example, the explosion of the space shuttle Challenger is discussed in [78] according to a data quality perspective; the analysis reports more than ten different categories of data quality problems having a role in the disaster.

Such errors are motivations at the basis of the several initiatives that are being launched in the public and private sectors, with data quality having a leading role, as detailed in Chapter 1; the initiatives include, for instance, the Data Quality Act effected by the United States government in 2002 [149].

Electronic data are only to a certain extent of better quality than data stored in paper documents. Indeed, electronic data benefit from a defined and regulated representation, but processes that originate such data are often out of control, and consequently errors in data proliferate.

In the last decades, information systems have been migrating from a hierarchical/monolithic to a network-based structure, where the potential sources that organizations can use for the purpose of their businesses is dramatically increased in size and scope. Data quality problems have been further worsened by this evolution. In networked information systems, processes are involved in complex information exchanges and often operate on input obtained from other external sources, frequently unknown a priori.

As a consequence, the overall quality of the information that flows between information systems may rapidly degrade over time if both processes and their inputs are not themselves subject to quality control. On the other hand, the same networked information system offers new opportunities for data quality management, including the possibility of selecting sources with better quality data, and of comparing sources for the purpose of error localization and correction, thus facilitating the control and improvement of data quality in the system.

Due to the described above motivations, researchers and organizations more and more need to understand and solve data quality problems, and thus need answering the following questions: What is, in essence, data quality? Which techniques, methodologies, and data quality issues are at a consolidated stage? Which are the well-known and reliable approaches? Which problems are open? This book is an attempt to respond to all these questions.

Goals

The goal of this book is to provide a systematic and comparative description of the vast number of research issues related to quality of data, and thus to illustrate the state of the art in the area of data quality. While being a real problem in a vast number of activities in the private and public sectors, data quality recently resulted in a significant number of contributions to the research community. There are several international conferences promoted by the database and information system communities that have data quality as their main topic; the International Conference on Information Quality (ICIQ) [95], organized traditionally at the Massachusetts Institute of

Technology (MIT) in Boston, started in 1996; the International workshop on Information Quality in Information Systems (IQIS) [99], held in conjunction with the SIGMOD conference since 2004; the international workshop on Data and Information Quality (DIQ), held in conjunction with the Conference on Advanced Information Systems Engineering (CAiSE) since 2004 [98]; and the international workshop on Quality of Information Systems (QoIS), held in conjunction with the Entity Relationship (ER) conference since 2005 [100]. There are also national conferences, held in France, Germany, and the US.

On the practical side, many data quality software tools are advertised and used in various data-driven applications, such as data warehousing, and to improve the quality of business processes. Frequently, their scope is limited and domain dependent, and it is not clear how to coordinate and finalize their use in data quality processes.

On the research side, the gap, still present between the need for techniques, methodologies, and tools, and the limited maturity of the area, has led so far to the presence of fragmented and sparse results in the literature, and the absence of a systematic view of the area.

Furthermore, in the area of data quality we highlight the existence of a dichotomy, typical of many other research areas that have a deep impact on real life, between practice-oriented approaches and formal research contributions. This book tries to address such a dichotomy, providing not only comparative overviews and explanatory frameworks of existing proposals, but also original solutions that combine the concreteness of practical approaches and the soundness of theoretical formalisms. By understanding the motivations and the different backgrounds of solutions, we have figured out the paradigms and forces contributing to the data quality environment.

Our main concern in this book is to provide a sound, integrated, and comprehensive picture of the state of the art and of future evolutions of data quality, in the database and information systems areas. This book includes an extensive description of techniques which constitute the core of data quality research, including record matching, data integration, error localization, and correction; such techniques are examined in a comprehensive and original methodological framework. Quality dimension definitions and adopted models are also deeply analyzed, and differences between the proposed solutions are highlighted and discussed. Furthermore, while systematically describing data quality as an autonomous research area, we highlight the paradigms and influences deriving from other areas, such as probability theory, statistical data analysis, data mining, knowledge representation, and machine learning. Our book also provides very practical solutions, such as methodologies, benchmarks for the most effective techniques, case studies, and examples.

The rigorous and formal foundation of our approach to data quality issues, presented with practical solutions, renders this book a necessary complement to books already published. Some books adopt a formal and research-oriented approach but are focused on specific topics or perspectives. Specifically, Dasu and Johnson [50] approach data quality problems from the perspective of data mining and machine learning solutions. Wang et al. [206] provide a general perspective on data quality, by compiling a heterogeneous collection of contributions from different projects and research groups. Jarke et al. [104] describe solutions for data quality issues in the data warehouse environment. Wang et al. [203] is a survey of research contributions, including new methods for measuring data quality, for modeling quality improvement processes, and for organizational and educational issues related to information quality.

Some other books give much more room to practical aspects rather than to formal ones. In particular, leading books in the practitioners field are Redman' [167] and [169], and English' [68]. The two Redman' books provide an extensive set of data quality dimensions, and discuss a vast set of issues related to management methodologies for data quality improvement. English's book provides a detailed methodology for data quality measurement and improvement, discussing step-by-step issues related to data architectures, standards, process- and data-driven improvement methodologies, costs, benefits, and managerial strategies.

Organization

The book is organized into nine chapters. Figure 0.1 lists the chapters and details interdependencies.

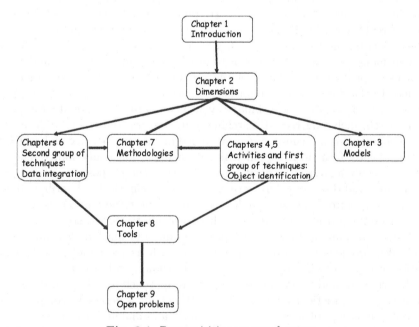

Fig. 0.1. Prerequisities among chapters

We initially provide basic concepts and establish coordinates to explore the area of data quality (Chapter 1). Then, we focus on dimensions that allow for the measurement of the quality of data values and data schemas (Chapter 2). These two chapters are preparatory to the rest of the book.

Models to express the quality of data in databases and information systems are investigated in Chapter 3. Chapter 4 describes the main activities for measuring and improving data quality. Some activities, such as error localization and correction, are introduced and fully described in Chapter 4; two specific chapters are dedicated to the most important activities and related research areas, namely object identification (Chapter 5) and data integration (Chapter 6), which are extensively investigated from the perspectives of relevant research paradigms and available techniques. Dimensions, models, activities, and techniques are the ingredients of any methodology for data quality measurement and improvement, and methodologies are the subject of Chapter 7. Specifically, in this chapter existing methodologies are examined and compared, and an original, comprehensive methodology is proposed, with an extensive case study. Tools, frameworks, and toolboxes proposed in the research literature for the effective use of techniques are described in Chapter 8. The book ends with Chapter 9, which puts all the ideas discussed in previous chapters in perspective and speculates on open problems and possible evolutions of the area.

Intended Audience

The book is intended for those interested in a comprehensive introduction to the wide set of issues related to data quality. It has been written primarily for researchers in the fields of databases and information systems interested in investigating properties of data and information that have impact on the quality of processes and on real life. This book introduces the reader to autonomous research in the field of data quality, providing a wide spectrum of definitions, formalisms, and methods, with critical comparisons of the state of the art. For this reason, this book can help establish the most relevant research areas in data quality, consolidated issues and open problems.

A second category of potential readers are data and information system administrators and practitioners, who need a systematization of the field. This category also includes designers of complex cooperative systems and services, such as e-Business and e-Government systems, that exhibit relevant data quality problems.

Figures 0.2 and 0.3 suggest possible paths, which can be followed by the above audiences.

The *researcher path*, for researchers interested in the core research areas in data quality, skips chapters on methodologies (Chapter 7) and tools (Chapter 8). The *information system administrator path* skips models (Chapter 3), data integration issues (Chapter 6) and open problems (Chapter 9).

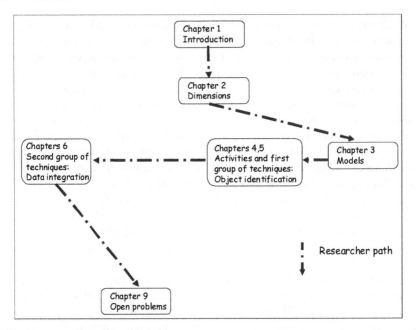

Fig. 0.2. Reading path for the researcher

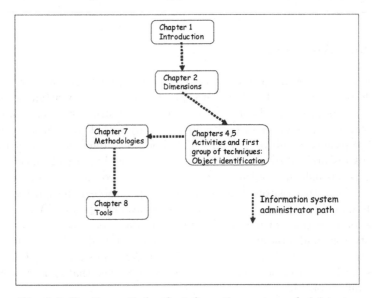

Fig. 0.3. Reading path for the information system administrator

Guidelines for Teaching

To the best of our knowledge, data quality is not a usually considered topic in undergraduate and graduate courses. Several PhD courses include data quality issues, while the market for professional, often expensive courses is rapidly increasing. However, recent initiatives are in the direction of introducing data quality in undergraduate and graduate courses [1]. We have organized the book to be used in an advanced course on the quality of databases and information systems. The areas of databases and information systems are currently lacking consolidated textbooks on data quality; we have tried to cover this demand. Although this book cannot be defined a textbook, it can be adopted, with some effort, as basic material for a course in data quality. Due to the undeniable importance of these topics, what happened in the 1980's for other database areas, e.g., database design, could happen for data quality: the plethora of textbooks which favored the introduction of this area in university courses.

Data quality can be the topic of self-contained courses, or else of cycles of seminars in courses on databases and information systems management. Data integration courses would also benefit from data quality seminars. With regards to information systems management, data quality can be taught in connection with topics such as information management, information economics, business process reengineering, process and service quality, and cost and benefit analysis. Data quality techniques can be offered also in specific courses on data warehousing and data mining.

The material of this book is sufficiently self-contained for students who are able to attend a course in databases. As students' prerequisites, it is useful, but not mandatory, to have notions of mathematics and, to some extent, probability theory, statistics, machine learning, and knowledge representation.

The book provides enough material to cover all the necessary topics without the need for other textbooks. In the case of a PhD course, the references are a good starting point for assigning students in-depth analysis activities on specific issues.

In terms of exercises, a useful approach for students is to develop a complex data quality project that can be organized into two parts. The first part could be devoted to the assessment of the quality of two or more databases jointly used in several business processes of an organization. The second part could focus on the choice and application of methodologies and techniques described in Chapters 4, 5, 6, and 7 to improve data quality levels of the databases to a fixed target. This approach gives students a taste of the problems to face within a real-life environment.

---

[1] As an example, in 2005 the University of Arkansas at Little Rock promoted a Master of Science in Information Quality (MS IQ).

Acknowledgements

First of all, we would like to thank several friends and researchers whose long-term frequentation and fruitful discussions on the topics covered in this book have positively influenced us; they are Daniele Barone, Laure Berti-Equille, Elisa Bertino, Paola Bertolazzi, Federico Cabitza, Cinzia Cappiello, Tiziana Catarci, Fabrizio De Amicis, Luca De Santis, Ahmed K. Elmagarmid, Markus Helfert, Domenico Lembo, Maurizio Lenzerini, Andrea Maurino, Massimo Mecella, Diego Milano, Paolo Missier, Felix Naumann, Davide Orlandi, Barbara Pernici, Louiqa Rashid, Ruggero Russo, Divesh Srivastava, Carlo Vaccari, and Richard Wang. Among students of our courses concerning data quality, we are particularly grateful to Matteo Strazzullo for his contributions on cost and benefit classifications.

Special mention should be given to the editors of this book series, Stefano Ceri and Mike Carey. We would also like to thank Ralf Gerstner of Springer-Verlag, who initially had the idea of considering data quality as a consolidated issue to be described in a book.

Carlo Batini
Monica Scannapieco

July 2006

Contents

1

Introduction to Data Quality

A Web search of the terms "data quality" through the search engine Google, returns about three millions of pages, an indicator that data quality issues are real and increasingly important (often, in the following, the term data quality will be shortened to the acronym DQ). The goal of this chapter is to introduce the relevant perspectives that make data quality an issue worth being investigated and understood. We first introduce the notion of data quality (Section 1.1), highlighting its relevance in real life and some of the main related initiatives in the public and private domains. Then, in Section 1.2, we show by means of several examples the multidimensional nature of data quality. Sections 1.3 and 1.4 analyze the different types of data, and the different types of information systems for which DQ can be investigated. In Section 1.5, we address the main research issues in DQ, application domains and related research areas. The research issues (Section 1.5.1) concern dimensions, models, techniques, methodologies, and tools; together, they provide the agenda for the rest of the book. Application domains are large sets, since data and information are fundamental ingredients of all the activities of people and organizations. We focus (Section 1.5.2) on three of the most relevant application domains, e-Government, Life Sciences, and the World Wide Web, highlighting the role that DQ plays in each of them. Research areas related to DQ will be examined in Section 1.5.3.

1.1 Why Data Quality is Relevant

The consequences of poor quality of data are often experienced in everyday life, but, often, without making the necessary connections to their causes. For example, the late or mistaken delivery of a letter is often blamed on a malfunctional postal service, although a closer look often reveals data-related causes, typically an error in the address, originating in the address database. Similarly, the duplicate delivery of automatically generated mail is often indicative of a database record duplication error.

Data quality has serious consequences, of far-reaching significance, for the efficiency and effectiveness of organizations and businesses. As already mentioned in the preface, the report on data quality of the Data Warehousing Institute (see [52]) estimates that data quality problems cost U.S. businesses more than 600 billion dollars a year. The findings of the report were based on interviews with industry experts, leading edge customers, and survey data from 647 respondents. In the following, we list further examples of the importance of data quality in organizational processes.

- *Customer matching.* Information systems of public and private organizations can be seen as the result of a set of scarcely controlled and independent activities producing several databases very often characterized by overlapping information. In private organizations, such as marketing firms or banks, it is not surprising to have several (sometimes dozens!) of customers registries, updated with different organizational procedures, resulting in inconsistent, duplicate information. As an example, it is very complex for banks to provide clients with a unique list of all their accounts and funds.
- *Corporate house-holding.* Many organizations establish separate relationships with single members of households, or, more generally, related groups of people; either way, they like, for marketing purposes, to reconstruct the household relationships in order to carry on more effective marketing strategies. This problem is even more complex than the previous one, since in that case the data to match concerned the same person, in this case it concerns groups of persons corresponding to the same household. For a detailed discussion on the relationship between corporate house holding information and various business application areas, see [200].
- *Organization fusion.* When different organizations or different units of an organization merge, it is necessary to integrate their legacy information systems. Such integration requires compatibility and interoperability at any layer of the information system, with the database level required to ensure both physical and semantic interoperability.

The examples above are indicative of the growing need to integrate information across completely different data sources, an activity in which poor quality hampers integration efforts. Awareness of the importance of improving the quality of data is increasing in many contexts. In the following, we summarize some of the major initiatives in both the private and public domains.

Private Initiatives

In the private sector, on the one hand, application providers and system integrators, and, on the other hand, direct users are experiencing the role of DQ in their own business processes.

With regard to application providers and systems integrators, IBM's recent (2005) acquisition of Ascential Software, a leading provider of data integration tools, highlights the critical role data and information stewardship plays in the enterprise. The 2005 Ascential report [208] on data integration provides a survey that indicates data quality and security issues as the leading inhibitors (55 % of respondents in a multi-response survey) to successful data integration projects. The respondents also emphasize that data quality is more than just a technological issue. It requires senior management to treat data as a corporate asset and to realize that the value of this asset depends on its quality.

In the last few years, SAP [84] has set up a project for testing in the area of DQ and to build an internal methodology, with important savings (documented in [84]) in several internal business processes.

The awareness of the relevance of data quality issues has led Oracle (see [151]) to recently enhance its suite of products and services to support an architecture that optimizes data quality, providing a framework for the systematic analysis of data, with the goals of increasing the value of data, easing the burden of data migration, and decreasing the risks inherent in data integration.

With regard to users, Basel2 is an international initiative in the financial domain that requires financial services companies to have a risk sensitive framework for the assessment of regulatory capital. The planned implementation date for Basel2 is December 2006, with parallel operation from January 2006. The regulatory requirements of Basel2 are demanding improvements in data quality. For example, the Draft Supervisory Guidance on Internal Ratings-Based Systems for Corporate Credit states (see [19]): "institutions using the Internal Ratings-Based approach for regulatory capital purposes will need advanced data management practices to produce credible and reliable risk estimates"; and "data retained by the bank will be essential for regulatory risk-based capital calculations and public reporting. These uses underscore the need for a well defined data maintenance framework and strong controls over data integrity."

Public Initiatives

In the public sector a number of initiatives address data quality issues at international, European, and national levels. We focus in the rest of the section on two of the main initiatives, the Data Quality Act in the US and the European directive on reuse of public data.

In 2001 the President of the US signed into law important new Data Quality legislation, concerning "Guidelines for Ensuring and Maximizing the Quality, Objectivity, Utility, and Integrity of Information Disseminated by Federal Agencies," in short the Data Quality Act. The Office of Management and Budget (OMB) issued guidelines referred for policies and procedures on data quality issues (see [149]). Obligations mentioned in the guidelines concern agencies, which are to report periodically to the OMB regarding the number and nature of data quality complaints received, and how such complaints were handled. OMB must also include a mechanism through which the public can petition agencies to correct information that does not meet the OMB standard. In the OMB guidelines data quality is defined as an encompassing term comprising utility, objectivity, and integrity. Objectivity is a measure to determine whether the disseminated information is accurate, reliable, and unbiased, and whether that information is presented in an accurate, clear, complete, and unbiased manner. Utility refers to the usefulness of the information for its anticipated purpose, by its intended audience. OMB is committed to disseminating reliable and useful information. Integrity refers to the security of information, namely protection of the information from unauthorized, unanticipated, or unintentional modification, to prevent it from being compromised by corruption or falsification. Specific risk-based, cost-effective policies are defined for assuring integrity.

The European directive 2003/98/CE on the reuse of public data (see [71]) highlights the importance of reusing the vast data assets owned by public agencies. The public sector collects, produces, and disseminates a wide range of information in many areas of activity, such as social, economic, geographical, metereological, business, and educational information. Making public all generally available documents held by the public sector, concerning not only the political process but also the legal and administrative processes, is considered a fundamental instrument for extending the right to information, which is a basic principle of democracy. Aspects of data quality addressed by such a directive are the accessibility of public data and availability in a format which is not dependent on the use of specific software. At the same time, a related and necessary step for public data reuse is to guarantee its quality in terms of accuracy and currency, through data cleaning campaigns. This makes it attractive to new potential users and customers.

1.2 Introduction to the Concept of Data Quality

From a research perspective, data quality has been addressed in different areas, including statistics, management, and computer science. Statisticians were the first to investigate some of the problems related to data quality, by proposing a mathematical theory for considering duplicates in statistical data sets, in the late 1960's. They were followed by researchers in management, who at the beginning of the 1980's focused on how to control data manufacturing systems in order to detect and eliminate data quality problems. Only at the beginning of the 1990's computer scientists begin considering the problem of defining, measuring, and improving the quality of electronic data stored in databases, data warehouses, and legacy systems.

When people think about data quality, they often reduce data quality just to accuracy. For example, let us consider the surname "Batini"; when this is spelled during a telephone call, several misspellings are reported by the other side, such as "Vatini," "Battini," "Barini," "Basini," all inaccurate versions of the original last name. Indeed, data are normally considered to be of poor quality if typos are present or wrong values are associated with a concept instance, such as an erroneous birth date or age associated with a person. However, data quality is more than simply data accuracy. Other significant dimensions such as completeness, consistency, and currency are necessary in order to fully characterize the quality of data. In Figure 1.1 we provide some examples of these dimensions, which are described in more detail among others in Chapter 2. The relation in the figure describes movies, with title, director, year of production, number of remakes, and year of the last remake.

Id	Title	Director	Year	#Remakes	LastRemakeYear
1	Casablanca	Weir	1942	3	1940
2	Dead poets society	Curtiz	1989	0	NULL
3	Rman Holiday	Wylder	1953	0	NULL
4	Sabrina	null	1964	0	1985

Fig. 1.1. A relation Movies with data quality problems

In the figure, the cells with data quality problems are shaded. At first, only the cell corresponding to the title of movie 3 seems to be affected by a data quality problem. In fact, there is a misspelling in the title, where Rman stands for Roman, thus causing an accuracy problem. Nevertheless, another accuracy problem is related to the exchange of the director between movies 1 and 2; Weir is actually the director of movie 2 and Curtiz the director of movie 1. Other data quality problems are a missing value for the director of movie 4, causing a completeness problem, and a 0 value for the number of remakes of movie 4, causing a currency problem because a remake of the movie has actually been proposed. Finally, there are two consistency problems: first, for movie 1, the value of LastRemakeYear cannot be lower than Year; second, for movie 4 the value of LastRemakeYear cannot be different from null, because the value of #Remakes is 0.

The above examples of dimensions concern the *quality of data* represented in the relation. Besides data, a large part of the design methodologies for the relational model addresses properties that concern the *quality of the schema*; for example, several normal forms have been proposed with the aim of capturing the concept of good relational schema, free of anomalies and redundancies. For instance, the relational schema of Figure 1.1 is in the Boyce Codd normal form, since all attributes that do not belong to a superkey are functionally dependent on the superkeys (Id and Title). Other data quality and schema quality dimensions will be discussed in Chapter 2. The above examples and considerations show that:

- Data quality is a multifaceted concept, as in whose definition different dimensions concur.
- The quality dimensions, e.g., accuracy, can be easily detected in some cases (e.g., misspellings) but are more difficult to detect in other cases (e.g., where admissible but not correct values are provided).
- A simple example of a completeness error has been shown, but as with accuracy, completeness can also be very difficult to evaluate (e.g., if a tuple representing a movie is entirely missing from the relation `Movie`).
- Consistency detection does not always localize the errors (e.g., for movie 1, the value or the `LastRemakeYear` attribute is wrong).

The above example concerned a relational table of a single database. Problems change significantly when other *types of data* are involved, and more complex *types of information systems* than a single database are considered. We now address these two aspects.

1.3 Data Quality and Types of Data

Data represent real world objects, in a format that can be stored, retrieved, and elaborated by a software procedure, and communicated through a network. The process of representing the real world by means of data can be applied to a large number of phenomena, such as measurements, events, characteristics of people, the environment, sounds, and smells. Data are extremely versatile in such representation. Besides data, other types of *information* are used in real-life and business processes, such as paper-based information, and information conveyed by the voice. We will not deal with all these types of information, and we concentrate on data.

Since researchers in the area of data quality must deal with a wide spectrum of possible data representations, they have proposed several classifications for data. First, several authors distinguish, implicitly or explicitly, three types of data:

1. *Structured*, when each data element has an associated fixed structure. Relational tables are the most popular type of structured data.
2. *Semistructured*, when data has a structure which has some degree of flexibility. Semistructured data are also "schemaless" or "self-describing" (see [1], [35], and [40]). XML is the markup language commonly used to represent semistructured data. Some common characteristics are (i) data can contain fields not known at design time; for instance, an XML file does not have an associated XML schema file; (ii) the same kind of data may be represented in multiple ways; for example, a date might be represented by one field or by multiple fields, even within a single set of data; and (iii) among fields known at design time, many fields will not have values.
3. *Unstructured*, when data are expressed in natural language and no specific structure or domain types are defined.

It is intuitive that dimensions and techniques for data quality have to be adapted for the three types of data described above, and are progressively more complex to conceive and use from structured to unstructured data.

A second point of view sees data as a product. This point of view is adopted, for example, in the IP-MAP model (see [177]), an extension of the Information Manufacturing Product model [201], which will be discussed in detail in Section 3.4; the IP-MAP model identifies a parallelism between the quality of data, and the quality of products as managed by manufacturing companies. In this model, three different types of data are distinguished:

- *raw data items* are considered smaller data units. They are used to construct information and component data items that are semi-processed information;
- while the raw data items may be stored for long periods of time, the *component data items* are stored temporarily until the final product is manufactured. The component items are regenerated each time an information product is needed. The same set of raw data and component data items may be used (sometimes simultaneously) in the manufacturing of several different products;
- *information products*, which are the result of a manufacturing activity performed on data.

Looking at data as a product, as discussed in Chapters 3 and 7, methodologies and procedures used over a long period, with suitable changes having been made to them, can be applied to data for quality assurance in manufacturing processes.

The third classification, proposed in [133], addresses a typical distinction made in information systems between elementary data and aggregated data. *Elementary* data are managed in organizations by operational processes, and represent atomic phenomena of the real world (e.g., social security number, age, sex). *Aggregated* data are obtained from a collection of elementary data by applying some aggregation function to them (e.g., the average income of tax payers in a given city). This classification is useful to distinguish different levels of severity in measuring and achieving the quality of data. As an example, the accuracy of an attribute Sex changes dramatically if we input M (male) instead of F (female); if the age of a single person is wrongly recorded as 25 instead of 35, the accuracy of the average age of a population of millions of inhabitants is minimally affected.

Dasu and Johnson in [50] investigate new types of data that emerge from the diffusion of networks and Internet, and observe that the definition of data itself has changed dramatically to include "any kind of information that is analyzed systematically." They distinguish several new types of data, among them are relevant in this book:

- *federated data*, which come from different heterogeneous sources, and, consequently, require disparate data sources to be combined with approximate matches;

- *web data*, that are "scraped" from the Web and, although characterized by unconventional formats and low control on data, more often constitute the primary source of information for several activities.

Previous classifications were not interested in the time dimension of data, investigated in [30]. According to its change frequency, we can classify source data into three categories:

- *stable* data is data that is unlikely to change. Examples are scientific publications; although new publications can be added to the source, older publications remain unchanged;
- *long-term-changing data* is data that has very low change frequency. Examples are addresses, currencies, and hotel price lists. The concept of low frequency is domain dependent; in an e-trade application, if the value of a stock quote is tracked once an hour, it is considered to be a low frequency change, while a shop that changes its goods weekly has a high-frequency change for clients;
- *frequently-changing data* is data that has intensive change, such as real-time traffic information, temperature sensor measures, and sales quantities. The changes can occur with a defined frequency or they can be random.

For this classification, the procedures for establishing the time dimension qualities of the three types of data, i.e., stable, long-term-changing, and frequently-changing data, are increasingly more complex.

Among the different types of data resulting from the above classification, we are mainly interested in focusing our attention on *structured* and *semistructured elementary data*, and on *information products*. Such types of data have been deeply investigated in the literature, and, to a certain extent, consolidated techniques and methodologies have been concieved. This does not mean that we will exclude other types of data from our analysis: dimensions for time-dependent data will be introduced and discussed in Chapter 2, and web data will be considered in Chapter 9, dedicated to open problems.

As a terminological note, when we give generic examples of structured data, we use the term *tuple* to indicate a set of *fields* or *cell values*, corresponding usually to different *definition domains* or *domains*, describing properties or *attributes* of a specific real world object; we use interchangeably the terms *relational table* or *table* or *relation* to indicate a set of tuples. As a consequence, *tuple* can be used in place of *record* and *table/relation* can be used in place of *structured file*. When we refer to generic data, we use the term *record* to indicate a set of fields, and we use interchangeably the terms *file* or *data set* to indicate a set of tuples.

1.4 Data Quality and Types of Information Systems

Data are collected, stored, elaborated, retrieved, and exchanged in *informa-tion systems* used in organizations to provide services to business processes. Different criteria can be adopted for classifying the different types of informa-tion systems, and their corresponding architectures; they are usually related to the overall organizational model adopted by the organization or the set of the organizations that make use of the information system. In order to clarify the impact of data quality on the different *types of information systems*, we adapt the classification criteria proposed in [153] for distributed databases. Three different criteria are proposed: distribution, heterogeneity, and autonomy.

Distribution deals with the possibility of distributing the data and the applications over a network of computers. For simplicity, we adopt a <yes, no> domain for distribution. *Heterogeneity* considers all types of semantic and technological diversities among systems used in modeling and physically representing data, such as database management systems, programming lan-guages, operating systems, middleware, markup languages. For heterogeneity we also adopt a simple <yes,no> domain. *Autonomy* has to do with the de-gree of hierarchy and rules of coordination, establishing rights and duties, defined in the organization using the information system. The two extremes are: (i) a fully hierarchical system, where only one subject decides for all, and no autonomy at all exists; and (ii) a total anarchy, where no rule exists, and each component organization is totally free in its design and management decisions. In this case we adopt a three-value <no, semi, totally> domain.

The three classifications are represented together in the classification space of Figure 1.2. Among all possible combinations, five main types of information systems are highlighted in the figure: Monolithic, Distributed, Data Ware-houses, Cooperative, and Peer-to-Peer.

- In a *monolithic information system* presentation, application logic, and data management are merged into a single computational node. Many monolithic information systems are still in use. While being extremely rigid, they provide advantages to organizations, such as reduced costs due to the homogeneity of solutions and centralization of management. In monolithic systems, data flows have a common format, and data quality control is facilitated by the homogeneity and centralization of procedures and management rules.
- A *data warehouse* (DW) is a centralized set of data collected from differ-ent sources, designed to support management decision making. The most critical problem in DW design concerns the cleaning and integration of the different data sources that are loaded into the DW, in that much of the implementation budget is spent on data cleaning activities.
- A *distributed information system* relaxes the rigid centralization of mono-lithic systems, in that it allows the distribution of resources and applica-tions across a network of geographically distributed systems. The network

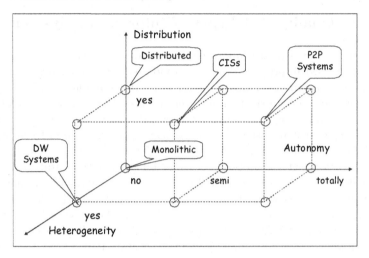

Fig. 1.2. Types of information systems

can be organized in terms of several tiers, each made of one or more computational nodes. Presentation, application logic, and data management are distributed across tiers. Usually, the different tiers and nodes have a limited degree of autonomy, data design is usually performed centrally, but to a certain extent some degree of heterogeneity can occur, due to the impossibility of establishing unified procedures. Problems of data management are more complex than in monolithic systems, due to the reduced level of centralization. Heterogeneities and autonomy usually increase with the number of tiers and nodes.

- A *cooperative information system* (CIS) can be defined as a large-scale information system that interconnects various systems of different and autonomous organizations, while sharing common objectives. According to [58], the manifesto of cooperative information systems, "an information system is cooperative if it shares goals with other agents in its environment, such as other information systems, human agents, and the organization itself, and contributes positively toward the fulfillment of these common goals." The relationship between cooperative information systems and DQ is double-faced: on the one hand it is possible to profit the cooperation between agents in order to choose the best quality sources, and thus improve the quality of circulating data. On the other hand, data flows are less controlled than in monolithic systems, and the quality of data, when not controlled, may rapidly decrease in time. Integration of data sources is also a relevant issue in CISs, especially when partners decide to substitute a group of databases, that have been independently developed, with an integrated in-house database. In *virtual data integration* a unique virtual integrated schema is built to provide unified access. This case is affected by data quality problems, because inconsistencies in data stored at different sites make it difficult to provide integrated information.

- In a *peer-to-peer information system* (usually abbreviated P2P), the traditional distinction between clients and servers typical of distributed systems is disappearing. A P2P system can be characterized by a number of properties: peers are higly autonomous and higly heterogeneous, they have no obligation for the quality of their services and data, no central coordination and no central database exist, no peer has a global view of the system, global behavior emerges from local interactions. It is clear that P2P systems are extremely critical from the point of view of data quality, since no obligation exists for agents participating in the system. It is also costly for a single agent to evaluate the reputation of other partners.

In the rest of the book, we will examine DQ issues mainly conceived for monolithic, distributed, data warehouses, and cooperative information systems, while issues for P2P systems will be discussed in Chapter 9 on open problems.

1.5 Main Research Issues and Application Domains in Data Quality

Due to the relevance of data quality, its nature, and the variety of data types and information systems, achieving data quality is a complex, multidisciplinary area of investigation. It involves several research topics and real-life application areas. Figure 1.3 shows the main ones.

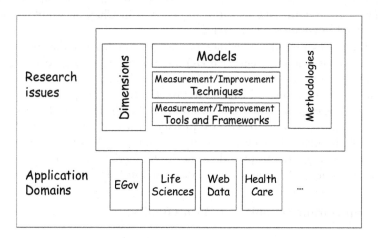

Fig. 1.3. Main issues in data quality

Research issues concern models, techniques, and tools, and two "vertical" areas, that cross the first three, i.e. dimensions and methodologies. We will discuss them in Section 1.5.1. Three of the application domains mentioned in Figure 1.3, namely e-Government, Life Sciences, and the World Wide Web, in which DQ is particularly relevant, are discussed in Section 1.5.2.

Research issues in DQ originate from research paradigms initially developed in other areas of research. The relationship between data quality and these related research areas will be discussed in Section 1.5.3.

1.5.1 Research Issues in Data Quality

Choosing *dimensions* to measure the level of quality of data is the starting point of any DQ-related activity. Though measuring the quality of ICT technologies, artifacts, processes, and services is not a new issue in research, for many years several standardization institutions have been operating (e.g. ISO, see [97]) in order to establish mature concepts in the areas of quality characteristics, measurable indicators, and reliable measurement procedures. Dimensions are discussed in Chapter 2. Dimensions are applied with different roles in models, techniques, tools, and frameworks.

Models are used in databases to represent data and data schemas. They are also used in information systems to represent business processes of the organization; these models have to be enriched in order to represent dimensions and other issues related to DQ. Models are investigated in Chapter 3.

Techniques correspond to algorithms, heuristics, knowledge-based procedures, and learning processes that provide a solution to a specific DQ problem or, as we say, to a *data quality activity*, as defined in Chapter 4. Examples of DQ activities are identifying if two records of different databases represent the same object of the real world or not; or finding the most reliable source for some specific data. DQ activities are defined in Chapter 4 and tecniques are discussed in Chapters 4, 5, and 6.

Methodologies provide guidelines to choose, starting from available techniques and tools, the most effective DQ measurement and improvement process (and hopefully, most economical for comparable results) within a specific information system. Methodologies are investigated in Chapter 7.

Methodologies and techniques, in order to be effective, need the support of *tools*, i.e., automatized procedures, provided with an interface, that relieve the user of the manual execution of some techniques. When a set of coordinated tools is integrated to provide a set of DQ services, we will use the term *framework*. Tools and frameworks are discussed in Chapter 8.

1.5.2 Application Domains in Data Quality

In this section, we analyze three distinct application domains of DQ. Their importance has been growing over the last few years, because of their relevance in daily lives of people and organizations: e-Government, Life Sciences, the World Wide Web.

e-Government

The main goal of all e-Government projects is the improvement of the relationship between the government, agencies, and citizens, as well as between agencies and businesses, through the use of information and communication technologies. This ambitious goal is articulated in different objectives:

1. the complete automation of those government administrative processes that deliver services to citizens and businesses, and that involve the exchange of data between government agencies;
2. the creation of an architecture that, by connecting the different agencies, enables them to fulfill their administrative processes without any additional burden to the users that benefit from them; and
3. the creation of portals that simplify access to services by authorized users.

e-Government projects must face the problem that similar information about one citizen or business is likely to appear in multiple databases. Each database is autonomously managed by the different agencies that historically has never been able to share data about citizens and businesses.

The problem is worsened by the many errors usually present in the databases, for many reasons. First, due to the nature of the administrative flows, several citizens' data (e.g. addresses) are not updated for long periods of time. This happens because it is often impractical to obtain updates from subjects that maintain the official residence data. Also, errors may occur when personal data on individuals is stored. Some of these errors are not corrected and a potentially large fraction of them is not detected. Furthermore, data provided by distinct sources differ in format, following local conventions, that can change in time and result in multiple versions. Finally, many of the records currently in the database were entered over years using legacy processes that included one or more manual data entry steps.

A direct consequence of this combination of redundancy and errors in data is frequent mismatches between different records that refer to the same citizen or business. One major outcome of having multiple disconnected views for the same information is that citizens and businesses experience consistent service degradation during their interaction with the agencies. Furthermore, misalignment brings about additional costs. First, agencies must make an investment to reconcile records using clerical review, e.g., to manually trace citizens and businesses that cannot be correctly and unequivocally identified. Secondly, because most investigation techniques, e.g., tax fraud prevention techniques, rely on cross-referencing records of different agencies, misalignment results in undetected tax fraud and reduced revenues.

Life Sciences

Life sciences data and specifically biological data are characterized by a diversity of data types, very large volumes, and highly variable quality. Data are available through vastly disparate sources and disconnected repositories. Their quality is difficult to assess and often unacceptable for the required usage. Biologists typically search several sources, for good quality data, for instance, in order to perform reliable in-silico experiments. However, the effort to actually assess the quality level of such data is entirely in the hands of the biologists; they have to manually analyze disparate sources, trying to integrate and reconcile heterogeneous and contradictory data in order to identify the best information. Let us consider, as an example, a gene analysis scenario. Figure 1.4 shows an example of a simple data analysis pipeline. As the result of a micro-array experiment, a biologist wants to analyze a set of genes, with the objective of understanding their functions.

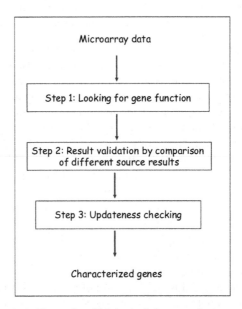

Fig. 1.4. Example of biological data analysis process

In Step 1, the biologist performs a Web search on a site that is known to contain gene data for the particular organism under consideration. Once the data is obtained, the biologist must assess its reliability. Therefore, in Step 2 the biologist performs a new web search in order to check if other sites provide the same gene information. It may happen that different sites provide conflicting results. Then (Step 3) the biologist also has to check that the provided results are up-to-date, i.e., if a gene is unknown in the queried sites, or no recent publication on that gene is available, e.g. through Pubmed (see [192]). The described scenario has many weaknesses:

1. the biologist must perform a time-consuming manual search for all the sources that may provide the function of the interested gene. This process

is also dependent on the user having personal knowledge about which sites must be queried;

2. the biologist has no way of assessing the trustworthiness of a result;
3. in Step 2, the biologist has no way of evaluating the quality of the results provided by different sites.
4. in Step 3, a new web search must be performed which again can be very time consuming.

In order to overcome such weaknesses, life sciences and biology need robust data quality techniques.

World Wide Web

Web information systems are characterized by the presentation of a large amount of data to a wide audience, the quality of which can be very heterogeneous. There are several reasons for this variety. First, every organization and individual can create a Web site and load every kind of information without any control on its quality, and sometimes with a malicious intent. A second reason lies in the conflict between two needs. On the one hand information systems on the web need to publish information in the shortest possible time after it is available from information sources. On the other hand, information has to be checked with regard to its accuracy, currency, and trustworthiness of its sources. These two requirements are in many aspects contradictory: accurate design of data structures, and, in the case of Web sites, of good navigational paths between pages, and certification of data to verify its correctness are costly and lengthy activities. However, the publication of data on Web sites is subject to time constraints.

Web information systems present two further aspects in connection to data quality that differentiate them from traditional information sources: first, a Web site is a continuously evolving source of information, and it is not linked to a fixed release time of information; second, in the process of changing information, additional information can be produced in different phases, and corrections to previously published information are possible, creating, in such a way, further needs for quality checks. Such features lead to a different type of information than with traditional media.

As a final argument, in Web information systems it is practically impossible to individuate a subject, usually called *data owner*, responsible for a certain data category. In fact, data are typically replicated among the different participating organizations, and one does not know how to state that an organization or subject has the primary responsibility for some specific data.

All previously discussed aspects make it difficult to certify the quality of data sources, and, for a user, to assess the reputation of other users and sources.

1.5.3 Research Areas Related to Data Quality

Data quality is fairly a new research area. Several other areas (see Figure 1.5) in computer science and other sciences have in the past treated related and overlapping problems; at the same time, such areas have developed in the last decades (in the case of statistics, in the last centuries) paradigms, models, and methodologies that have proved to be of major importance in grounding the data quality research area. We now discuss such research areas.

1. *Statistics* includes a set of methods that are used to collect, analyze, present, and interpret data. Statistics has developed in the last two centuries a wide spectrum of methods and models that allow one to express predictions and formulate decisions in all contexts where uncertain and imprecise information is available for the domain of interest. As discussed in [121], statistics and statistical methodology as the basis of data analysis are concerned with two basic types of problems: (i) summarizing, describing, and exploring data, (ii) using sampled data to infer the nature of the process that produced the data. Since low quality data are an inaccurate representation of the reality, a variety of statistical methods have been developed for measuring and improving the quality of data. We will discuss some statistical methods in Chapters 4 and 5.

2. *Knowledge representation* (see [144] and [54] for insightful introductions to the area) is the study of how knowledge about an application domain can be represented, and what kinds of reasoning can be done with that knowledge (this is called *knowledge reasoning*). Knowledge about an application domain may be represented procedurally in form of program code, or implicitly as patterns of activation in a neural network. Alternatively, the area of knowledge representation assumes an explicit and declarative representation, in terms of a *knowledge base*, consisting of logical formulas or rules expressed in a representation language. Providing a rich representation of the application domain, and being able to reason about it, is becoming an important leverage in many techniques for improving data quality; we will see some of these techniques in Chapters 5 and 8.

3. *Data mining* (see [92]) is an analytic process designed to explore usually large sets of data in search of consistent patterns and/or systematic relationships between attributes/variables. *Exploratory data mining* is defined in [50] as the preliminary process of discovering structure in a set of data using statistical summaries, visualization, and other means. In this context, achieving good data quality is an intrinsic objective of any data mining activity (see [46]), since otherwise the process of discovering patterns, relationships and structures is seriously deteriorated. From another perspective, data mining techniques may be used in a wide spectrum of activities for improving the quality of data; we will examine some of them in Chapter 4.

4. *Management information systems* (see [53]) are defined as systems that provide the information necessary to manage an organization effectively. Since data and knowledge are becoming relevant resources both in operational and decision business processes, and poor quality data result in poor quality processes, it is becoming increasingly important to supply management information systems with functionalities and services that allow one to control and improve the quality of the data resource.

5. *Data integration* (see [116]) has the goal of building and presenting a unified view of data owned by heterogeneous data sources in distributed, cooperative, and peer-to-peer information systems. Data integration will be considered in Chapter 4 as one of basic activities whose purpose is improving data quality, and will be discussed in detail in Chapter 6. While being an autonomous and well-grounded research area, data integration will be considered in this book as strictly related to data quality, regarding two main issues, providing query results on the basis of a quality characterization of data at sources, and identifying and solving conflicts on values referring to the same real-world objects.

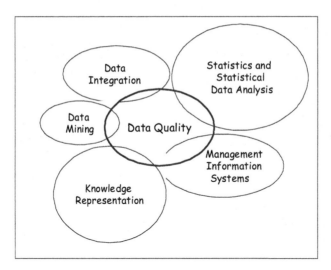

Fig. 1.5. Research areas related to data quality

1.6 Summary

In this chapter we have perceived that data quality is a multidisciplinary area. This is not surprising, since data, in a variety of formats and with a variety of media, are used in every real-life or business activity, and deeply influence the quality of processes that use data. Many private and public organizations have perceived the impact of data quality on their assets and missions, and have consequently launched initiatives of large impact. At the same time, while in monolithic information systems data are processed within controlled activities, with the advent of networks and the Internet, data are created and exchanged with much more "turbulent" processes, and need more sophisticated management.

The issues discussed in this chapter introduce to the structure of the rest of the book: dimensions, models, techniques, methodologies, tools, and frameworks will be the main topics addressed. While data quality is a relatively new research area, other areas, such as statistical data analysis, have addressed in the past some aspects of the problems related to data quality; with statistical data analysis, also knowledge representation, data mining, management information systems, and data integration share some of the problems and issues characteristic of data quality, and, at the same time, provide paradigms and techniques that can be effectively used in data quality measurement and improvement activities.

2

Data Quality Dimensions

In Chapter 1 we provided an intuitive concept of data quality and we informally introduced several data quality dimensions, such as accuracy, completeness, currency, and consistency.

This chapter investigates data quality in more depth, and presents multiple associated *dimensions*. Each dimension captures a specific aspect included under the general umbrella of data quality. Both data and schema dimensions are important. Data of low quality deeply influences the quality of business processes, while a schema of low quality, e.g., an unnormalized schema in the relational model, results in potential redundancies and anomalies during the lifecycle of data usage. Data dimensions can be considered more relevant in real-life applications and processes than schema dimensions.

More specifically, quality dimensions can refer either to the *extension* of data, i.e., to data values, or to their *intension*, i.e., to their schema. Both data dimensions and schema dimensions are usually defined in a qualitative way, referring to general properties of data and schemas, and the related definitions do not provide any facility for assigning values to dimensions themselves. Specifically, definitions do not provide quantitative measures, and one or more *metrics* are to be associated with dimensions as separate, distinct properties. For each metric, one or more *measurement methods* are to be provided regarding (see [169]) (i) where the measurement is taken, (ii) what data are included, (iii) the measurement device, and (iv) the scale on which results are reported. According to the literature, at times we will distinguish between dimensions and metrics, while other times we will directly provide metrics.

The quality of conceptual and logical schemas is very important in database design and usage. Conceptual schemas are typically produced within the first phase of the development of an information system. Erroneous conceptual schema design strongly impacts the system development and must be detected as soon as possible. Logical schemas are at the base of the implementation of any database application. Methods and techniques for assessing, evaluating, and improving conceptual schemas and logical schemas in different application domains is still a fertile research area.

Despite such recognized importance, the prevalent attention to the definitions of data quality dimensions has been devoted to data values, which, more extensively than schemas, are used in business and administrative processes. As a consequence, in this chapter we deal especially with data dimensions, but we also discuss some of the most relevant schema dimensions.

In the following sections we describe in detail data dimensions in order to understand the different possible meanings and metrics. Some definitions of data dimensions are independent of the data model used to represent the data. Specifically, the definitions provided for accuracy and time-related dimensions are model independent. Where some specific features of dimensions will require referring to the data model, it will be explicitly highlighted. Most examples refer to the relational model, and thus the relational terminology introduced in Chapter 1 is adopted. More specifically, we provide detailed descriptions of accuracy (Section 2.1), completeness (Section 2.2), currency and other time dimensions (Section 2.3), and finally consistency (Section 2.4). Section 2.5 discusses other dimensions which are mainly related to the evolution of information systems toward networked, web-based information systems. Some proposals of comprehensive classifications of dimensions are first illustrated and then compared in Section 2.6. Section 2.7 deals with schema dimensions, briefly describing correctness, minimality, completeness, and pertinence, and, in more detail, readability and normalization.

2.1 Accuracy

Accuracy is defined as the closeness between a value v and a value v′, considered as the correct representation of the real-life phenomenon that v aims to represent. As an example if the name of a person is John, the value v′ = John is correct, while the value v = Jhn is incorrect. Two kinds of accuracy can be identified, namely a syntactic accuracy and a semantic accuracy.

Syntactic accuracy is the closeness of a value v to the elements of the corresponding definition domain D. In syntactic accuracy we are not interested in comparing v with the true value v′; rather, we are interested in checking whether v is any one of the values in D, whatever it is. So, if v = Jack, even if v′ = John, v is considered syntactically correct, as Jack is an admissible value in the domain of persons' names. Syntactic accuracy is measured by means of functions, called *comparison functions*, that evaluate the distance between v and the values in D. Edit distance is a simple example of a comparison function, taking into account the minimum number of character insertions, deletions, and replacements to convert a string s to a string s′. More complex comparison functions exist, for instance taking into account similar sounds or character transpositions. In Chapter 5, a detailed description of the main comparison functions will be provided.

Let us consider the relation Movies introduced in Chapter 1, shown in Figure 2.1.

Id	Title	Director	Year	#Remakes	LastRemakeYear
1	Casablanca	Weir	1942	3	1940
2	Dead Poets Society	Curtiz	1989	0	NULL
3	Rman Holiday	Wylder	1953	0	NULL
4	Sabrina	NULL	1964	0	1985

Fig. 2.1. A relation Movies

The value Rman Holiday in movie 3 for Title is syntactically inaccurate, since it does not correspond to any title of a movie. Roman Holiday is the closest movie name to Rman Holiday; indeed, the edit distance between Rman Holiday and Roman Holiday is equal to 1 and simply corresponds to the insertion of the char o in the string Rman Holidays. Since 1 is the edit distance, the measure of syntactic accuracy is 1. More precisely, given a comparison function C, we may define a measure of syntactic accuracy of a value v with respect to a definition domain D, as the minimum value of C, when comparing v with all the values in D. Such a measure will be in the domain $[0, \ldots, n]$, where n is the maximum possible value that the comparison function may have.

Semantic accuracy is the closeness of the value v to the true value v'. Let us consider again the relation Movies of Figure 2.1. The exchange of directors' names in tuples 1 and 2 is an example of a semantic accuracy error: indeed, for movie 1, a director named Curtiz would be admissible, and thus it is syntactically correct. Nevertheless, Curtiz is not the director of Casablanca; therefore a semantic accuracy error occurs.

The above examples clearly show the difference between syntactic and semantic accuracy. Note that, while it is reasonable to measure syntactic accuracy using a distance function, semantic accuracy is measured better with a <yes, no> or a <correct, not correct> domain. Consequently, semantic accuracy coincides with the concept of *correctness*. In contrast with what happens for syntactic accuracy, in order to measure the semantic accuracy of a value v, the corresponding true value has to be known, or, else, it should be possible, considering additional knowledge, to deduce whether that the value v is or is not the true value.

From the above arguments, it is clear that semantic accuracy is typically more complex to calculate than syntactic accuracy. When it is known a priori that the rate of errors is low, and the errors result typically from typos, then syntactic accuracy tends to coincide with semantic accuracy, since typos produce values close to the true ones. As a result, semantic accuracy may be achieved by replacing an inaccurate value with the closest value in the definition domain, under the assumption that it is the true one.

In a more general context, a technique for checking semantic accuracy consists of looking for the same data in different data sources and finding the correct data by comparisons. This latter approach also requires the solution of the *object identification problem*, i.e., the problem of understanding whether two tuples refer to the same real-world entity or not; this problem will be discussed extensively in Chapter 5. The main issues to be addressed for solving the object identification problem are

- *Identification*: tuples in one or several sources may not have unique identifiers, and thus they need to be put in correspondence by means of appropriate *matching keys*.
- *Decision strategy*: once tuples are linked on the basis of a matching key, a decision must be made to state whether it corresponds to the same entity or not.

The accuracy above discussed is referred to a single value of a relation attribute. In practical cases, coarser accuracy definitions and metrics may be applied. As an example, it is possible to calculate the accuracy of an attribute called *attribute* (or *column*) *accuracy*, of a relation (*relation accuracy*), or of a whole database (*database accuracy*).

When considering accuracy for sets of values instead of single values, a further notion of accuracy can be introduced, namely duplication. *Duplication* occurs when a real-world entity is stored twice or more in a data source. Of course, if a primary key consistency check is performed when populating a relational table, a duplication problem does not occur if the primary key assignment has been made with a reliable procedure. The duplication problem is more relevant for files or other data structures that do not allow the definition of key constraints. A typical cost of duplication is, for example, the additional mailing cost enterprises pay for mailing customers, when customers are stored more than once in the their database. An indirect cost must be added to this direct cost, which consists of the loss of reputation of the enterprise in the eyes of its customers who may be bothered by having to receive the same material more than once.

For relation and database accuracy, for both syntactic and semantic accuracy, a *ratio* is typically calculated between accurate values and the total number of values. For instance, the accuracy of a relation can be measured as the ratio between the number of correct cell values and the total number of cells in the table. More complex metrics can be defined that consider comparison functions; for instance, as we said before, a typical process for syntactic accuracy evaluation is to match tuples from the source under examination with tuples of another source which is supposed to contain the same, but correct tuples.

In such a process, accuracy errors on attribute values can be either those that do not affect the tuple matching, or those that can stop the process itself, not allowing the matching. For instance, an accuracy error on an attribute SocialSecurityNumber (SSN) value can seriously affect the matching attempt; instead, given that SSNs are used for matching, an accuracy error on an attribute with a minor identification power, such as Age, cannot prevent the identification process from being carried out correctly. In the rest of this section we illustrate a few metrics (see [74]) taking these aspects into account.

Let us consider a relation schema R consisting of K attributes and a relational table r consisting of N tuples. Let q_{ij} ($i = 1..N$, $j = 1..K$) be a boolean variable defined to correspond to the cell values y_{ij} such that q_{ij} is equal to 0 if y_{ij} is syntactically accurate, while otherwise it is equal to 1.

In order to identify whether or not accuracy errors affect a matching of a relational table r with a reference table r' containing correct values, we introduce a further boolean variable s_i equal to 0 if the tuple t_i matches a tuple in r', and otherwise equal to 1. We can introduce three metrics to distinguish the relative importance of value accuracy in the context of the tuple. The first two metrics have the purpose of giving a different importance to errors on attributes that have a higher identification power, in line with the above discussion.

The first metric is called *weak accuracy error*, and is defined:

$$\sum_{i=1}^{N} \frac{\beta((q_i > 0) \bigwedge (s_i = 0))}{N},$$

where $\beta(.)$ is a boolean variable equal to 1 if the condition in parentheses is true, 0 otherwise, and $q_i = \sum_{j=1}^{K} q_{ij}$. Such metric considers the case in which for a tuple t_i accuracy errors occur ($q_i > 0$) but do not affect identification ($s_i = 0$).

The second metric is called *strong accuracy error*, and is defined as

$$\sum_{i=1}^{N} \frac{\beta((q_i > 0) \bigwedge (s_i = 1))}{N},$$

where $\beta(.)$ and q_i have the same meaning as above. Such a metric considers the case in which accuracy errors occur ($q_i > 0$) for a tuple t_i and actually do affect identification ($s_i = 1$).

The third metric gives the percentage of accurate tuples matched with the reference table. It is expressed by the degree of syntactic accuracy of the relational instance r

$$\sum_{i=1}^{N} \frac{\beta((q_i = 0) \bigwedge (s_i = 0))}{N}$$

by actually considering the fraction of accurate ($q_i = 0$) matched ($s_i = 0$) tuples.

2.2 Completeness

Completeness can be generically defined as "the extent to which data are of sufficient breadth, depth, and scope for the task at hand" [205]. In [161], three types of completeness are identified. *Schema completeness* is defined as the degree to which concepts and their properties are not missing from the schema. *Column completeness* is defined as a measure of the missing values for a specific property or column in a table. *Population completeness* evaluates missing values with respect to a reference population.

If focusing on a specific data model, a more precise characterization of completeness can be given. In the following we refer to the relational model.

2.2.1 Completeness of Relational Data

Intuitively, the completeness of a table characterizes the extent to which the table represents the corresponding real world. Completeness in the relational model can be characterized with respect to: (i) the presence/absence and meaning of null values, and (ii) the validity of one of the two assumptions called *open world assumption* and *closed world assumption*. We now introduce the two issues separately.

In a model *with* null values, the presence of a null value has the general meaning of a missing value, i.e., a value that exists in the real world but for some reason is not available. In order to characterize completeness, it is important to understand *why* the value is missing. Indeed, a value can be missing either because it exists but is unknown, or because it does not exist at all, or because it may exist but it is not actually known whether it exists or not. For a general discussion on the different types of null values see [11]; here we describe the three types of null values, by means of an example.

Let us consider a `Person` relation with the attributes `Name`, `Surname`, `BirthDate`, and `Email`. The relation is shown in Figure 2.2. For the tuples with `Id` equal to 2, 3, and 4, the `Email` value is NULL. Let us suppose that the person represented by tuple 2 has no e-mail: no incompleteness case occurs. If the person represented by tuple 3 has an e-mail, but its value is not known then tuple 3 presents an incompleteness. Finally, if it is not known whether the person represented by tuple 4 has an e-mail or not, incompleteness may not be the case.

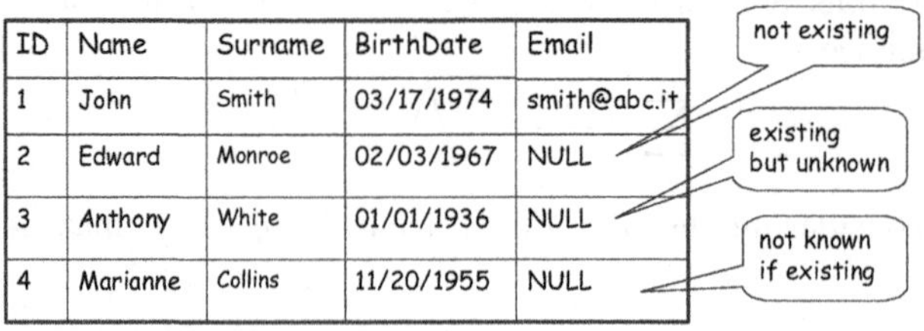

ID	Name	Surname	BirthDate	Email
1	John	Smith	03/17/1974	smith@abc.it
2	Edward	Monroe	02/03/1967	NULL
3	Anthony	White	01/01/1936	NULL
4	Marianne	Collins	11/20/1955	NULL

not existing

existing but unknown

not known if existing

Fig. 2.2. The `Person` relation, with different null value meanings for the e-mail attribute

In logical models for databases, such as the relational model, there are two different assumptions on the completeness of data represented in a relation instance r. The *closed world assumption* (CWA) states that only the values actually present in a relational table r, and no other values represent facts of the real world. In the *open world assumption* (OWA) we can state neither the truth nor the falsity of facts not represented in the tuples of r.

From the four possible combinations emerging from (i) considering or not considering null values, and (ii) OWA and CWA, we will focus on the following two most interesting cases:

1. model without null values with OWA;
2. model with null values with CWA.

In a model *without* null values with OWA, in order to characterize completeness we need to introduce the concept of *reference relation*. Given the relation r, the reference relation of r, called ref(r), is the relation containing all the tuples that satisfy the relational schema of r, i.e., that represent objects of the real world that constitute the present true extension of the schema.

As an example, if Dept is a relation representing the employees of a given department, and one specific employee of the department is not represented as a tuple of Dept, then the tuple corresponding to the missing employee is in ref(Dept), and ref(Dept) differs from Dept in exactly that tuple. In practical situations, the reference relations are rarely available. Instead their cardinality is much easier to get. There are also cases in which the reference relation is available but only periodically (e.g., when a census is performed).

On the basis of the reference relation, the completeness of a relation r is measured in a model without null values as the fraction of tuples actually represented in the relation r, namely, its *size* with respect to the total number of tuples in ref(r):

$$C(r) = \frac{|r|}{|ref(r)|}$$

As an example, let us consider the citizens of Rome. Assume that, from the personal registry of Rome's municipality, the overall number is six million. Let us suppose that a company stores data on Rome's citizens for the purpose of its business; if the cardinality of the relation r storing the data is 5,400,000, then $C(r)$ is equal to 0.9.

In the model with null values with CWA, specific definitions for completeness can be provided by considering the granularity of the model elements, i.e., value, tuple, attribute and relations, as shown in Figure 2.3. Specifically, it is possible to define

- a *value completeness*, to capture the presence of null values for some fields of a tuple;
- a *tuple completeness*, to characterize the completeness of a tuple with respect to the values of all its fields;

- an *attribute completeness*, to measure the number of null values of a specific attribute in a relation;
- a *relation completeness*, to capture the presence of null values in a whole relation.

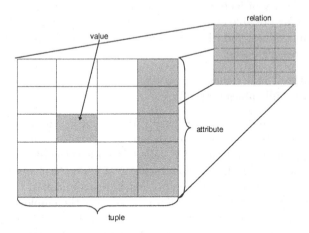

Fig. 2.3. Completeness of different elements in the relational model

As an example, in Figure 2.4, a `Student` relation is shown. The tuple completeness evaluates the percentage of specified values in the tuple with respect to the total number of attributes of the tuple itself. Therefore, in the example, the tuple completeness is 1 for tuples 6754 and 8907, 0.8 for tuple 6587, equal to 0.6 for tuple 0987, and so on. One way to see the tuple completeness is as a measure of the information content of the tuple, with respect to its maximum potential information content. With reference to this interpretation, we are implicitly assuming that all values of the tuple contribute equally to the total information content of the tuple. Of course, this may not be the case, as different applications can weight the attributes of a tuple differently.

The attribute completeness evaluates the percentage of specified values in the column corresponding to the attribute with respect to the total number of values that should have been specified. In Figure 2.4, let us consider an application calculating the average of the votes obtained by students. The absence of some values for the `Vote` attribute simply implies a deviation in the calculation of the average; therefore, a characterization of `Vote` completeness may be useful.

The relation completeness is relevant in all applications that need to evaluate the completeness of a whole relation, and can admit the presence of null values on some attributes. Relation completeness measures how much information is represented in the relation by evaluating the content of the information actually available with respect to the maximum possible content, i.e., without null values. According to this interpretation, completeness of the relation Student in Figure 2.4 is 53/60.

StudentID	Name	Surname	Vote	ExaminationDate
6754	Mike	Collins	29	07/17/2004
8907	Anne	Herbert	18	07/17/2004
6578	Julianne	Merrals	NULL	07/17/2004
0987	Robert	Archer	NULL	NULL
1243	Mark	Taylor	26	09/30/2004
2134	Bridget	Abbott	30	09/30/2004
6784	John	Miller	30	NULL
0098	Carl	Adams	25	09/30/2004
1111	John	Smith	28	09/30/2004
2564	Edward	Monroe	NULL	NULL
8976	Anthony	White	21	NULL
8973	Marianne	Collins	30	10/15/2004

Fig. 2.4. Student relation exemplifying the completeness of tuples, attributes and relations.

2.2.2 Completeness of Web Data

Data that are published in Web information systems can be characterized by evolution in time. While in the traditional paper-based media, information is published once and for all, Web information systems are characterized by information that is continuously published.

Let us consider the Web site of a university, where a list of courses given at that university in the current academic year is published. At a given moment, the list can be considered *complete* in the sense that it includes all the courses that have been officially approved. Nevertheless, it is also known that more courses will be added to the list, pending their approval. Therefore, there is the need to apprehend how the list will evolve in time with respect to completeness. The *traditional* completeness dimension provides only a static characterization of completeness. In order to consider the temporal dynamics of completeness, as needed in Web information systems, we introduce the notion of completability.

We consider a function $C(t)$, defined as the value of completeness at the instant t, with $t \in [\text{t\_pub}, \text{t\_max}]$, where t_pub is the initial instant of publication of data and t_max corresponds to the maximum time within which the series of the different scheduled updates will be completed. Starting from the function $C(t)$, we can define the *completability* of the published data as

$$\int_{t\_curr}^{t\_max} C(t),$$

where t_curr is the time at which completability is evaluated and t_curr <
t_max.

Completability, as shown in Figure 2.5, can be graphically depicted as an
area Cb of a function that represents how completeness evolves between an
instant t_curr of observation and t_max. Observe that the value corresponding
to t_curr is indicated as c_curr; c_max is the value for completeness estimated
for t_max. The value c_max is a real reachable limit that can be specified for
the completeness of the series of elements; if this real limit does not exist,
c_max is equal to 1. In Figure 2.5, a reference area A is also shown, defined as

$$(t\_max - t\_curr) * \frac{c\_max - c\_pub}{2},$$

that, by comparison with Cb, allows us to define ranges [High, Medium, Low]
for completability.

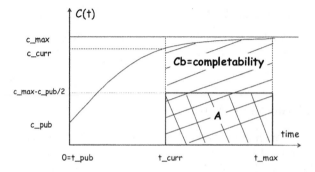

Fig. 2.5. A graphical representation of completability

With respect to the example above, considering the list of courses published on a university Web site, the completeness dimension gives information
about the current degree of completeness; the completability information gives
the information about how fast this degree will grow in time, i.e., how fast
the list of courses will be completed. The interested reader can find further
details in [159].

2.3 Time-Related Dimensions: Currency, Timeliness, and Volatility

An important aspect of data is their change and update in time. In Chapter
1 we provided a classification of types of data according to the temporal
dimension, in terms of stable, long-term-changing, and frequently changing
data. The principal time-related dimensions proposed for characterizing the
above three types of data are currency, volatility, and timeliness.

Currency concerns how promptly data are updated. As an example in Figure 2.1, the attribute **#Remakes** of movie 4 has low currency because a remake of movie 4 has been done, but this information did not result in an increased value for the number of remakes. Similarly, if the residential address of a person is updated, i.e., it corresponds to the address where the person lives, then the currency is high.

Volatility characterizes the frequency with which data vary in time. For instance, stable data such as birth dates have volatility equal to 0, as they do not vary at all. Conversely, stock quotes, a kind of frequently changing data, have a high degree of volatility due to the fact that they remain valid for very short time intervals.

Timeliness expresses how current data are for the task at hand. The timeliness dimension is motivated by the fact that it is possible to have current data that are actually useless because they are *late* for a specific usage. For instance, the timetable for university courses can be current by containing the most recent data, but it cannot be timely if it is available only after the start of the classes.

We now provide possible metrics of time-related dimensions. Currency can be typically measured with respect to *last update* metadata, which correspond to the last time the specific data were updated. For data types that change with a fixed frequency, last update metadata allow us to compute currency straightforwardly. Conversely, for data types whose change frequency can vary, one possibility is to calculate an average change frequency and perform the currency computation with respect to it, admitting errors. As an example, if a data source stores residence addresses that are estimated to change every five years, then an address with its last update metadata reporting a date corresponding to one month before the observation time can be assumed to be *current*; in contrast, if the date reported is ten years before the observation time, it is assumed to be *not current*.

Volatility is a dimension that inherently characterizes certain types of data. A metric for volatility is given by the length of time (or its inverse) that data remain valid.

Timeliness implies that data not only are current, but are also in time for events that correspond to their usage. Therefore, a possible measurement consists of (i) a currency measurement and (ii) a check that data are available *before* the planned usage time.

More complex metrics can be defined for time-related dimensions. As an example, we cite the metric defined in [17], in which the three dimensions currency, volatility, and timeliness are linked by defining timeliness as a function of currency and volatility. More specifically,

1. Currency is defined as

$$Currency = Age + (DeliveryTime - InputTime),$$

where *Age* measures how old the data unit is when received, *DeliveryTime* is the time the information product is delivered to the customer, and *InputTime* is the time the data unit is obtained. Therefore, currency is the sum of how old data are when received (*Age*), plus a second term that measures how long data have been in the information system, (*DeliveryTime − InputTime*);

2. Volatility is defined as the length of time data remains valid;
3. Timeliness is defined as,

$$\max\{0, 1 - \frac{currency}{volatility}\}.$$

Timeliness ranges from 0 to 1, where 0 means bad timeliness and 1 means good timeliness.

Observe that the relevance of currency depends on volatility: data that are highly volatile must be current, while currency is less important for data with low volatility.

2.4 Consistency

The consistency dimension captures the violation of semantic rules defined over (a set of) data items, where items can be tuples of relational tables or records in a file. With reference to relational theory, *integrity constraints* are an instantiation of such semantic rules. In statistics, *data edits* are another example of semantic rules that allow for the checking of consistency.

2.4.1 Integrity Constraints

The interested reader can find a detailed discussion on integrity constraints in the relational model in [11]. The purpose of this section is to summarize the main concepts, useful for introducing the reader to consistency-related topics.

Integrity constraints are properties that must be satisfied by all instances of a database schema. Although integrity constraints are typically defined on schemas, they can at the same time be checked on a specific instance of the schema that presently represents the extension of the database. Therefore, we may define integrity constraints for schemas, describing a schema quality dimension, and for instances, representing a data dimension. In this section, we will define them for instances, while in section 2.7 we will define them for schemas.

It is possible to distinguish two main categories of integrity constraints, namely, *intrarelation constraints* and *interrelation constraints*. Intrarelation integrity constraints can regard single attributes (also called *domain constraints*) or multiple attributes of a relation.

Let us consider an `Employee` relation schema, with the attributes `Name`, `Surname`, `Age`, `WorkingYears`, and `Salary`. An example of the domain constraint defined on the schema is "`Age` is included between 0 and 120." An example of a multiple attribute integrity constraint is: "If WorkingYears is less than 3, than Salary could not be more than 25.000 Euros per year."

Interrelation integrity constraints involve attributes of more than one relation. As an example, consider the Movies relation instance in Figure 2.1. Let us consider another relation, OscarAwards, specifying the Oscar awards won by each movie, and including an attribute Year corresponding to the year when the award was assigned. An example of interrelation constraint states that " Year of the Movies relation must be equal to Year of OscarAwards."

Most of the considered integrity constraints are *dependencies*. The following main types of dependencies can be considered:

- *Key Dependency.* This is the simplest type of dependency. Given a relation instance r, defined over a set of attributes, we say that for a subset K of the attributes a key dependency holds in r, if no two rows of r have the same K-values. For instance, an attribute like SocialSecurityNumber can serve as a key in any relation instance of a relation schema Person. When key dependency constraints are enforced, no duplication will occur within the relation (see also Section 2.1 on duplication issues).
- *Inclusion Dependency.* Inclusion dependency is a very common type of constraint, and is also known as *referential constraint*. An inclusion dependency over a relational instance r states that some columns of r are contained in other columns of r or in the instances of another relational instance s. A *foreign key constraint* is an example of inclusion dependency, stating that the referring columns in one relation must be contained in the primary key columns of the referenced relation.
- *Functional Dependency.* Given a relational instance r, let X and Y be two nonempty sets of attributes in r. r satisfies the functional dependency $X \rightarrow Y$, if the following holds for every pair of tuples t_1 and t_2 in r:

$$\text{If } t_1.X = t_2.X, \text{ then } t_1.Y = t_2.Y,$$

where the notation $t_1.X$ means the projection of the tuple t_1 onto the attributes in X. In Figure 2.6, examples of relations respectively satisfying and violating a functional dependency $AB \rightarrow C$ are shown. In the figure, the relation r_1 satisfies the functional dependency, as the first two tuples, having the same values for the attribute A and the attribute B, also have the same value for the attribute C. The relation r_2 does not satisfy the functional dependency, since the first two tuples have a different C field.

2.4.2 Data Edits

In the previous section, integrity constraints were discussed within the relational model as a specific category of consistency semantic rules. However, where data are not relational, consistency rules can still be defined. As an example, in the statistical field, data coming from census questionnaires have

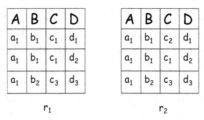

Fig. 2.6. Example of functional dependencies

a structure corresponding to the *questionnaire schema*. The semantic rules are thus defined over such a structure in a way very similar to relational constraints. Such rules, called *edits*, are less powerful than integrity constraints because they do not rely on a data model like the relational one. Nevertheless, data editing has been done extensively in the national statistical agencies since the 1950s, and has revealed a fruitful and effective area of application. *Data editing* is defined as the task of detecting inconsistencies by formulating rules that must be respected by every correct set of answers. Such rules are expressed as *edits*, which denote error conditions.

As an example, an inconsistent answer to a questionnaire can be to declare

```
marital status = ''married'', age = ''5 years old''
```

The rule to detect this kind of errors could be the following:

```
if marital status is married, age must not be less than 14.
```

The rule can be put in the form of an edit, which expresses the error condition, namely,

$$\text{marital status} = \text{married} \land \text{age} < 14$$

After the detection of erroneous records, the act of correcting erroneous fields by restoring correct values is called *imputation*. The problem of localizing errors by means of edits and imputing erroneous fields is known as the *edit-imputation problem.*In Chapter 4 we will examine some issues and methods for the edit-imputation problem.

2.5 Other Data Quality Dimensions

In the previous section, a description of the principal data quality dimensions was provided. However, in the data quality literature, several further dimensions have been proposed in addition to the four described ones.

There are general proposals for sets of dimensions that aim to fully specify the data quality concept in a general setting (see Section 2.6). Some other proposals are related to specific domains that need ad hoc dimensions in order to capture the peculiarities of the domain. For instance, specific data quality dimensions are proposed in the following domains:

1. The *archival domain* (see [217] and [111]) and the Interpares project [101], which makes use of dimensions such as *condition* (of a document) that refers to the physical suitability of the document for scanning.
2. The *statistical domain*; every National bureau of census and international organizations such as the European Union or the International Monetary Fund define several dimensions for statistical and scientific data (see [96]), such as *integrity*, on the notion that statistical systems should be based on adherence to the principle of objectivity in the collection, compilation, and dissemination of statistics.
3. The *geographical and geospatial domain* (see [152], [89], and [101]), where the following dimensions are proposed: (i) *positional accuracy*, defined as a quality parameter indicating the accuracy of geographical positions, and (ii) *attribute/thematic accuracy*, defined as the positional and/or value accuracy of properties such as sociodemographic attributes in thematic maps.

In the following we will describe some new dimensions that are gaining increasing importance in networked information systems. With the advent of Web information systems, and peer-to-peer information systems, the number of sources of data increases dramatically, and provenance on available data is difficult to evaluate in the majority of cases. This is a radical change from old, centralized systems (still widespread in some organizations, such as banks), where data sources and data flows are accurately controlled and monitored. In this context, new quality dimensions arise; among them we now discuss interpretability, synchronization in time series, and, in more detail, accessibility and (the set of) dimensions proposed for characterizing the quality of an information source. Other dimensions are introduced and discussed in [50].

Interpretability concerns the documentation and metadata that are available to correctly interpret the meaning and properties of data sources. In order to maximize interpretability, the following types of documentation should be available:

1. the conceptual schema of the file(s) or database(s) made available;
2. the integrity constraints that hold among data;
3. a set of metadata for cross-domain information resource description, such as the one described in the standard Dublin core (see [63] for an exhaustive introduction to this standard including, among others, metadata like *creator*, *subject*, *description*, *publisher*, *date*, *format*, *source*, and *language*);
4. a certificate describing available measures of data quality dimensions and schema dimensions; and
5. information on the history and provenance of data, i.e., how and where it has been created, produced, and maintained. For a discussion on provenance of data, see Chapter 3.

Synchronization between different time series concerns proper integration of data having different time stamps. Synchronization is a major problem for organizations that produce statistics, and in which data come from different sources of collected data with different time stamps. For example, if in a company we are combining data on expenditures and data on revenues, it is important to get the data synchronized correctly, otherwise the analysis could produce incorrect results. Statistical methods, the discussion of which is out of the scope of this book, are used to synchronize the data and allow their fusion. We refer again to [50] for more details on this point.

2.5.1 Accessibility

Publishing large amounts of data in Web sites is not a sufficient condition for its availability to everyone. In order to access it, a user needs to access a network, to understand the language to be used for navigating and querying the Web, and to perceive with his or her senses the information made available. *Accessibility* measures the ability of the user to access the data from his or her own culture, physical status/functions, and technologies available. We focus in the following on causes that can reduce physical or sensorial abilities, and, consequently, can reduce accessibility, and we briefly outline corresponding guidelines to achieve accessibility. Among others, the World Wide Web Consortium [198] defines the individuals with disabilities as subjects that,

1. may not be able to see, hear, move, or process some types of information easily or at all;
2. may have difficulty reading or comprehending text;
3. may not have to or be able to use a keyboard or mouse;
4. may have a text-only screen, a small screen, or a slow Internet connection;
5. may not speak or understand a natural language fluently.

Several guidelines are provided by international and national bodies to govern the production of data, applications, services, and Web sites in order to guarantee accessibility. In the following, we describe some guidelines related to data provided by the World Wide Web Consortium in [198].

The first, and perhaps most important, guideline addresses providing equivalent alternatives to auditory and visual content, called *text equivalent content*. In order for a text equivalent to make an image accessible, the text content can be presented to the user as synthesized speech, braille, and visually displayed text. Each of these three mechanisms uses a different sense, making the information accessible to groups affected by a variety of sensory and other disabilities. In order to be useful, the text must convey the same function or purpose as the image. For example, consider a text equivalent for a photographic image of the continent of Africa as seen from a satellite. If the purpose of the image is mostly that of decoration, then the text "Photograph of Africa as seen from a satellite" might fulfill the necessary function. If the purpose of the photograph is to illustrate specific information about African geography, such as its organization and subdivision into states, then the text equivalent should convey that information with more articulate and informative text. If the photograph has been designed to allow the user to select the image or part of it (e.g., by clicking on it) for information about Africa, equivalent text could be "Information about Africa", with a list of items describing the parts that can be selected. Therefore, if the text conveys the same function or purpose for the user with a disability as the image does for other users, it can be considered a text equivalent.

Other guidelines suggest

- avoiding the use of color as the only means to express semantics, helping daltonic people appreciate the meaning of data;
- usage of clear natural language, by providing expansions of acronyms, improving readability, a frequent use of plain terms;
- designing a Web site that ensures device independence using features that enable activation of page elements via a variety of input devices;
- providing context and orientation information to help users understand complex pages or elements.

Several countries have enacted specific laws to enforce accessibility in public and private Web sites and applications used by citizens and employees in order to provide them effective access and reduce the digital divide.

2.5.2 Quality of Information Sources

Several dimensions have been proposed for characterizing the quality of an information source as a whole.

In Wang and Strong [205], three dimensions model how "trustable" is the information source providing the data. These dimensions are believability, reputation, and objectivity. Believability considers whether a certain source provides data that can be regarded as true, real and credible. Reputation considers how trustable is the information source. Objectivity takes into account impartiality of sources in data provisioning.

Similarly to the above described dimensions, reliability (or credibility) is also proposed as a dimension for representing whether a source provides data conveying the right information (e.g., in Wand and Wang [199]).

More recently, with the increasing interest in peer-to-peer systems, the quality characterization of a source (or peer) is gaining importance. Indeed, in such systems that are completely open, there is the need to assess and filter data that circulate in the system, and one possibility is to rely on the trustability of each peer. As an example, in [59], a trust model for information peers is proposed, in which a trust level is associated to a certain peer for each typology of data provided to the community. The interested reader can find more details on trust issues in peer-to-peer systems in Chapter 9.

2.6 Approaches to the Definition of Data Quality Dimensions

In this section we focus on the general proposals for dimensions by illustrating some of them. There are three main approaches adopted for proposing comprehensive sets of the dimension definitions, namely, theoretical, empirical, and intuitive. The *theoretical approach* adopts a formal model in order to define or justify the dimensions. The *empirical approach* constructs the set of dimensions starting from experiments, interviews, and questionnaires. The *intuitive approach* simply defines dimensions according to common sense and practical experience.

In the following, we summarize three main proposals that clearly represent the approaches to dimension definitions: Wand and Wang [199], Wang and Strong [205], and Redman [167].

2.6.1 Theoretical Approach

A theoretical approach to the definition of data quality is proposed in Wand and Wang [199]. This approach considers an information system (IS) as a representation of a *real-world system* (RW); RW is *properly represented* in an IS if (i) there exists an exhaustive mapping $RW \rightarrow IS$, and (ii) no two states in RW are mapped into the same state in an IS, i.e., the inverse mapping is a function (see Figure 2.7).

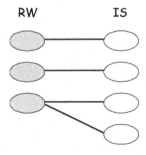

Fig. 2.7. Proper representation of the real world system in the theoretical approach from [199]

All deviations from proper representations generate deficiencies. They distinguish between *design deficiencies* and *operation deficiencies*. Design deficiencies are of three types: *incomplete representation, ambiguous representation,* and *meaningless states.* They are graphically represented in Figure 2.8.

Only one type of operation deficiency is identified, in which a state in RW might be mapped to a wrong state in an IS; this is referred to as *garbling*.

Garbling with a map to a meaningless state is dangerous, as it will preclude a map back to a real world state (see Figure 2.9a). Garbling to a meaningful but wrong state will allow the user to map back to a real world state (see Figure 2.9b).

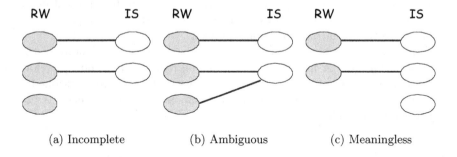

(a) Incomplete   (b) Ambiguous   (c) Meaningless

Fig. 2.8. Incomplete, ambiguous, and meaningless representations of the real world system in the theoretical approach

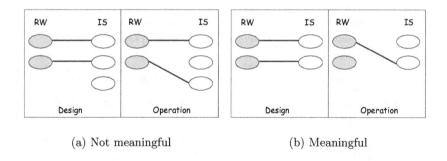

(a) Not meaningful   (b) Meaningful

Fig. 2.9. Garbling representations of the real world system from [199]

A set of data quality dimensions are defined by making references to described deficiencies. More specifically, the identified dimensions are (the quoted text is from [199])

- *Accuracy*: "inaccuracy implies that the information system represents a real world state different from the one that should have been represented." Inaccuracy refers to a garbled mapping into a wrong state of the IS, where it is possible to infer a valid state of the real world though not the correct one (see Figure 2.9b).

- *Reliability* indicates "whether the data can be counted on to convey the right information; it can be viewed as correctness of data." No interpretation in terms of data deficiencies is given.
- *Timeliness* refers to "the delay between a change of the real-world state and the resulting modification of the information system state." Lack of timeliness may lead to an IS state that reflects a past RW state.
- *Completeness* is "the ability of an information system to represent every meaningful state of the represented real world system." Completeness is of course tied to incomplete representations.
- *Consistency* of data values occurs if there is more than one state of the information system matching a state of the real-world system; therefore "inconsistency would mean that the representation mapping is one-to-many." This is captured by representation, so the inconsistency is not considered a result of a deficiency.

Category	Dimension	Definition: the extent to which ...
Intrinsic	Beleivability	data are accepted or regardedas true, real and credible
	Accuracy	data are correct, reliable and certified free of error
	Objectivity	data are unbiased and impartial
	Reputation	data are trusted or highly regarded in terms of their source and content
Contextual	Value-added	data are beneficial and provide advantages for their use
	Relevancy	data are applicable and useful for the task at hand
	Timeliness	the age of the data is appropriate for the task at hand
	Completeness	data are of sufficient depth, breadth, and scope for the task at hand
	Appropriate amount of data	the quantity or volume of available data is appropriate
Representational	Intepretability	data are in appropriate language and unit and the data definitions are clear
	Ease of understanding	data are clear without ambiguity and easily comprehended
	Representational consistency	data are always presented in the same format and are compatible with the previous data
	Concise representation	data are compactly represented without behing overwhelmed
Accessibility	Accessibility	data are available or easily and quickly retrieved
	Access security	access to data can be restricted and hence kept secure

Fig. 2.10. Dimensions proposed in the empirical approach

2.6.2 Empirical Approach

In the proposal discussed in Wang and Strong [205], data quality dimensions have been selected by interviewing data consumers. Starting from 179 data quality dimensions, the authors selected 15 different dimensions, represented in Figure 2.10 with their definitions. A two-level classification is proposed, in which each of four *categories* is further specialized into a number of *dimensions*. The four categories are

- *intrinsic data quality*, capturing the quality that data has on its own. As an example, accuracy is a quality dimension that is intrinsic to data;
- *contextual data quality* considers the context where data are used. As an example, the completeness dimension is strictly related to the context of the task;
- *representational data quality* captures aspects related to the quality of data representation, e.g., interpretability;
- *accessibility data quality* is related to the accessibility of data and to a further non-functional property of data access, namely, the level of security.

2.6.3 Intuitive Approach

Redman [167] classifies data quality dimensions according to three categories, namely, conceptual schema, data values, and data format. *Conceptual schema* dimensions correspond to what we called schema dimensions. *Data value* dimensions refer specifically to values, independently of the internal representation of data; this last aspect is covered by *data format* dimensions. Our focus here is on data extension; therefore, in Figure 2.11, we provide the definitions for data value and format dimensions only.

2.6.4 A Comparative Analysis of the Dimension Definitions

According to the definitions described in the previous section, there is no general agreement either on which set of dimensions defines data quality or on the exact meaning of each dimension. In fact, in the illustrated proposals, dimensions are not defined in a measurable and formal way. Instead, they are defined by means of descriptive sentences in which the semantics are consequently disputable. Nevertheless, we attempt to make a comparison between the different definitions provided with the purpose of showing possible agreements and disagreements in the different proposals. In order to cover a larger number of proposals, besides the previously described Wand and Wang [199], Wang and Strong [205], and Redman [167], we also consider Jarke et al. [104], Bovee et al. [31], Naumann [139], and Liu [120]. Hereafter we will refer to the proposals with the name of the first author of the work.

With regard to time-related dimensions, in Figure 2.12, definitions for currency, volatility, and timeliness by different authors are illustrated. In the figure, Wand and Redman provide very similar definitions but for different dimensions, i.e., for timeliness and currency, respectively. Wang and Liu assume the same meaning for timeliness, Naumann proposes a very different definition for it, and Bovee only provides a definition for timeliness in terms of currency and volatility. Bovee's currency corresponds to timeliness as defined

Dimension Name	Type of dimension	Definition
Accuracy	data value	Distance between v and v', considered as correct
Completeness	data value	Degree to which values are present in a data collection
Currency	data value	Degree to which a datum is up-to-date
Consistency	data value	Coherence of the same datum, represented in multiple copies, or different data to respect integrity constraints and rules
Appropriateness	data format	One format is more appropriate than another if it is more suited to user needs
Interpretability	data format	Ability of the user to interpret correctly values from their format
Portability	data format	The format can be applied to as a wide set of situations as possible
Format precision	data format	Ability to distinguish between elements in the domain that must be distinguished by users
Format flexibility	data format	Changes in user needs and recording medium can be easily accommodated
Ability to represent null values	data format	Ability to distinguish neatly (without ambiguities) null and default values from applicable values of the domain
Efficient use of memory	data format	Efficiency in the physical representation. An icon is less efficient than a code
Representation consistency	data format	Coherence of physical instances of data with their formats

Fig. 2.11. Dimensions proposed in the intuitive approach [167]

by Wang and Liu. Volatility has a similar meaning in Bovee and Jarke. The comparison shows that there is no substantial agreement on the names to use for time-related dimensions; indeed, currency and timeliness are often used to refer to the same concept. There is not even agreement on the semantics of a specific dimension; indeed, for timeliness, different meanings are provided by different authors.

With regard to completeness, in Figure 2.13, different proposals for completeness definitions are shown. By comparing such definitions, it emerges that there is substantial agreement on what completeness is, although it often refers to different granularity levels and different data model elements, e.g., information system in Wand, data warehouse in Jarke, and entity in Bovee.

2.6.5 Trade-offs Between Dimensions

Data quality dimensions are not independent, i.e., correlations exist between them. If one dimension is considered more important than the others for a specific application, then the choice of favoring it may imply negative consequences for the other ones. In this section, we provide some examples of possible trade-offs.

First, trade-offs may need to be made between timeliness and any one of the three dimensions: accuracy, completeness, and consistency. Indeed, hav-

Reference	Definition
Wand 1996	Timeliness refers only to the delay between a change of a real world state and the resulting modification of the information system state
Wang 1996	Timeliness is the extent to which age of the data is appropriate for the task at hand
Redman 1996	Currency is the degree to which a datum is up-to-date. A datum value is up-to-date if it is correct in spite of possible discrepancies caused by time-related changes to the correct value
Jarke 1999	Currency describes when the information was entered in the sources and/or the data warehouse. Volatility describes the time period for which information is valid in the real world
Bovee 2001	Timeliness has two componenets: age and volatility. Age or currency is a measure of how old the information is, based on how long ago it was recorded. Volatility is a measure of information instability-the frequency of change of the value for an entity attribute
Naumann 2002	Timeliness is the average age of the data in a source
Liu 2002	Timeliness is the extent to which data are sufficiently up-to-date for a task

Fig. 2.12. Time-related dimensions definitions

Reference	Definition
Wand 1996	The ability of an information system to represent every meaningful state of the represented real world system.
Wang 1996	The extent to which data are of sufficient breadth, depth and scope for the task at hand
Redman 1996	The degree to which values are present in a data collection
Jarke 1999	Percentage of the real-world information entered in the sources and/or the data warehouse
Bovee 2001	Deals with information having all required parts of an entity's information present
Naumann 2002	It is the quotient of the number of non-null values in a source and the size of the universal relation
Liu 2002	All values that are supposed to be collected as per a collection theory

Fig. 2.13. Completeness dimensions definitions

ing accurate (or complete or consistent) data, may need checks and activities that require time, and thus timeliness is negatively affected. Conversely, having timely data may cause lower accuracy (or completeness or consistency). A typical situation in which timeliness can be preferred to accuracy, completeness, or consistency is given by most Web applications: as the time constraints are often very stringent for Web data, it is possible that such data are deficient with respect to other quality dimensions. For instance, a list of courses published on a university Web site must be timely though there could be accuracy or consistency errors and some fields specifying courses could be missing.

Conversely, when considering an administrative application, accuracy, consistency, and completeness requirements are more stringent than timeliness, and therefore delays are mostly admitted in dimensions other than timeliness.

Another significant case of trade-off is between consistency and completeness [15]. Here the question is "Is it better to have less but consistent data, i.e., poor completeness, or to have more but inconsistent data?". This choice is again very domain specific. As an example, statistical data analysis typically requires a significant and representative amount of data in order to perform the analysis; in this case, the approach is to favor completeness, tolerating inconsistencies, or adopting techniques to solve them. Conversely, when considering the publishing of a list of votes obtained by students as the result of an exam, it is more important to have a list of consistency checked votes than a complete one, possibly deferring the publication of the complete list.

2.7 Schema Quality Dimensions

In the previous sections, we provided an in-depth characterization of data quality dimensions. In this section, the focus is on schema quality dimensions. However, there is a strict relationship between quality of schemas and quality of data, as highlighted in the next example. Let us suppose we want to model residence addresses of people; in Figure 2.14, there are two possibilities to model such a concept. Specifically, in Figure 2.14a, the residence addresses are modeled as attributes of a relation Person, while in Figure 2.14b, the residence addresses are modeled as a relation Address, with the fields Id, StreetPrefix, StreetName, Number, City, and a relation ResidenceAddress storing the address at which the person lives. The solution in Figure 2.14a has some problems. First, representing addresses as a single field creates ambiguity on the meaning of the different components; for instance, in tuple 3 of the Person relation, is 4 a civic number or the number of the avenue (it is actually part of the name of the square)? Second, the values of the attribute Address can also contain information that is not explicitly required to be represented (e.g., the floor number and zip code of tuples 1 and 2 of the Person relation). Third, as the Person relation is not normalized, a redundancy problem occurs and hence further errors on the Address attribute may be potentially introduced (see the same address values for tuples 1 and 2 of the Person relation). On the other hand, the solution in Figure 2.14b is more complex. In real implementation there is often the need to manage trade-offs between the two modeling solutions.

A comprehensive proposal on schema dimensions is described in the book of Redman [167], and includes six dimensions and 15 subdimensions referring to schema quality. Here, we focus on seven subdimensions, which we call dimensions in the following section. In the definitions we are going to provide, we assume that the database schema is the result of the translation of a set of requirements, expressed usually in natural language, into a set of concep-

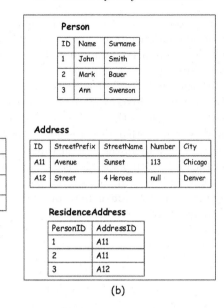

Person

ID	Name	Surname
1	John	Smith
2	Mark	Bauer
3	Ann	Swenson

Address

ID	StreetPrefix	StreetName	Number	City
A11	Avenue	Sunset	113	Chicago
A12	Street	4 Heroes	null	Denver

ResidenceAddress

PersonID	AddressID
1	A11
2	A11
3	A12

(b)

Person

ID	Name	Surname	Address
1	John	Smith	113 Sunset Avenue 60601 Chicago
2	Mark	Bauer	113 Sunset Avenue 60601 Chicago
3	Ann	Swenson	4 Heroes Street Denver

(a)

Fig. 2.14. Two ways of modeling residence addresses

tual (or logical) structures, expressed in terms of a conceptual (or logical) database model. Two of these dimensions, namely, *readability* and *normalization*, will be discussed in specific sections. We briefly introduce the remaining five dimensions.

1. *Correctness with respect to the model* concerns the correct use of the categories of the model in representing requirements. As an example, in the Entity Relationship model we may represent the logical link between persons and their first names using the two entities **Person** and **FirstName** and a relationship between them. The schema is not correct wrt the model since an entity should be used only when the concept has a unique existence in the real world and has an identifier; this is not the case with **FirstName**, which would be properly represented as an attribute of the entity **Person**.

2. *Correctness with respect to requirements* concerns the correct representation of the requirements in terms of the model categories. Assume that in an organization each department is headed by exactly one manager and each manager may head exactly one department. If we represent **Manager** and **Department** as entities, the relationship between them should be one-to-one; in this case, the schema is correct wrt requirements. If we use a one-to-many relationship, the schema is incorrect.

3. *Minimalization.* A schema is minimal if every part of the requirements is represented only once in the schema. In other words, it is not possible to eliminate some element from the schema without compromising the in-

formation content. Consider the schema in Figure 2.15, which represents several relationships between concepts **Student**, **Course**, and **Instructor**. We represent also minimum and maximum cardinalities of entities in relationships, except in one case, where we indicate the maximum cardinality with the symbol "?". The schema is redundant in the case in which the direct relationship **Assigned to** between **Student** and **Instructor** has the same meaning as the logical composition of the two relationships **Attends** and **Teaches**; otherwise, it is nonredundant. Notice that the schema can be redundant only in the case in which the unspecified maximum cardinality of the entity **Course** is "1", since only in this case does a unique instructor correspond to each course, and the composition of the two relationships **Attends** and **Teaches** may provide the same result as the relationship **Assigned to**.

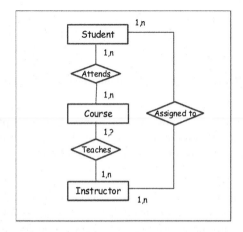

Fig. 2.15. A possibly redundant schema

4. *Completeness* measures the extent to which a conceptual schema includes all the conceptual elements necessary to meet some specified requirements. It is possible that the designer has not included certain characteristics present in the requirements in the schema, e.g., attributes related to an entity **Person**; in this case, the schema is incomplete.

5. *Pertinence* measures how many unnecessary conceptual elements are included in the conceptual schema. In the case of a schema that is not pertinent, the designer has gone too far in modeling the requirements, and has included too many concepts.

Completeness and pertinence are two faces of the same issue, i.e., obtaining a schema at the end of the conceptual design phase that is the *exact* correspondence in the model of the reality described by requirements.

2.7.1 Readability

Intuitively, a schema is readable whenever it represents the meaning of the reality represented by the schema in a clear way for its intended use. This simple, qualitative definition is not easy to translate in a more formal way, since the evaluation expressed by the word *clearly* conveys some elements of subjectivity. In models, such as the Entity Relationship model, that provide a graphical representation of the schema, called *diagram*, readability concerns both the diagram and the schema itself. We now discuss them.

With regard to the diagrammatic representation, readability can be expressed by a number of *aesthetic criteria* that human beings adopt in drawing diagrams: crossings between lines should be avoided as far as possible, graphic symbols should be embedded in a grid, lines should be made of horizontal or vertical segments, the number of bends in lines should be minimized, the total area of the diagram should be minimized, and, finally, hierarchical structures such as generalization hierarchies among, say, an entity E1 and two entities E2 and E3 should be such that E1 is positioned at a higher level in the diagram in respect to E2 and E3. Finally, the children entities in the generalization hierarchy should be symmetrical with respect to the parent entity. For further discussion on aesthetic criteria, see [22], and [186].

The above criteria are not respected in the case of the Entity Relationship diagram of Figure 2.16. We can see in the diagram many crossings between lines. Most objects are placed casually in the area of the schema, and it is difficult to identify the group of entities related by generalization hierarchy. The schema, in a few words, has a "spaghetti style."

Following the aesthetic rules described above, we may completely restructure the diagram, leading to the new diagram shown in Figure 2.17. Here, most relevant concepts have a larger dimension, there are no bends in lines, and the generalization hierarchy is more apparent.

The second issue addressed by readability is the simplicity of schema representation. Among the different conceptual schemas that equivalently represent a certain reality, we prefer the one or the ones that are more compact, because compactness favors readability. As an example, in the left hand side of Figure 2.18, we see a schema where the represented entity City is related to the three children entities in the generalization hierarchy. Due to the inheritance property [66], which states that all concepts related to the parent entity are also related to all the children entities, we can drop the three occurrences of relationships involving the entity City and change them into a single relationship with the entity Employee, resulting in a more compact and readable schema.

2.7.2 Normalization

The property of *normalization* has been deeply investigated, especially in the relational model, although it expresses a model-independent, general property of schemas.

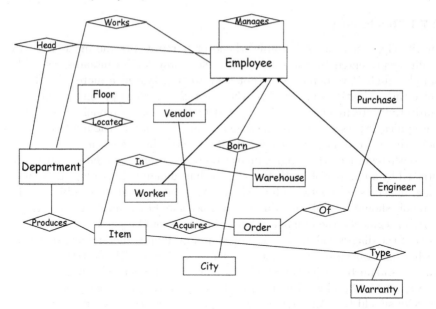

Fig. 2.16. "Spaghetti style" Entity Relationship schema

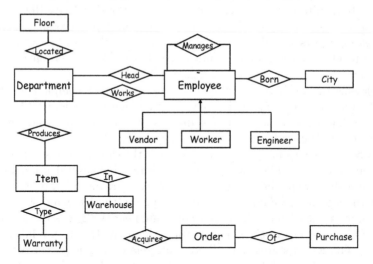

Fig. 2.17. An equivalent readable schema

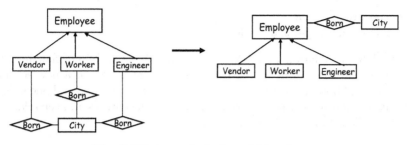

Fig. 2.18. An equivalent readable schema

In the relational model, normalization is strictly related to the structure of functional dependencies. Several degrees of normalization have been defined in the relational model, such as first, second, third, Boyce Codd, fourth, and other normal forms. The most popular and intuitive normal form is the *Boyce Codd normal form* (BCNF). A relation schema R is in BCNF if for every non trivial functional dependency X -> Y defined on R, X contains a key K of R, i.e., X is a superkey of R. For more details on the BCNF and other normal forms, see [11] and [66].

To exemplify, a relational schema R is in BCNF if all nontrivial functional dependencies have a key in the left hand side of the dependency, so, all non key attributes depend on a unique key. The interpretation of this property is that the relational schema represents a unique concept, with which all nontrivial functional dependencies are homogeneously associated, and whose properties are represented by all non-key attributes.

As already mentioned, normalization is a property that can be defined in every conceptual or logical model; as an example of normalization not applied to the relational model, Figure 2.19 shows an unnormalized schema in the Entity Relationship model. It is made of a unique entity Employee-Project, with five attributes; two of them, the underlined ones, define the identifier of the entity. Following [20], we can define the concept of normalized ER schema

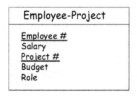

Fig. 2.19. An unnormalized Entity Relationship schema

by associating the functional dependencies defined among the attributes of the entity, and adapting the above definition of BCNF to the entities and the relationships. We define the following functional dependencies in the schema:

- EmployeeId → Salary

- `ProjectId` $\rightarrow$ `Budget`
- `EmployeeId,ProjectId` $\rightarrow$ `Role`

that lead to a violation of BCNF. With the objective of normalizing the schema, we can transform the entity `Employee-Project` into a new schema (see Figure 2.20) made of two entities, `Employee` and `Project`, and one many-to-many relationship defined between them. Now the entities and the relationship are in BCNF, as is the whole schema.

Fig. 2.20. A normalized schema

2.8 Summary

In this chapter we have seen a variety of dimensions and metrics that characterize the concept of data quality. These dimensions provide a reference framework to those organizations interested in the quality of data, and allow them to characterize and to some extent measure the quality of data sets. Furthermore, fixing and measuring data quality dimensions allow comparison with reference thresholds and values that may be considered target quality values to be achieved in the organization. As a consequence, quality dimensions are at the basis of any process of measurement and improvement of data quality in an organization. As an example, in contracts related to sale of data, the issue of quality of service is crucial, expressing precisely and unambiguously the demand for quality data. Finally, dimensions may be mentioned in laws and rules concerning data usage in government for citizen/business relationships.

It is not surprising that there are many dimensions, since data aim to represent all kinds of spatial, temporal, and social phenomena of the real world; furthermore, in databases, data are represented at two different levels, the intension and the extension, and, consequently, different dimensions have to be conceived. Moreover, we have seen that dimensions may be domain independent, i.e., of general application, or else domain dependent, referring to phenomena characteristic of specific domains. As long as, on one end, ICT technologies evolve, and, on the other end they are applied increasingly to new sciences and applications of the real world, data quality dimensions will evolve and new dimensions will arise. The concept of data is rapidly evolving, from structured data typical of relational databases, to semistructured data, unstructured data, documents, images, sounds, and maps resulting in a continuous change of the concept of data quality.

Due to the above evolutive phenomena, and the relative immaturity of the data quality research area, another issue that is not surprising, and that is significant in the area, is the absence of enforced de facto standards enacted by international organizations on classifications and definitions of data dimensions and metrics.

Dimensions are the core of any investigation in data quality, and they will be used throughout in the rest of the book.

3

Models for Data Quality

3.1 Introduction

In Chapter 2 we introduced several dimensions which are useful to describe and measure data quality in its different aspects and meanings. In order to use database management systems (DBMSs) we represent data, and the relative operations on it, in terms of a *data model* and a *data definition and manipulation language*, i.e., a set of structures and commands that can be represented, interpreted, and executed by a computer. We could follow the same process to represent, besides data, their quality dimensions. This means that in order to represent data quality, we have to extend data models.

Models are widely used in databases for various purposes, such as analyzing a set of requirements and representing it in terms of a conceptual description, called *conceptual schema*; such a description is translated into a *logical schema*; queries and transactions are expressed on such a logical schema.

Models are also used in the wider area of information systems to represent business processes of organizations in terms of subprocesses, their inputs and outputs, causal relationships between them, and functional/non-functional requirements related to processes. Such models are needed in order to help the analyst, e.g., to analyse and foresee process behaviour, measure performance, and design possible improvements.

In this chapter we investigate the principal extensions of traditional models for databases and information systems, proposed to deal with data quality dimensions issues. In Section 3.2 we investigate proposed extensions of conceptual and logical database models for structured data typical of relational DBMSs. Logical models are considered both from the perspective of data description models, and as related to data manipulation and data provenance. Then we discuss models for semistructured data, with specific attention to XML schemas (Section 3.3). In Section 3.4 we move on to management information system models; here, we investigate two "orthogonal" issues: (i) extensions of models for process descriptions to issues related to sources, users involved in data checks, etc., and (ii) proposals for joint representation of elementary and aggregated data and related qualities. In all the models that we are going to describe, we will see that the extensions of models to data quality issues lead to structures characterized by high complexity.

3.2 Extensions of Structured Data Models

The principal database models are the Entity Relationship model, the most common for conceptual database design (see [20]), and the relational model, adopted by a wide range of database management systems.

3.2.1 Conceptual Models

Several solutions exist for extending the Entity Relationship model with quality characteristics (see [184] and [183]). The different proposals focus on *attributes*, the unique representation structure in the model with which data values may be associated. A possibility is to model the quality of attribute values as another attribute of the same entity. For example, if we want to express a dimension (e.g., accuracy or completeness) for the attribute Address of an entity Person, we may add (see Figure 3.1) a new attribute AddressQualityDimension to the entity.

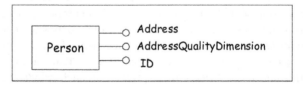

Fig. 3.1. A first example of quality dimension represented in the Entity Relationship Model

The drawback of this solution is that now the entity is no longer normalized, since the attribute AddressQualityDimension is dependent upon Address, which is dependent upon Id. Another problem is that if we want to define several dimensions for an attribute, we have to define a new attribute for each dimension, resulting in a proliferation of attributes.

A second possibility is to introduce two types of entities, explicitly defined for expressing quality dimensions and their values: a data quality dimension entity and a data quality measure entity.

The goal of the DataQualityDimension entity is to represent all possible pairs of dimensions and corresponding ratings; the pairs <DimensionName, Rating> constitute the set of dimensions and possible corresponding values resulting from measurements. In the previous definition, we have implicitly assumed that the scale of rating is the same for all attributes. If the scale depends on the attribute, then we have to extend the properties of the DataQualityDimension entity to <Dimension-Name, Attribute, Rating>.

In order to represent metrics for dimensions, and its relationship with entities, attributes, and dimensions, we have to adopt a more complex structure than the one shown in Figure 3.2, in which we introduce the DataQualityMeasure entity; its attributes are Rating, in which the values depend on the specific dimension modeled, and DescriptionofRating. The complete *data quality schema*, which we show by means of the example in Figure 3.2, is made up of

1. The original *data schema*, made in the example of the entity Class with all its attributes (here, we represent only the attribute Attendance).
2. The DQ Dimension entity with a pair of attributes <DimensionName, Rating>.
3. The relationship between the entity Class, the related attribute Attendance, and the DQ Dimension entity with a many-to-many relationship ClassAttendanceHas; a distinct relationship has to be introduced for each attribute of the entity Class.
4. The relationship between the previous structure and the DQ Measure entity with a new representation structure that extends the Entity Relationship model, and relates entities and relationships.

The overall structure adopted in Figure 3.2 has been proposed in [184].

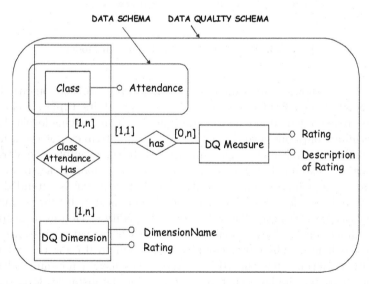

Fig. 3.2. A first example of quality dimension represented in the Entity Relationship Model

The above example shows how complex a schema becomes extended with the above structures to describe qualities.

3.2.2 Logical Models for Data Description

[204] and [206] extend the relational model with quality values associated with each attribute value, resulting in the *quality attribute model*. We explain the model with an example, shown in Figure 3.3.

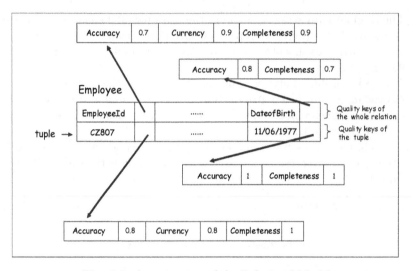

Fig. 3.3. An extension of the Relational Model

The figure shows a relational schema `Employee`, defined on attributes `EmployeeId`, `DateofBirth`, and others, and one of its tuples. Relational schemas are extended adding an arbitrary number of underlying levels of *quality indicators* (only one level in the figure) to the attributes of the schema, to which they are linked through a quality key. In the example, the attribute `EmployeeId` is extended with three quality attributes, namely accuracy, currency, and completeness, while the attribute `DateofBirth` is extended with accuracy and completeness, since currency is not meaningful for permanent data such as `DateofBirth`. The values of such quality attributes measure the quality dimensions' values associated with the whole relation instance (top part of the figure). Therefore, completeness equal to 0.7 for the attribute `DateofBirth` means that the 70 % of the tuples have a non-null value for such an attribute. Similar structures are used for the instances level quality indicator relations (bottom part of the figure); if there are n attributes of the relational schema, n quality tuples will be associated to each tuple in the instance.

3.2.3 The Polygen Model for Data Manipulation

In principle, in every process of data collection and analysis, such as medical or biological experiments, data originating from different sources are manipulated in different stages; new data produced at each stage inherit the quality of ancestor data according to histories that depend on the execution plan. In Chapter 4, for several quality dimensions and relational algebra operations, we will investigate the functional relationships between the quality values of the input data and the quality values of the output data. In this section we investigate an extension of the relational model, called *Polygen model* ([202] and [206]), proposed for explicitly tracing the origins of data and the intermediate sources. The model is targeted to heterogeneous distributed systems; the name of the model is derived from "multiple" "sources" (respectively, "poly" and "gen" in Greek). Now we briefly discuss the model, relevant for its pioneer role in the area. A *polygen domain* is a set of ordered triples:

1. a datum drawn from a simple domain in a schema of a local database;
2. a set of *originating databases* denoting the local databases from which the datum originates; and
3. a set of *intermediate databases* in which the data led to the selection of the datum.

A *polygen relation* is a finite set of time varying tuples, each tuple having the same set of attribute values from the corresponding polygen domains. A *polygen algebra* is a set of relational algebra operators whose semantics allows annotation propagation. The five primitive operators in the model are project, cartesian product, restrict, union, and difference. More precisely:

1. *project, cartesian product, union*, and *difference* are extended from the relational algebra. The difference operator over two Polygen relations r_1 and r_2 is extended as follows (for the remaining operators see [202] and [206]). A tuple t in r_1 is selected if the data part of t is not identical to those of the tuples of r_2. Since each tuple in r_1 has to be compared with all the tuples in r_2, it follows that all the originating sources of the data in r_1 are to be included in the intermediate source set produced by the difference operator.
2. The *restrict* operator is introduced to select tuples in a polygen relation that satisfy a given condition, and such tuples populate intermediate sources.
3. *Select* and *join* are defined in terms of the restrict operator, so they also involve intermediate sources.
4. New operators are introduced, e.g. *coalesce*, which takes two columns as input and merges them into one column (no inconsistency is admitted).

Note that in general in heterogeneous multidatabase systems, the values coalesced may be inconsistent. This issue is not considered in the Polygen approach; it will be discussed in detail in Section 6.4.3 dedicated to instance-level conflict resolution techniques.

3.2.4 Data Provenance

The Polygen model is a first attempt to represent and analyze the provenance of data, which has been recently investigated in a more general context. *Data provenance* is defined in [36] as the "description of the origins of a piece of data and the process by which it arrived in the database." The typical mechanism to trace the provenance is the use of *annotations* that can be exploited to represent a wide spectrum of information about data, such as comments or other types of metadata, and, in particular, data representing the quality of data. Annotations can be used in a variety of situations including

1. systematically trace the provenance and flow of data, namely even if the data has undergone a complex process of transformation steps, we can determine the origins by examining the annotations;
2. describe information about data that would otherwise have been lost in the database, e.g. an error report about a piece of data;
3. enable the user to interpret the data semantics more accurately, and to resolve potential conflicts among the data retrieved from different sources. This capability is useful in the field of data integration (see Chapter 6), where we are interested in understanding how data in different databases with heterogeneous semantics and different quality levels can be integrated;
4. filter the data retrieved from a database according to quality requirements;
5. improve the management of data trustworthiness through annotations referring to the reputation of a source or to a certification procedure.

Two types of provenance are defined in the literature, *why provenance* and *where provenance* (see [49], [36], and [47] as the main references in this area). We introduce them by means of an example. Assume we issue the following query:

```
SELECT StudentId, LastName, Sex
FROM Student
WHERE Age > SELECT AVERAGE Age FROM Student
```

over the relational schema Student (StudentId, LastName, Sex, Age).

If the output is the tuple <03214, Ngambo, Female>, the provenance of the tuple can be related to two distinct data items:

1. The set of tuples in the input relation that contributed to the final result. In this case, all the tuples have to be selected as contributing tuples, since any modification in one tuple may affect the presence of <03214, Ngambo, Female> in the result. This kind of provenance is called *why provenance*, since we are looking for the tuples that explain the shape of the output.

2. The tuple(s) in the input relation that originated the values 03214, Ngambo, and Female in the output tuple. In this case, the set is made up of the unique tuple with StudentId = 03214. This kind of provenance is called *where provenance*, since in this case we are interested in finding from where annotations are propagated. In the case of a join between two tuples, both would be considered part of the input set.

The where provenance is particularly useful in the data quality context. In the case where annotations represent quality values, control of the process of quality dimension propagation is allowed by identifying the sources that are responsible for quality degradation. For the above reasons, in the following we focus on the where provenance.

We will discuss the concept of the where provenance and its different meanings in the following context: given a relational database D, with a set of annotations associated with tuples in D, and a query Q over D, compute the provenance of an output tuple t in the result of Q.

If we think of possible meanings, i.e., methods to compute the where provenance (similar considerations can be made for the why provenance), two different approaches exist: the *reverse query* (or lazy) approach and the *forward propagation* (or eager) approach.

In the *reverse query approach* (see [49]) and [36]), a "reverse" query Q' is generated in which the result is the tuple or set of tuples that contribute, when Q has been executed, in producing it.

In the *forward propagation approach*, when applying Q, an enriched query Q* is generated and executed that computes how annotations are propagated in the result of Q. The approach is called *eager*, since provenance is immediately made available, together with the output of Q. The forward propagation approach, in turn, has three possible types of execution or *propagation schemes* [47], called the *default scheme*, the *default-all scheme*, and the *custom propagation scheme*. We introduce the three schemes by means of an example. Assume (see Figure 3.4) we have a database of clients made up of two different tables, Client1 and Client2 and a mapping table between identifiers of clients in Client1 and Client2, (a typical situation in many organizations).

Intuitively, the default propagation scheme propagates annotations of data according to where data is copied from. Assume that the following query Q_1 is computed on the database of Figure 3.4:

```
SELECT DISTINCT c.Id, c.Description
FROM Client1 c
WHERE c.Id = 071
```

The result of Q_1 executed against the relation Client1 in the default propagation scheme is the unique tuple

$$< 071[ann_1]; Cded[ann_2] >$$

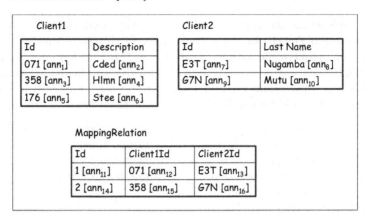

Fig. 3.4. Two `Client` relations and a mapping relation

The semantics of the default scheme is quite natural, but it has a drawback, in that two equivalent queries (i.e., queries that return the same output for every database) may not propagate the same annotations to the output. Consider the two queries, Q_2:

```
SELECT DISTINCT c2.Id AS Id, c2.LastName AS LastName
FROM Client2 c2, MappingRelation m
WHERE c2.Id = m.Client2Id
```

and Q_3:

```
SELECT DISTINCT m.Id AS Id,  c2.LastName AS LastName
FROM Client2 c2 , MappingRelation m
WHERE c2.Id = m.Client2Id
```

The results of running Q_2 and Q_3 under the default propagation scheme are shown in Figure 3.5. For Q_2 the annotations for the `Id` attribute are from the `Client2` relation while for Q_3 the annotations for the `Id` attribute are from the `MappingRelation`.

The *default scheme* propagates the annotation for equivalent queries differently. We need a second propagation scheme, where propagations are invariant under equivalent queries. This scheme is called the *default-all propagation scheme* in [47]; it propagates annotations according to where data is copied from among all equivalent formulations of the given query. In case a user wants to bear the responsibility to specify how annotations should propagate, a third scheme can be adopted, the *custom scheme*, where annotation propagations are explicitly declared in the query.

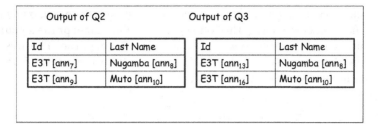

Fig. 3.5. The output of two queries

The above schemes can be applied flexibly, whatever the type of the annotated information, i.e., it could be the source relation, the exact location within the source, or a comment on the data.

3.3 Extensions of Semistructured Data Models

In [175], a model for associating quality values to data-oriented XML documents is proposed. The model, called *Data and Data Quality* (D^2Q), is intended to be used in the context of a cooperative information system (CIS). In such systems, the cooperating organizations need to exchange data each other, and it is therefore critical for them to be aware of the quality of such data. D^2Q can be used in order to certify the accuracy, consistency, completeness, and currency of data. The model is semistructured, thus allowing each organization to export the quality of its data with a certain degree of flexibility. More specifically, quality dimension values can be associated with various elements of the data model, ranging from the single data value to the whole data source. The main features of the D^2Q model are summarized as follows:

- A *data class* and a *data schema* are introduced to represent the *domain* data portion of the D^2Q model, namely, the data values that are specific to a given cooperating organization's domain.
- A *quality class* and a *quality schema* correspond to the quality portion of the D^2Q model.
- A *quality association function* that relates nodes of the graph corresponding to the data schema to nodes of the graph corresponding to the quality schema. Quality associations represent biunivocal functions among all nodes of a data schema and all non-leaf nodes of a quality schema.

In Figure 3.6, an example of a D^2Q schema is shown. On the left-hand side of the figure, a data schema is shown representing enterprises and their owners. On the right-hand side, the associated quality schema is represented. Specifically, two quality classes, `Enterprise_Quality` and `Owner_Quality` are associated with the `Enterprise` and `Owner` data classes. Accuracy nodes are shown for both data classes and related properties. For instance, `Code_accuracy` is an accuracy node associated with the `Code` property, while `Enterprise_accuracy` is an accuracy node associated with the data class `Enterprise`. The arcs connecting the data schema and the quality schema with the `quality labels` represent the quality association functions.

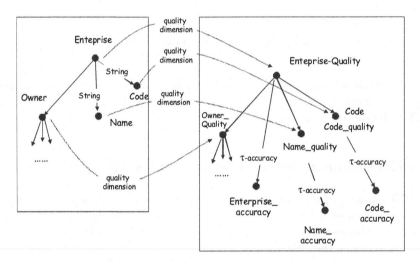

Fig. 3.6. Example of D^2Q quality schema

The D^2Q model is intended to be easily translated into the XML data model. This is important for meeting the interoperability requirements that are particularly stringent in cooperative systems. Once translated into XML, the model can be queried by means of an extension of the XQuery language that queries quality values in the model. XQuery allows users to define new functions. Quality values represented according to the D^2Q model can be accessed by a set of XQuery functions, called *quality selectors*. Quality selectors are defined for accuracy, completeness, consistency, currency and for the overall set of quality values that can be associated with a data node.

In Figure 3.7, the implementation of the quality selector *accuracy*() is shown as an example. `Searchroot` is a function defined to reach the root of a document containing the input node.

```
define function accuracy($n as node*) as node* {
let $root := searchroot($n), qualitydoc:=document(string($root/@qualityfile))
for $q in $n/@quality
for $r in $qualitydoc//*[@qOID eq $q]/accuracy
return $r }
```

Fig. 3.7. Accuracy selector implementation as an XQuery function

The D^2Q model represents quality values to be associated with generic data. XML is used as a language for modeling quality dimensions in a growing number of contributions. For example, see in [126] a proposal for modeling quality of data by means of six quality measures meaningful in the biological domain. Being domain specific, such a proposal also includes metrics that allow the computation of node quality values across the XML graph, by considering the interdependencies between quality values of the various nodes in the graph.

3.4 Management Information System Models

In this section we discuss management information system models in their relation to data quality issues. We discuss process models in Sections 3.4.1 and Section 3.4.2, introducing the IP-MAP model and its extensions. Issues related to data models are discussed in Section 3.4.3.

3.4.1 Models for Process Description: the IP-MAP model

The Information Production Map (IP-MAP) model [177] is based on the principle that data can be seen as a particular product of a manufacturing activity, and so descriptive models (and methodologies) for data quality can be based on models conceived in the last two centuries for manufacturing traditional products. The IP-MAP model is centered on the concept of *information product (IP)*, introduced in Chapter 1.

An *information production map* is a graphical model designed to help people comprehend, evaluate, and describe how an information product such as an invoice, customer order, or prescription is assembled in a business process. The IP-MAP is aimed at creating a systematic representation for capturing the details associated with the manufacturing of an information product. IP-MAPs are designed to help analysts to visualize the information production process, identify ownership of process phases, understand information and organizational boundaries, and estimate time and quality metrics associated with the current production process. There are eight types of construct blocks that can be used to form the IP-MAP. Each construct block is identified by a unique name and is further described by a set of attributes (metadata). The content of metadata varies depending on the type of construct block. In Figure 3.8, the possible types of construct blocks are shown, together with the symbol used for their representation.

An example of information production map is shown in Figure 3.9. Information products (IP in the figure) are produced by means of processing activities and data quality checks on *raw data* (RD), and semi-processed information or *component data* (CD), introduced in Chapter 2. In the example, we assume that high schools and universities of a district have decided to cooperate in order to improve their course offering to students, avoiding

Concept name	Symbol	Description
Source (raw input data)		Represents the source of each raw (input) data that must be available in order to produce the information product expeceted by the customer
Customer (output)		Represents the consumer of the information product. The consumer specifies the data elements that constitute the "finished" information products.
Data quality		Represents the checks for data quality on those data items that are essential in producing a "defect-free" information product.
Processing		Represents any calculations involving some or all of the raw input data items or component data items required to ultimately produce the information block.
Data Storage		It is any data item in a database.
Decision		It used to describe the different decision conditions t obe avaluated and the corresponding procedures for handling the incoming data items,based on the evaluation.
Business Boundary		Specifies the movement of the information product accross departmental or organization boundaries.
Information system boundary		Reflects the changes to the raw data items or component data items as they move form one information system to another type of information system. These system changes could be inter or intra business units.

Fig. 3.8. IP-MAP construct blocks

overlappings and being more effective in the education value chain. To this end, high schools and universities have to share historical data on students and their curricula. Therefore, they perform a record linkage activity that matches students in their education life cycle. To reach this objective, high schools periodically supply relevant information on students; in case it is in paper format, the information has to be converted in electronic format. At this point invalid data are filtered and matched with the database of university students. Unmatched students are sent back to high schools for clerical checks, and matched students are analyzed; the result of the analysis on curricula and course topics are sent to the advisory panel of the universities.

3.4.2 Extensions of IP-MAP

The IP-MAP model has been extended in several directions. First, more powerful mechanisms have been provided in [160] and [174], called *event process chain diagrams* representing the *business process overview*, the *interaction model* (how company units interact), the *organization model* (who does what), the *component model* (what happens), and the *data model* (what data is needed). This is done by modeling

- the event that triggers the use of data by a process;
- the communication structure between sources, consumers, and organizational groups;

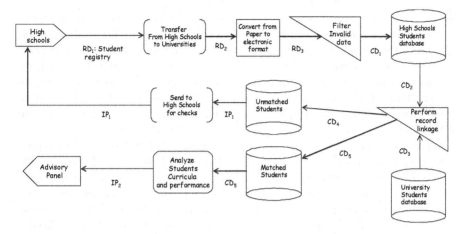

Fig. 3.9. An example of IPMAP

- the hierarchy of organizational groups/functions;
- the relationship between products, storages, and other data components;
- logical relationships between events and processes.

A modeling formalism is proposed in [174], called IP-UML, extending UML with a data quality profile based on IP-MAP. The use of UML instead of the IP-MAP formalism has the following advantages:

1. UML is a standard language, and computer-aided tools have been implemented for it;
2. UML is a language supportive of analysis, design, and implementation artifacts, so the same language can be used in all the phases of analysis and development;
3. the expressive power of UML is higher with reference to the process modelling constructs.

We briefly recall that in UML (see [150], and [79]) the specification of analysis and design elements is based on the notion of a *model element*, defined as an abstraction drawn from the system being modeled; the principal model elements are *classes* and *relationships* between classes. A *constraint* is a semantic restriction that can be attached to a model element. A *tag definition* specifies new kinds of properties that may be attached to model elements. A *tagged value* specifies the actual values of tags of individual model elements. A *stereotype* is a new model element that extends previously defined model elements through a precise semantics. According to the UML specification [148] "a coherent set of such extensions, defined for a specific purpose, constitutes a *UML profile*."

The starting concepts of IP-UML are the ones defined in the IP-MAP framework; the result of the proposed extension is a UML profile called data quality profile. The *data quality profile* consists of three different models, namely, the data analysis model, the quality analysis model and the quality design model.

The *data analysis model* specifies which data are important for consumers, as its quality is critical for the organization's success. In the data analysis model information products, raw data and component data are represented as a stereotyped UML class. A *quality data class* is a class labeled with this a that generalizes Information product classes, Raw data classes, and Component data classes.

The *quality analysis model* consists of modeling elements that can represent quality requirements of data, related to one of the dimensions typically defined for data quality. The set of dimensions proposed consists of four categories; for example the *intrinsic information quality category* includes accuracy, objectivity, believability, and reputation. In order to model the overall set of dimension-related requirements, the following stereotypes are introduced:

1. A *quality requirement* class generalizes the set of quality requirements that can be specified on a quality data class.
2. A *quality association* class associates a quality requirement class with a quality data class. Quality requirements on data need to be verified so that, if they are not satisfied, improvement actions can be taken; therefore, a constraint is specifically introduced on the quality association.

The specification of a distinct stereotype for each quality requirement has the advantage of clearly fixing the types of requirements that can be associated with data.

The *quality design model* specifies IP-MAPs. The IP-MAP dynamic perspective, in which processes are described together with exchanged data, can be obtained by combining *UML activity diagrams* with *UML object flow diagrams*. Activity diagrams are a special case of state diagrams in which the states are action or subactivity states and in which the transitions are triggered by completion of the actions or subactivities in the source states. Object flows are diagrams in which objects that are input or output from an action may be shown as object symbols. The following UML extensions need to be introduced, to represent IP-MAP elements:

- *stereotyped activities*, to represent processing and data quality blocks;
- *stereotyped actor*, to represent customer, source, and data storage blocks;
- *stereotyped dependency relationships*, to give a precise semantics to the relationships between some elements.

Notwithstanding the rich set of new structures introduced in the extensions of IP-MAP, such extensions suffer from different limitations, discussed in the next section, with new models that attempt to override such limitations.

3.4.3 Data Models

A first limitation of IP-MAP (and IP-MAP extensions) lies in the fact that it does not distinguish between or provide specific formalisms for *operational processes*, which make use of *elementary data*, and *decisional processes*, which use *aggregated data*. The information system of an organization is composed of both types of data, that present different quality problems. So, it seems relevant to enrich data models for management information systems to explicitly provide a uniform formalism to represent both types of data and their quality dimensions.

Secondly, IP-MAP does not take specific features of cooperative information systems (CIS) into account. In a CIS, as Figure 3.10 shows, an organization can be modeled as a collection of processes that transform input information flows into output information flows, and that carry a stream of information products. In Figure 3.10, three organizations are represented that exchange four information flows: two of them are composed of two information products each; the two remaining flows exchange one single information product. In the domain of a specific organization, an input flow to a process can be transformed into (i) an internal flow, (ii) an input to another intra-organizational process, or (iii) an output flow to one or more external organizations.

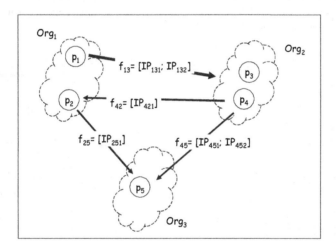

Fig. 3.10. Organizations, processes, and information flows in a Cooperative Information System

In [131], [130], and [132], a comprehensive approach to overcome the above limitations is presented, discussed in the following sections.

A Data Model of the Information Flows of an Organization

We first distinguish two different roles for organizations exchanging information flows in a CIS, namely, a *producer (organization)* when it produces flows for other organizations, and a *consumer (organization)* when it receives flows from other organizations. Every organization usually plays both roles. Following traditional manufacturing practice, we characterize the quality of the individual items produced on the producer side; by extension, we associate a *quality offer profile* to a producer organization. Such a profile represents the quality that the organization is willing to offer to its customers, i.e., to other consumer organizations that require that information for use in a cooperative process. Symmetrically, on the consumer side we define the notion of *quality demand profile* to express acceptable quality levels for the information items that consumers will acquire. Ultimately, we frame the problem of managing information quality within an organization as the problem of matching the quality profile offered by that organization to the quality requested by the consumers of the organization. At this point, we are able to define a framework for expressing quality offer and demand in a CIS context. The framework models both the structure of a cooperative organization (*data schema*) and its quality profiles (*quality schema*, see next section) in a uniform, hierarchical way.

We start by associating quality profiles with the elementary information items that the organization produces and consumes during the execution of processes (see Figure 3.11 for the metaschema of the data schema, represented with a class diagram in UML).

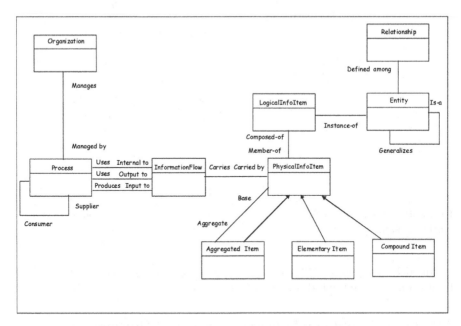

Fig. 3.11. Data, process, and organization schema

An *information flow* f is a sequence of *physical information items* (PII), that are streamed from a producer process to one or more consumer processes. For instance, given a domain entity `Address`, and its instance 4 `Heroes` `Street` (suitably identified using keys defined for `Address`), a PII would be a specific copy of J. Smith's address, produced at a particular time t by a process p_1 and sent to a process p_2 over flow f. All PIIs produced by any process at any time, referring to the same data, homogeneous in meaning, are associated with a single *logical information item* 4 `Heroes` `Street`.

Physical information items and logical information items describe *atomic* (or *elementary*) information items and their flow in time. As the metaschema in Figure 3.11 shows, a *compound item* is obtained recursively from other compound or elementary items using composition functions, such as the record type function (e.g. an `Address` is composed of `Street`, `City`, and `ZipCode`). An *aggregated item* is obtained from a collection of elementary and compound items by applying an aggregation function to them (e.g., the average income of tax payers in a given town).

With the above representation structures we are able to model both information flows made of elementary items and flows made of aggregated items. Finally, we associate information flows between processes, and processes with organizations. Information flows are of three types: input to, output from, and internal to processes. We enrich the set of representation structures with other structures, typical of a conceptual model, such as *entity*, *relationship* among entities, and *generalization* among entities, as done in the schema in Figure 3.11, with usual meanings in the Entity Relationship model.

A Quality Profile Model

In order to represent and compute quality profiles, associated with all the classes in the previous schema, we model the quality profile of an organization as a *data cube* on a given set of dimensions, using the *multidimensional database model* proposed in [3]. We view the quality profile of a single item as one point in a *multidimensional cube*, in which the axes include a hierarchy of entities consisting of physical and logical information items, flows, processes, organizations, and quality dimensions.

The information carried by each quality point in the resulting *quality cube* is the single quality measurement at the finest level of granularity, i.e., the quality descriptor associated with a single physical data item and for a single dimension. Figure 3.12 shows the *star schema*, in the data warehouse approach; it has the quality values as fact entity, and the remaining ones as the dimension entities; attributes of fact and dimension entities are not shown.

The quality profiles for information flows, processes, and entire organizations are computed as appropriate aggregations from a base quality cube. Thus, once an appropriate set of *aggregation functions* (e.g., average) is defined over quality descriptors, quality profiles at each level of granularity in an organization are described within an established framework for multidimensional data. As an example, consider again Figure 3.10, where two organizations, five processes and four flows are defined. We may aggregate quality

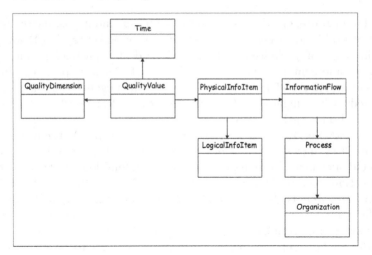

Fig. 3.12. Star schema of the data quality cube

values along the following chain: (i) physical information item, (ii) information flow, (iii) process, (iv) organization; and, using aggregation functions, we
may associate quality values with each one of the above information flows,
processes, and organizations, according to the perspective we choose.

3.5 Summary

In this chapter we have seen several proposals for extending data and process
models, to provide them with structures for representing quality dimensions
and for using them to measure and improve data quality profiles of single
information flows, processes, and entire organizations. In the following chapters we will address the core topics of research in and experience with data
quality, i.e., techniques and methodologies proposed for DQ measurement and
improvement. We anticipate that such techniques and methodologies seldom
rely on the proposals presented in this chapter on model extensions, with
the distinctive exception of the IP-MAP model. Furthermore, only a few pro-
totypical DBMSs have experienced the adoption of some of the approaches
mentioned, among them [6]. This feeble connection is due to the complexity of
the overall equipment of the representational structures proposed in the different approaches, and the lack of consolidated tools and DBMSs to manage
them.

The future of research on models appears to be in provenance and trustworthiness issues. In cooperative information systems, and peer-to-peer information systems, knowing the provenance and the trustworthiness of data is
crucial for the user, who may trace the history of data and increase his or her
awareness in accessing and using them.

4

Activities and Techniques for Data Quality: Generalities

In Chapter 1 we noticed that data quality is a multifaceted concept, and the cleaning of poor quality data can be performed by measuring different dimensions and setting out on several different activities, with different goals. A *data quality activity* is any process we perform directly on data to improve their quality. An example of "manual" data quality activity is the process we perform when we send an e-mail message, and the e-mail bounces back because of an unknown user; we check the exact address in a reliable source, and we type the address on the keyboard more carefully to avoid further mistakes. An example of "computerized" data quality activity is the matching of two files in which inaccurate records are included, in order to find similar records that correspond to the same real-world entity through an approximate method. Other activities for improving data quality act on processes; they will be discussed and compared with data quality activities in Chapter 7.

Data quality activities are performed using different techniques that result in different efficiency and effectiveness for measuring and improving data quality dimensions. The final goal of this chapter, and of Chapters 5 and 6, is to define the data quality activities and introduce the most relevant techniques proposed to support each of them. In this chapter we first define the activities (Section 4.1) and provide the reader a map of the book sections where the different activities are dealt with. The two most investigated data quality activities, namely object identification and data integration, will be discussed in Chapter 5 and Chapter 6. In this chapter we discuss two of the activities, namely, quality composition (Section 4.2), and error localization and correction (Section 4.3). The final section (Section 4.4) opens the discussion on costs and benefits of data quality, introducing and comparing proposed classifications for costs/benefits; this material will be applied in Chapter 7 on methodologies.

4.1 Data Quality Activities

Although a large quantity of algorithms, heuristics, and knowledge-based techniques have been proposed that are classified as *data quality activities*, a limited number of categories can be identified. They are listed in the following, providing temporary definitions that will be detailed later in this chapter, as well as in Chapters 5 and 6:

1. *New data acquisition* is a process of data acquisition performed with the goal of refreshing the database with new quality data. The manual example discussed above falls in this category.
2. *Standardization* (or *normalization*) is the modification of data with new data according to defined standard or reference formats, e.g., change of Bob to Robert, change of Channel Str. to Channel Street.
3. *Object identification* (or *record linkage, record matching, entity resolution*), given one or more tables, has the purpose of identifying those records in the tables that represent the same real-world object. When the table is unique this activity is also called *deduplication*.
4. *Data integration* is the task of presenting a unified view of data owned by heterogeneous and distributed data sources. Data integration has different goals resulting in two specific activities:
   - *quality-driven query processing* is the task of providing query results on the basis of a quality characterization of data at sources;
   - *instance-level conflict resolution* is the task of identifying and solving conflicts of values referring to the same real-world objects.
5. *Source trustworthiness* has the goal of rating sources on the basis of the quality of data they provide to other sources in an open or peer-to-peer context, where no or little control exists on the quality of data.
6. *Quality composition* defines an algebra for composing data quality dimension values, for instance, given two relations in which the completeness values are known, and an operator, e.g., the union, computes the completeness of the union, starting from the completeness of the operand relations.
7. *Error localization* (or *error detection*), that given one or more tables, and a set of semantic rules specified on them, finds tuples that do not respect such rules.
8. *Error correction*, that, given one or more tables, a set of semantic rules, and a set of identified errors in tuples, corrects erroneous values in tuples in order to respect the overall set of rules.
9. *Cost optimization* has the goal to optimize a given target on data quality, according to a cost objective. For example, among different providers of data sets characterized by different costs and quality dimension metrics, we could be interested in selecting the provider with the optimal cost/quality ratio for a given data demand.

Other activities that more loosely pertain to data quality are

- *Schema matching*, which takes two schemas as input and produces a mapping between semantically correspondent elements of the two schemas.
- *Schema cleaning*, which provides rules for transforming the conceptual schema in order to achieve or optimize a given set of qualities (e.g., readability, normalization) while preserving other properties (e.g., equivalence of content).
- *Profiling* analyzes data in the database in order to infer intensional properties, such as the structure of the database, fields with similar values, join paths, and join sizes.

Since schema matching, schema cleaning, and schema profiling primarily involve data schemas, they will not be considered in the following. Two of the activities, namely, object identification/record linkage and data integration are of crucial importance in current business scenarios, and have been widely investigated from a research and industrial perspective. As already mentioned, two specific chapters are dedicated to them; Chapter 5 will describe object identification and Chapter 6 will describe data integration. In addition,

1. New data acquisition will be dealt with in Chapter 7 in the context of data quality improvement methodologies, where it will be discussed as one of the data driven strategies.
2. Standardization is usually performed as a preprocessing activity in error localization, object identification, and data integration. However, as standardization is mostly included in object identification techniques, we describe in detail in Chapter 5 as one of the steps of object identification.
3. Source trustworthiness is an emerging research issue in open and peer-to-peer systems. When dealing with such systems, trust and data quality become two crucial concepts. We will discuss such issues in Chapter 9, dedicated to open research problems.
4. Cost optimization covers four different aspects: (i) cost trade-offs between quality dimensions, discussed in Chapter 2; (ii) cost and benefit classifications for characterizing data quality in business processes, addressed in Section 4.4.1; (iii) cost/benefit analysis of data quality improvement processes, described in Chapter 7; and (iv) cost-based selection of data sources, illustrated in Chapter 9, in which the cost of data will be one of the parameters that guide the decision process.

In the rest of this chapter, we briefly describe the remaining activities. The following sections deal with quality composition (Section 2), error localization and correction (Section 3), and, finally with cost and benefit classifications (Section 4).

4.2 Quality Composition

In several contexts, including e-Business and e-Government, especially when data is replicated across different sources, it is usual to obtain new data by combining data sets extracted from one or more sources. In these contexts, it is important to be able to calculate a quality dimension or the set of qualities of the new resulting data, starting from the quality dimension values of the original sources, if available. Furthermore, in order to enhance the quality of data, it is often not enough to consider single sources and independently orchestrate improvement actions on them; instead, such actions should be properly complemented by composing data from different sources.

Let us consider a set of public administrations that cooperate with each other in an e-Government scenario, and let us focus on a specific data quality dimension, namely, the completeness dimension. In some countries, in every municipality the following registries are held: (i) a personal data registry for residents and (ii) a separate registry for the civil status of the residents. At the regional level, we may assume that there are local income tax payer registries, while at central level there are usually national social insurance, accident insurance and other registries. These sources usually have different levels of completeness in representing the corresponding reality of interest, and in many administrative processes, these sources are combined. It would be interesting to directly calculate the completeness of the combined result starting from the completeness of the sources, if known, without performing on the result a costly process of quality measurement. This is the goal of the data quality composition activity.

The general problem statement for the definition of the quality composition problem is represented in Figure 4.1. The data source, or the set of data sources, X, described according to a data model M, is processed by a generic composition function F. It is defined on a set of operators $O = [o_1, \ldots, o_k]$ defined in the model M. Also, a function Q_D calculates the value of the quality dimension D for X, i.e., $Q_D(X)$ and the value of D for Y equals F(X), i.e. $Q_D(Y)$. We aim to define the function $Q_D^F(X)$ that calculates $Q_D(Y)$ starting from $Q_D(X)$, instead of calculating such a value directly on Y by applying the function $Q_D(Y)$.

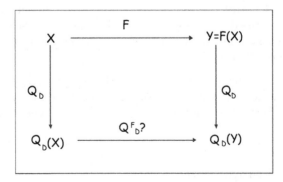

Fig. 4.1. The general problem of quality composition

We will consider the case of this problem in which

- M is the relational model;
- O corresponds to the set of relational algebraic operators, such as Union, Intersection, Cartesian product, Projection, Selection, and Join;
- D is a specific data quality dimension, e.g. completeness or accuracy; and
- Q_D^F is a function that evaluates the quality of the relations under different hypotheses and for different relational operators.

The problem of defining a *composition algebra* for data quality dimensions has been considered in several papers in the literature, namely, Motro and Ragov [136]; Wang et al. [206]; Parsiann et al. [157], [155], [156]; Naumann et al. [140], and Scannapieco and Batini [173]. In Figure 4.2 these approaches are compared on the basis of (i) the adopted model, (ii) the quality dimensions considered, (iii) the relational algebra operators taken into account, and (iv) the specific assumptions on the sources. In the following section we comment all the issues dealt with in Figure 4.2; when describing the approaches, we will use the names of the authors in the first column of the table.

Paper	Model	Specific assumptions on the sources	Quality dimensions considered	Algebraic operators
Motro 1998	Relational model with OWA (implicit)	No assumption	Soundness Completeness	Cartesian Product Selection Projection
Parssiann 2002	Relational model with OWA (implicit)	Uniformely distributed errors in identifier attributes Error probabilites for all attributes independent of each other Uniformly distributed errors in non identifier attributes for mismember and other tuples	Accuracy Inaccuracy Mismembership Incompletness	Selection Projection Cartesian Product Join
Wang 2001	Relational model	Uniformly distributed errors	Accuracy	Selection Projection
Naumann 2004	Data integration system Set of data sources + Universal relation with CWA	Set relationships between sources - Disjointness - Quantified overlap - Independence (coincidential overlap) - Containment	Coverage Density Completeness	Join merge Full outer join merge Left outer join merge Right outer join merge
Scannapieco 2004	Relational model with OWA and CWA	Open world vs closed world assumption Set relationships between sources - Disjointness - Non quantified overlap - Containment	Completeness	Union Intersection Cartesian product

Fig. 4.2. Comparison between approaches to quality composition

We recall that in Chapter 2 we have introduced the concepts of *closed world assumption, open world assumption, reference relation,* and the related dimension definitions of *value completeness*, *tuple completeness*, and *relation completeness*.

4.2.1 Models and Assumptions

Motro and Parssian consider a model in which an ideal (called conceptual by Parssian) relation *r-ideal* and the corresponding real relation *r-real* can be constructively defined; as a consequence, they may distinguish common and non common tuples between them. Motro defines dimensions in terms of the differences between r-ideal and r-real, measured considering, respectively, common tuples and uncommon ones. Parssian goes further, distinguishing, between the two types of tuples, between pairs of tuples that differ in the primary keys (called *identifiers* in the Parssian approach and in the following), and tuples that are identical on the keys and differ on the non key attributes (*non-identifier* attributes in the following). The assumptions dealt with by Parssian on error probabilities both on identifier and non identifier attributes are described in Figure 4.2. Wang is not interested in completeness issues. He does not consider tuples that are in the ideal relation and are not members of the real relation; furthermore, he assumes that the tuples that appear in the real relation are only there by mistake, called *mismember tuples*. Wang, within his simplified model, assumes uniform distribution of errors in the relation.

Naumann, differently from other authors, investigates quality composition in the context of a data integration system. Naumann adopts a model where data sources correspond to local relations and databases. A global source exists, called *universal relation*, that corresponds to the set of all tuples that can be obtained through the sources at hand. Naumann considers four different cases of set relationships between sources: (i) disjointness, (i) containment, (iii) independence, corresponding to coincidental overlap, and (iv) quantified overlap, where the number of common tuples among sources is known. In the following, we will describe the set of operators adopted by Naumann, both in expressing the relationship between the sources and the universal relation, and in the characterization of quality composition. Naumann is interested in evaluating the quality of the process of composing sources, in order to put together information that is split into different sources. For this reason, he is interested in evaluating the behavior of join operators.

The *full outer join merge* operator is defined as a suitable adaptation of the full outer join operator of relational algebra (see [66]) to the context in which conflicts in tuples are taken into account. In the proposed model, it is assumed that tuples of different sources have been identified as corresponding to the same object of the real world. When we merge two tuples t_1 and t_2 referring to the same object, depending on the situations common attributes can have (i) both null values, (ii) t_1 a null value and t_2 a specified value, (iii) the inverse, i.e., t_1 a specified value and t_2 a null value, (iv) the same specified value, and (v) different specified values. In the last case, it is assumed that a *resolution function* is provided. Let us consider two given sources, corresponding to relations r_1 and r_2 The *join merge* operator may be defined as an extension of the join operator by further applying the resolution function. The *full* (and the *left/right*) *outer join merge* operator(s) are defined as an extension of the outer join operators, where join merge is used instead of join. The *universal relation* is defined as the full outer join merge of r_1 and r_2. Within this model, Naumann adopts the closed world assumption, since only tuples in the sources may exist in the universal relation.

Scannapieco adopts both closed world and open world assumptions; in this way, all the types of completeness discussed in Chapter 2 may be defined. Furthermore, in the open world assumption, given two distinct relations r_1 and r_2, two different hypotheses can be made on the reference relations: (i) the two reference relations of r_1 and r_2 are the same, and (ii) the reference relations differ. This is due to the fact that, when composing relations with composition operators such as union or join, we may give (see Figure 4.3) two different interpretations to the operations, according to the following assumptions:

- if the two reference relations are the same (left-hand side of Figure 4.3), incompleteness concerns the lack of objects with sources referring to the same reality of interest; and
- if the two reference relations are different (right-hand side of Figure 4.3), the interpretation of the composition results in the integration of different realities of interest.

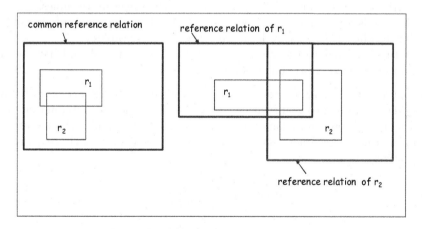

Fig. 4.3. Assumptions for reference relations

In the two previous cases, the evaluation of the resulting completeness has to be different. With reference to set relationships between sources, Scannapieco considers overlap, containment, and a weaker notion of overlap, where the number of common tuples is not known.

4.2.2 Dimensions

In this section we first discuss dimensions comparatively, then we focus on two specific dimensions, namely accuracy and completeness.

In Motro, given an ideal relation `r-ideal` and the corresponding real relation `r-real`, two dimensions are defined:

- *Soundness* measures the proportion of the real data that is true:

$$\frac{|\texttt{r-ideal}| \cap |\texttt{r-real}|}{|\texttt{r-real}|}$$

- *Completeness* measures the proportion of the true data that is stored in the real relation:

$$\frac{|\texttt{r-ideal}| \cap |\texttt{r-real}|}{|\texttt{r-ideal}|}$$

Parssian defines four different dimensions, depending on the pair of tuples considered in the relationship between the ideal relation and the real relation. More precisely

- A tuple in `r-real` is *accurate* if all of its attribute values are accurate, i.e., are identical to the values of a corresponding tuple of `r-ideal`. We call $S_{accurate}$ the set of accurate tuples.
- A tuple is *inaccurate* if it has one or more inaccurate (or null) values for its non-identifier attributes, and no inaccurate values for its identifier attribute (or attributes); $S_{inaccurate}$ is the set of inaccurate tuples.
- A tuple is a *mismember* if it should not have been captured into `r-real`, but has been; $S_{mismember}$ is the set of mismember tuples.
- A tuple belongs to the *incomplete* set $S_{incomplete}$ if it should have been captured into `r-real`, but has not been.

In Figure 4.4 we show an example of (i) an ideal relation `Professor`; (ii) a possible corresponding real relation, with accurate tuples in white, inaccurate tuples in pale gray, and mismember tuples in dark gray; and (iii) a set of incomplete tuples. Accuracy, inaccuracy, mismembership of `r-real` are defined, respectively, as

$$accuracy = \frac{|S_{accurate}|}{|\texttt{r-real}|},$$

$$inaccuracy = \frac{|S_{inaccurate}|}{|\texttt{r-real}|},$$

$$mismembership = \frac{|S_{mismember}|}{|\texttt{r-real}|}.$$

The completeness of **r-real** can be defined as

$$\frac{|S_{incomplete}|}{|\text{r-real}| - |S_{accurate}| + |S_{incomplete}|}$$

since, when considering **r-real**, we have to eliminate mismember tuples and add the set of incomplete tuples.

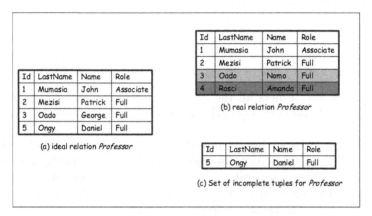

(a) ideal relation *Professor*

(b) real relation *Professor*

(c) Set of incomplete tuples for *Professor*

Fig. 4.4. Examples of accuracy/inaccuracy/mismember tuples and incomplete set in the Parssian approach

Wang, within the concept of accuracy, distinguishes between a *relation accuracy* and a *tuple accuracy*. In the hypothesis of uniform distribution of errors that cause inaccuracy, the tuple accuracy is defined as *probabilistic tuple accuracy*. It coincides numerically with the overall relation accuracy.

In Naumann, completeness is analyzed from three different points of views, corresponding to the coverage, density, and completeness dimensions.

1. The *coverage* of a source **s** captures the number of objects represented in the source **s** with respect to the total number of objects in the universal relation **ur**, and is defined as

$$\frac{|\,\mathbf{s}\,|}{|\,\mathbf{ur}\,|}.$$

2. The *density* of a source captures the number of *values* represented in the source, and is defined as the number of non-null values referred to by the attributes in the universal relation. More formally, we first define the *density of an attribute* **a** of **s** as

$$d(\mathbf{a}) = \frac{|\,(\mathbf{t} \in \mathbf{s} \mid \mathbf{t.a} \neq null)\,|}{|\,\mathbf{s}\,|}.$$

The *density* of the source s is the average density over the set of all attributes A of the universal relation ur:

$$\frac{1}{\mid A \mid} \sum_{a \in A} d(a).$$

3. The *completeness* of a source s captures the number of values represented in the source, with respect to the total potential amount of values of the real world; it is expressed by the formula

$$\frac{\mid (a_{ij} \neq null \mid a_{ij} \in s) \mid}{\mid ur \mid \times \mid A \mid},$$

where a_{ij} is the value of the j_{th} attribute of tuple t_i in s.

Scannapieco considers all the dimensions presented for completeness in Chapter 2, and also other ones (the interested reader can refer to [173]).

In the rest of the section, we provide various results on accuracy and completeness. Due to previously discussed heterogeneity of approaches, we will discuss each proposal separately. Due to the more significant contributions provided, in the following we focus on Wang, Parssian, Naumann, and Scannapieco. We adopt the symbols described in Figure 4.5.

Symbol	Meaning
r	input relation
$r_1, r_2, .., r_n$	a set of n input relations
s	output relation
$\mid r \mid$	size of the relation r
acc	accuracy
inacc	inaccuracy
cov	coverage
compl	completeness

Fig. 4.5. Symbols used in the exposition

4.2.3 Accuracy

Wang provides several results for selection and projection operators. We analyze selection, while for the more complex formulas related to projection, we refer you to [206]. Under the assumption that $\mid s \mid$, the size of the output relation, is available, the following formula easily derives from the hypothesis of uniform distribution of errors:

$$acc(s) = acc(r).$$

Other formulas are provided for the worst and best case scenarios; for instance, for the worst case, if $|r| \leq |s|$, then $\mathtt{acc(s)} = 0$. See [206] for more details.

Results provided by Parssian are richer, due to the the larger set of dimensions defined for the input relations. We provide details for accuracy and inaccuracy in the case of cartesian product and selection operations.

For cartesian product, applied to two relations r_1 and r_2, the following formulas can be simply derived:

$$\mathtt{acc(s)} = \mathtt{acc}(r_1) * \mathtt{acc}(r_2)$$

and

$$\mathtt{inacc(s)} = \mathtt{acc}(r_1) * \mathtt{inacc}(r_2) + \mathtt{acc}(r_2) * \mathtt{inacc}(r_1) + \mathtt{inacc}(r_1) * \mathtt{inacc}(r_2).$$

Concerning the selection operation, four different cases apply according to the structure of the condition in the selection: the selection condition applies to an identifier/non-identifier attribute and the selection is an equality/inequality. We will examine two of them.

In the case where the condition is an inequality applied to an identifier attribute, due to the assumption of uniform distribution of errors, the accuracy, inaccuracy, mismembership, and completeness values for s are identical to the ones for r. This is because the status of the selected tuples remains unchanged.

In the case where the condition is an equality applied to a non-identifier attribute A, tuples are selected or not selected depending on their being accurate or inaccurate in the values of A. To estimate the size of the various components of s, we need to estimate the probability that an accurate/inaccurate/mismember tuple is in one of the parts of r related to non identifier attributes appearing or not appearing in the condition. We call $P(t \in s)$ such probability. The formula for accuracy in this case is intuitively:

$$\mathtt{acc(s)} = \mathtt{acc}(r) * \frac{|r|}{|s|} * P(t \in s)$$

For a formal proof of the previous formula and details on all remaining cases, see [156].

4.2.4 Completeness

In the following we focus on the contributions by Naumann and Scannapieco. First, in the Naumann approach there is a functional relationship between completeness, coverage, and density of a relation r_1, namely,

$$\mathtt{compl}(r_1) = \mathtt{cov}(r_1) * \mathtt{density}(r_1).$$

This relationship results directly from the definitions provided. Naumann characterizes the composition functions, in the case of binary operators on two relations r_1 and r_2, for the three dimensions and all the previously defined operators under the assumptions defined in Section 4.2.1.

In Figure 4.6 we show several cases for the coverage dimension, which we discuss here; for other cases, see [140].

Assumption/ operator	r_1 and r_2 disjoint	Quantified overlapping (= x)	r_1 contained in r_2
Join merge	0	$|x| / |ur|$	cov(r_1)
Left outer join merge	cov(r_1)	cov(r1)	cov(r_1)
Full outer join merge	cov(r_1) + cov(r_2)	cov(r_1) + cov(r_2) − $|x| / |ur|$	cov(r_1)

Fig. 4.6. Coverage composition functions in Naumann

Looking at Figure 4.6, in the case of the join merge, the results of the operator under the different assumptions are, respectively, (i) no object, (ii) only the common objects, and (iii) only the objects of r_1, leading straightforwardly to the formulas. In the case of the left outer join merge, due to the property of the left outer join of maintaining all the tuples of the first source r_1 in the result, the coverage is independent of the assumptions, and is equal to cov(r_1). Similar considerations hold for the full outer join merge case. For all the other cases and properties not mentioned here, we refer to [140].

In the approach of Scannapieco, we consider the two cases of the open world assumption, in which given r_1 and r_2 input relations are defined, respectively, over (i) the same reference relation, or (ii) two different reference relations. Note that we assume to know the sizes of the reference relations themselves, and not the reference relations themselves. We consider the evaluation of completeness for the union operator.

Case 1: Same Reference Relation. We suppose that

$$\mathtt{ref(r_1)= ref(r_2)=ref(s)}.$$

In the case in which no additional knowledge on relations is available, we may only express an upper bound:

$$\mathtt{compl(r)} \geq \max\ (\mathtt{compl(r_1)},\ \mathtt{compl(r_2)}).$$

Behind this inequality, we can distinguish three more cases:

1. disjointness: if $r_1 \cap r_2 = 0$ then $\mathtt{compl(s)} = \mathtt{compl(r_1)} + \mathtt{compl(r_2)}$;
2. non quantified partial overlap: if $r_1 \cap r_2 \neq 0$ then $\mathtt{compl(s)} > \max(\mathtt{compl(r_1)}, \mathtt{compl(r_2)})$; and

Id	LastName	Name	Role
1	Ongy	Daniel	Full
2	Mezisi	Patrick	Full
3	Oado	George	Full
4	Rosci	Amanda	Full

(a) dept1

Id	LastName	Name	Role
1	Mumasia	John	Associate
2	Mezisi	Patrick	Full
3	Oado	George	Full
4	Gidoy	Nomo	Associate
5	Rosci	Amanda	Full

(b) dept2

Id	LastName	Name	Role
1	Mumasia	John	Associate
2	Oymo	Vusi	Associate
3	Msgula	Luyo	Associate
4	Keyse	Frial	Associate

(c) dept3

Id	LastName	Name	Role
1	Ongy	Daniel	Full
2	Oado	George	Full

(d) dept4

Fig. 4.7. Examples of input relations

3. containment: if $r_1 \subset r_2$ then $\mathtt{compl(s)} = \mathtt{compl}(r_2)$.

For example, Figures 4.7a and 4.7b show the two relations dept1 and dept2, each representing professors of a department and having the same reference relation, $\mathtt{ref\text{-}dept} = \mathrm{ref}(\mathtt{dept1}) = \mathrm{ref}(\mathtt{dept2})$, corresponding to all the professors of the department. Notice that dept1 represents only full professors. We have the following input data: (i) $|\mathtt{dept1}| = 4$, (ii) $|\mathtt{dept2}| = 5$, and (iii) $|\mathtt{ref\text{-}dept}| = 8$. Hence, $\mathtt{compl(dept1)} = 0.5$ and $\mathtt{compl(dept2)} = 0.625$. From this information we can derive

$$\mathtt{compl(dept1 \cup dept2)} \geq 0.625.$$

Figure 4.7c shows the relation dept3, the size of which is 4; this relation contains only associate professors; therefore, $\mathtt{dept3} \cap \mathtt{dept1}$ is $\varnothing$. In this case, we can easily compute

$$\mathtt{compl(dept1 \cup dept3)} = 0.5 + 0.5 = 1$$

Figure 4.7d shows the relation dept4, the size of which is 2; observe that $\mathtt{dept4} \subseteq \mathtt{dept1}$. In this case, we have

$$\mathtt{compl(dept1 \cup dept4)} = 0.5.$$

Case 2: Different Reference Relations. We consider a case that can occur in real scenarios, i.e., the reference relations are a disjoint and complete partition of a domain. This is the case, for example, when we merge two disjoint sets of citizens resident in differen cities. More specifically, we suppose that $\mathtt{ref}(r_1) \cap \mathtt{ref}(r_2) = \varnothing$ and $\mathtt{ref(s)} = \mathtt{ref}(r_1) \cup \mathtt{ref}(r_2)$. In this case, it is easy to show that the completeness of s for the union is

$$\mathtt{compl(s)} = \frac{|r_1| + |r_2|}{|\mathtt{ref}(r_1)| + |\mathtt{ref}(r_2)|} =$$

$$= \frac{\text{compl}(r_1) * |r_1| + \text{compl}(r_2) * |r_2|}{|\text{ref}(r_1)| + |\text{ref}(r_2)|}.$$

For other cases, related to intersection and cartesian product, we refer you to [173].

4.3 Error Localization and Correction

In the introduction of this chapter, error localization and error correction activities were identified as data quality activities. Error localization and correction are useful every time data have been collected from error-prone sources (e.g., those in which manual input has been performed) or acquired from sources whose reliability is not known at all.

In Chapter 2 we have seen that errors in data may be expressed in terms of a wide number of dimensions; for some of them we have provided measures and, in the case of consistency, formal models to characterize the dimension. We argue that corresponding methods for error localization and correction depend on the type of quality dimension we want to control and achieve. The following sections take into account such dimension dependence, and are hence organized as follows

1. localize and correct inconsistencies in Section 4.3.1;
2. localize and correct incomplete data in Section 4.3.2;
3. localize outliers, i.e., data values that are anomalous with respect to other data, and usually are an indicator of incorrect data, in Section 4.3.3.

4.3.1 Localize and Correct Inconsistencies

Historically, the problem of localizing inconsistencies has occurred in statistical surveys carried out by processing answers obtained through a collection of questionnaires, and is also typical of data collected in experiments and analyses (e.g., clinical) for medical diagnosis and care. Error localization and correction is becoming increasingly important when using sensor networks, e.g., for detection of harmful biological and chemical agents and in collecting data in monitoring environmental conditions. The error rate of these sensor networks is highly dependent on the current battery level of the device, interference, and other parameters.

A first formalization of the problem appears in [76]; more recent contributions appear in several papers (see [33], [215], and [163]). In the following, we will consider data collected through questionnaires as a reference case; as we will see, the approach can be generalized to other cases where more complex data models are defined, e.g., relational data model with integrity constraints.

When designing a questionnaire, the data provided as responses to the questionnaire must verify a set of properties, corresponding to the edits introduced in Chapter 2. In the statistical world, the set of all edits is called the *set of edit rules*, or *check plan*, or *compatibility plan*. Usually, such rules are known only to a certain extent, since collecting and expressing rules is a costly activity, and even a simple questionnaire can result in tens and hundreds of such rules. Errors, or inconsistencies between answers or out-of-range answers, can be due to low quality in the original design of the questionnaire, or can be introduced during any later phase of data production, such as data input or conversion.

When edits are collected, it is crucial that they be proven to be *consistent*, i.e. without contradictions, otherwise, every conceivable procedure to use edits in order to localize errors will fail. Furthermore, they should be *non-redundant*, i.e. no edit in the set can be logically derived from other edits.

As an example of an inconsistent set of edits, assume a survey is performed on the employees of a company. Consider the three edits (here, and in the following, we informally introduce the syntax and the semantics of edits):

1. `Salary = false`, which means "every employee has a salary."
2. `Has a desk = false`, which means "every employee has a desk."
3. `(Salary = true)` and `(Has a desk = true)`, which means "an employee is not allowed to have a salary and to have a desk."

There is an evident contradiction among the three edits. This is an indication that one of the edits, most probably edit 3, is wrong. An example of a redundant set of edits is:

1. `Role = professor` ∧ `AnnualIncome < 100.000`
2. `AnnualIncome < 100.000`

where the redundancy concerns the constraint on `AnnualIncome`.

Once we have a *valid*, i.e., at least consistent, set of edits, we can use them to perform the activity of *error localization*. This may be done by checking if the truth assignments associated with the values in the questionnaire satisfy the logic formula corresponding to the set of edits. In this activity, it would be obviously preferable to have a *non redundant* set of edits, because decreasing the number of edits while maintaining the same power of inconsistency detection can simplify the whole process.

After the localization of erroneous records, in order to correct errors, we could perform on them the activity called *new data acquisition* in Section 4.1. Unfortunately, this kind of activity is usually very costly, and, in all the contexts in which data are collected for statistical purposes, the use of edits is usually preferred to correct erroneous data. The activity of using edits to correct erroneous fields by restoring correct values is called *error correction* or *imputation*. The problem of localizing errors by means of edits and imputing erroneous fields is usually referred to as the *edit-imputation problem*. Fellegi and Holt in [76] provide a theoretical model for the edit-imputation problem. The main goals of the model are as follows

- The data in each record should satisfy all edits by changing the fewest fields possible. This is called the *minimum change principle*.

- When imputation is necessary, it is desirable to maintain the marginal and joint frequency distribution of values in the different fields.

The above two goals may be in conflict, as the following example shows. Consider a questionnaire that collects several properties of people, such as <Age, MaritalStatus, TypeofWork>. A "true" record such as <68, married, retired> could result due to some error into <6, married, retired>. Such a record does not respect an edit such as

Age < 15 ∧ MaritalStatus = married.

We may correct 6 into 15, respecting the minimum change principle for the age, but if we apply the rule in all similar cases we alter the distribution of values of Age. Even changing 6 (and analogous incorrect values) in order to respect the frequency distribution of correct values of Age, we could modify the joint distribution with MaritalStatus and TypeofWork. Thus, in general, we have to perform more complex and wide changes. Fellegi and Holt provide a solution to the edit imputation problem that finds the minimum number of fields to change in order to respect all the edits, thus achieving the first goal. They make an important assumption in their method: that implicit edit is known. *Implicit edits* are those that can be logically derived from explicitly defined edits. In *error localization* they were considered redundant edits, and so they were minimized; during *error correction* they cannot be ignored, since they express properties that do not fail for a record but may fail as values are changed. The following example adapted from [215] provides intuition for computational issues. Consider a record,

<Age, MaritalStatus, Relationship-to-Head-of-Household>,

and the following two edits:

edit1: Age < 15 ∧ MaritalStatus = married
edit2: MaritalStatus = not married ∧
Relationship-to-Head-of-Household = spouse

An implicit edit, as may easily be checked, is

edit3: Age < 15 ∧ Relationship-to-Head-of-Household = spouse

We initially assume that edit3 is hidden. Consider now a record $r_1 =$ <10, not married, spouse>. The record fails for edit2; in order to correct the record, we may change the marital status to married, to obtain a new record r_2 that now fails for edit1. So, we have to make a second attempt, that involves the value spouse. If we explicitly consider edit3, we immediately reach the conclusion that at least one of the two values <10,spouse> has to be changed.

Assuming availability of implicit edits, Fellegi and Holt formulate the problem as a set covering problem. Alternatively, if implicit edits are not available, then the edit-imputation problem can be solved by integer programming methods which are much slower. Probabilistic imputation methods have to be used to deal with the second goal, namely, to maintain the marginal and joint frequency distribution of variables. We refer to [33] for these issues.

4.3.2 Incomplete Data

In Chapter 2 we introduced completeness as a relevant data quality dimension, and we defined and provided metrics for it in the context of relational tables. Another type of incompleteness arises in the measurement of phenomena during a period of time, e.g., in time series. We consider now the two cases of completeness.

With regard to relational tables, enforcing explicit values for an attribute A, or for a set of attributes $A_1, A_2, \ldots, A_n$ in place of missing ones, can be expressed as the problem of conformance to edits of the form

A_1 = null or A_2 = null or ...or A_n = null.

In this case, the problem of finding the minimum number of values to be modified is trivial, since this number coincides with the set of missing values. Thus, the goal that becomes critical is to maintain the marginal and joint frequency distributions of the attributes. If the attributes to be considered are $A_1, A_2, \ldots, A_n$, an assumption can be made that attributes are missing monotonically, that is, A_i is not missing only if $A_{i-1}, A_{i-2}, \ldots, A_1$ are not missing. In this case, a regression method can be performed recursively, generating valid values from A_1 to A_n.

With regard to time series, two types of incompleteness can be identified, namely, truncated data and censored data. *Truncated data* corresponds to observations that are dropped from the analyzed data set. For example, customers that take at the most one flight a year might not be included in an airline customer database. *Censored data* correspond to data that we know for sure have not been collected before a certain time t_1 (*left censored data*) or after a certain time t_2 (*right censored data*). As an example of left censored data, assume we are interested in measuring the *mean time between failure* of a computer; we could have only historical data available after a certain time t_1, and we might not know at what time $t_0 < t_1$ the computer started operating. The possible situations are shown in Figure 4.8.

Note that truncated or censored data can also appear in relational tables with values not time stamped. For instance, a 64-bit integer cannot represent values higher than $2^{64} - 1$; so, integer overflows correspond to censored values. As another example, a sales invoice system may assign a default date for

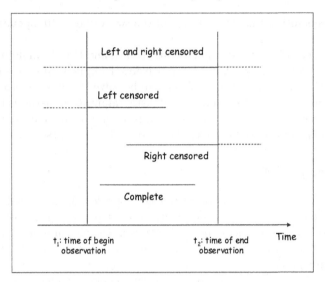

Fig. 4.8. Types of incomplete data in time series

missing date invoices. As a consequence, invoices with missing values all have exactly the same data, which has a high frequency.

Truncated and censored data can be detected with the help of histograms and frequency distributions. For example in the sales order system, corresponding to the default date a spike appears in the frequency distribution of dates.

4.3.3 Discovering Outliers

A value that is unusually larger or smaller in relation to other values in a set of data is called an *outlier*. As an example, consider the following data:

$$2, 5, 6, 3, 8, 76, 4, 3, 7.$$

Intuition tells us that 76 is a suspicious value, because all the other data are numbers between 0 and 10. Typically, an outlier is attributable to one of the following causes in the measurement of data:

1. it is incorrectly observed, recorded, or entered in a database;
2. it comes from a different population, in relation to other values; and
3. it is correct, but represents a rare event.

In our example, 76 could be a simple typo, where the separating comma between 7 and 6 is missing. This is an example of temporary false or spurious value, sometimes called *data glitch*, that corresponds to causes 1 and 2. It is important to distinguish between outliers of type 3, correct but rare data, and outliers of types 1 and 2, i.e., data glitches. As a consequence of the above discussion, methods for managing outliers are characterized by two phases, (i) discovering outliers and (ii) deciding between rare data and data glitches.

Outliers are detected by measuring the departure of values from what we expect them to be. We discuss the following methods that can be used for the detection of outliers: control charts, distributional outliers, and time series outliers. A comprehensive list of these methods is discussed in detail in [50].

- *Control charts* have been developed primarily by the manufacturing industry to measure the quality of products; several data samples are collected, and statistics, such as mean and standard error, are computed and analyzed. As an example, in Figure 4.9, the region inside the rectangle represents values that are inside single attribute error limits, while the ellipse represents the joint control limits based on the joint distribution of the two attributes. Some points that are inside control limits of the single attributes are outliers when the elliptic control area corresponding to the pair of attributes is considered.

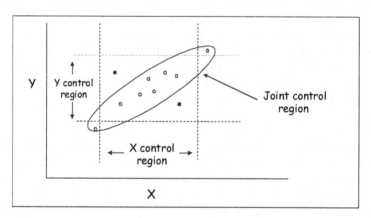

Fig. 4.9. Example of a control chart based on two attributes

Control charts are suitable for studying one or two attributes at a time. They cannot be used for capturing outliers based on interrelationships between attributes; it is possible that a value might be well suited in relation to any given attribute, but might be outside fixed error bounds in relation to the attributes taken together.

- *Distributional outliers.* According to this method, outliers are seen as points which are in a region of low density. Since these points are relatively isolated, they are "probably" outliers. The intuition is that outliers are likely to be at a large distance from the other data points. Starting from this intuition, distributional outliers can be found computing the value $F[d](x)$ for every point x in the set of values, which is the fraction of points in the set of values at distance d or more from x. The set of

$F[p, d]$ outliers is the set of points x such that $F[d](x) > p$, where p is a threshold value. Note that outliers could be clustered, e.g., because of default or censored values for some of the fields. The threshold p should be adjusted to take these fields into account.

- *Time series outliers.* These methods analyze outliers in time series. They consider relevant properties of time series, such as the fact that data which are close in time tend to be highly correlated. They also consider the presence of cyclic patterns in the data, such as credit card payments that may have peaks at certain hours in the week. A technique for time series starts with partitioning the group of attributes measured in series (such as, e.g., `<CreditCardNumber, Expense>`) into sections, using a space partitioning strategy. Each class of the partition is a state that a data point can have in time. A given time series is modeled as a trajectory of states, with transition probabilities between states. Thus transitions can be ranked by their likelihoods, and outliers correspond to low likelihood transitions.

Once the outliers are identified, we have to decide whether they represent an abnormal but legitimate behavior or a data glitch. In the time series methods, two different measures of deviation are considered for the decision. The *relative deviation* represents the movement of a data point relative to other data points over time. For instance the data points may represent the history of credit card purchases of a customer, with some customers purchasing at a faster rate, while other customers continue at the same rate at which they started. The *within deviation* measures the dynamics of a data point in relation to its own expected behavior.

We briefly compare the two strategies. The relative deviation is more robust, since state changes require significant changes in attributes. The within deviation is sensitive to minor changes and is better for analyzing long-term changes; thus, it is more suitable for discriminating between rare data and glitches. In fact, genuine changes are usually persistent over time, whereas glitches appear and disappear unpredictably. A drop in revenues at a single point in time is more likely to be a data problem, such as missing data, rather than a downward trend. Patterns in glitches reveal systematic causes, such as data in particular missing intervals.

4.4 Cost and Benefit Classifications

In this section we start to discuss how an organization can analyze whether it is convenient or not to engage DQ improvement campaigns. In other words, we will discuss how quantifying (i) the costs of current poor data quality, (ii) the costs of DQ initiatives to improve it, and (iii) the benefits that are gained from such initiatives. Cost-benefit analysis is an arduous task in many cost domains, and it is more arduous in the DQ area due to the less consolidated nature of the discipline. The existing proposals range from classifications provided for costs and benefits to methodologies for performing the cost-benefit analysis process. Classifications are either generic, or specific, e.g., for the financial domain. The advantages of generic classifications (see also [70]) range from establishing clearer terminology to providing consistent measurement metrics. They can be used as checklists during the cost-benefit analysis activity. We discuss in this section issues related to generic classifications, and postpone to Chapter 7 the discussion on methodologies. In the following we distinguish the differences between cost issues and benefit issues.

4.4.1 Cost Classifications

Three very detailed classifications for costs appear in English [68], Loshin [123], and Eppler and Helfert [70]. We first present the three classifications, discussing their original issues; then, we propose a common classification framework to compare them all.

The English classification is shown in Figure 4.10. Data quality costs correspond to costs of business processes and data management processes due to poor data quality. Costs for information quality assessment or inspection measure data quality dimensions to verify that processes are performing properly. Finally, process improvement and defect prevention costs involve activities to improve the quality of data, with the goal of eliminating, or reducing, the costs of poor data quality. Costs due to low data quality are analyzed in depth in the English approach, shown in the Figure 4.10, and are subdivided into three categories:

1. *Process failure costs* result when poor quality information causes a process not to perform properly. As an example, inaccurate mailing addresses cause correspondence to be misdelivered.
2. *Information scrap and rework.* When information is of poor quality, it requires several types of defect management activities, such as reworking, cleaning, or rejecting. Examples of this category are
   - redundant data handling, if the poor quality of a source makes it useless, time and money has to be spent to collect and maintain data in another database;
   - business rework costs, due to re-performing failed processes, such as resending correspondence, as in the previous example;
   - data verification costs, when data users do not trust the data, they have to perform their own quality inspection, to remove low quality data.
3. *Loss and missed opportunity costs* correspond to the revenues and profits not realized because of poor information quality. For example due to low accuracy of customer e-mail addresses, a percentage of customers already acquired cannot be reached in periodic advertising campaigns, resulting in lower revenues, roughly proportional to the decrease of accuracy in addresses.

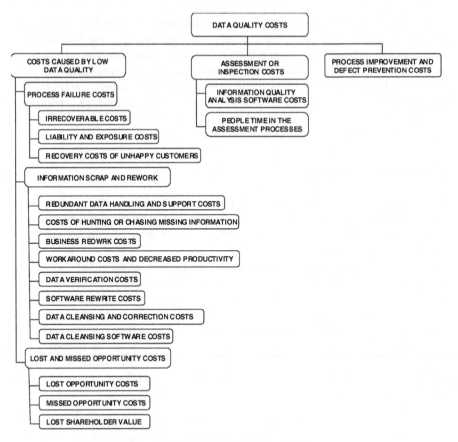

Fig. 4.10. The English classification

The Loshin classification is shown in Figure 4.11. Loshin analyzes the costs of low data quality, classifying it in different domain impacts, on

- the operational domain, which includes the components of the system used for processing information and the costs of maintaining the operation of the system;
- the tactical domain, which attempts to address and solve problems before they arise;
- the strategic domain, which stresses the decisions affecting the longer term.

For both the operational impact and tactical/strategic impact several cost categories are introduced. Here, we describe some of the operational impact costs:

- detection costs are incurred when a data quality problem provokes a system error or processing failure;
- correction costs are associated with the actual correction of a problem;

- rollback costs are incurred when work that has been performed needs to be undone;
- rework costs are incurred when a processing stage must be repeated;
- prevention costs arise when a new activity is implemented to take the necessary actions to prevent operational failure due to a detected data quality problem.

Examples of tactical/strategic costs are: (i) delay, due to inaccesible data resulting in a delayed decision process that, in turn, may cause productivity delays, (ii) lost opportunities, i.e., the negative impact on potential opportunities in strategic initiatives, and (iii) organizational mistrust, due to the decision of managers, unsatisfied by inconsistencies in data, to implement their own decision support system, resulting in redundancies and inconsistencies due to frequent use of the same sources.

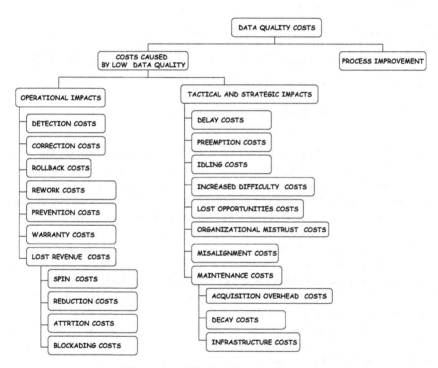

Fig. 4.11. The Loshin classification

The EpplerHelfert classification is shown in Figure 4.12. EpplerHelfert derives its classification with a bottom up approach; first, it produces a list of specific costs that have been mentioned in the literature, such as higher maintenance costs and data re-input costs. Then, it generates a list of direct costs associated with improving or assuring data quality, such as training

costs of improving data quality know-how. At this point it puts together the
two classifications corresponding to the two major classes of costs, namely
cost due to poor data quality and improvement costs. Costs due to poor data
quality are categorized in terms of their measurability or impact, resulting in
direct vs. indirect cost classes. *Direct costs* are those monetary effects that
arise immediately from low data quality, while *indirect costs* arise from the
intermediate effects. Improvement costs are categorized within the information
quality process.

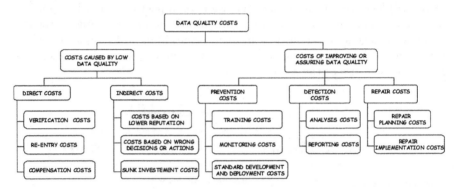

Fig. 4.12. The EpplerHelfert classification

For the purpose of producing a new classification that allows for the integration of the three classifications discussed above, we use a second classification proposed by Eppler and Helfert in [70]; such a classification produces a
conceptual framework that could be used in the cost-benefit analysis of data
quality programs. It is based on the data production life cycle approach, which
distinguishes between *data entry*, *data processing*, and *data usage* costs. The
iterative attribution of all the cost categories of the three previous classifications to this new high-level classification leads to the comparative classification of Figure 4.13; the different background patterns used for the English,
Loshin, and EpplerHelfert classification items are shown in the legend. When
comparing the three classifications, we notice that they have very few items
in common, all placed at an abstract level, namely *corrective* costs, *preventive*
costs, and *process improvement* costs and the two most similar classifications
are the English and Loshin ones.

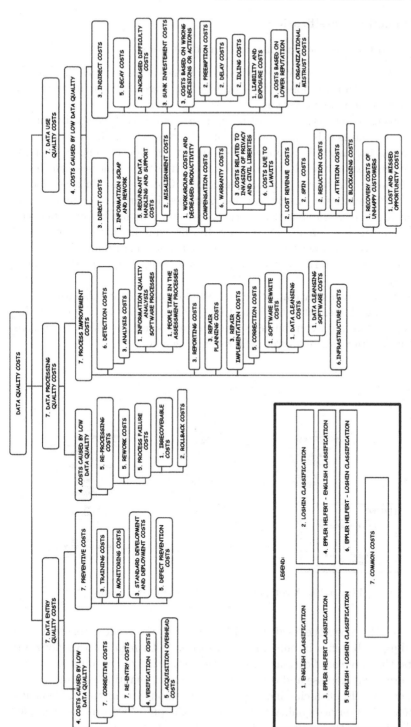

Fig. 4.13. A comparative classification for costs

4.4.2 Benefits Classification

Benefits can typically be classified into three categories:

1. *Monetizable*, when they correspond to values that can be directly expressed in terms of money. For example, improved data quality results in increased monetary revenues.
2. *Quantifiable*, when they cannot be expressed in terms of money, but one or more indicators exist that measure them, expressed in a different numeric domain. For example improved data quality in Government-to-Business relationships may result in reduced wasted time by businesses, which can be expressed in terms of a time indicator. Observe that in several contexts a quantifiable benefit can be expressed in terms of a monetizable benefit if a reasonable and realistic conversion function is found between the quantifiable domain and money. In our example, if the time wasted by business is productive time, the "wasted time" quantifiable benefit can be translated in terms of the monetizable benefit "unproductively spent money."
3. *Intangible*, when they cannot be expressed by a numeric indicator. A typical intangible benefit is the loss of image of an agency or a company due to inaccurate data communicated to customers, e.g., requests to citizens for undue tax payments from the revenue agency.

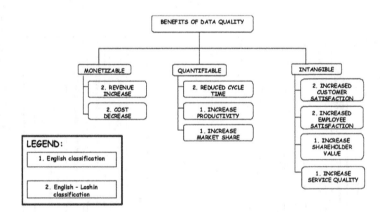

Fig. 4.14. A comparative classification for benefits

Figure 4.14 shows the English and Loshin items represented together, corresponding to benefits in the three categories. With regard to monetizable benefits, the two classifications agree in the indication of economic issues related to revenue increase and cost decrease, while in quantifiable and intangible benefits the English classification is richer; among the intangible benefits, the reference to service quality is relevant. In Chapter 7 we will see examples of applications of the above classifications in a real case study.

4.5 Summary

In this chapter we have introduced several data quality activities, discovering that the improvement of data quality in an organization can be performed with a variety of actions and strategies. All of the activities introduced apply to data, and produce data of improved quality according to a given process. Other improvement activities can rely on processes that manipulate data, modifying the process or introducing suitable controls in the process; we will discuss them in Chapter 7.

We have also started the discussion on activities while thoroughly analyzing (i) quality composition, and (ii) error localization and correction. Finally, we have discussed cost-benefit classifications in data quality, that can be used as check lists in the process of cost and benefit allocation. For quality composition and error localization and correction we introduced a spectrum of techniques for several possible cases, while for cost/benefit classifications we compared the different approaches. In such a way, we provided a framework for analysis that allows the reader to choose the specific approach to adopt based on the context of use.

5

Object Identification

In this chapter, we describe object identification, probably the most important and the most extensively investigated data quality activity.

In order to introduce critical issues, and justify the structure of the chapter, let us describe an example related to an e-Government application scenario. In such a scenario, different agencies manage administrative procedures related to different types of businesses in order to register their information on businesses in their respective national registries, authorize specific activities, and provide services, e.g. for collecting taxes. In each agency, the same set of businesses is represented, with some attributes common and other attributes specific to the agency. We have reported in Figure 5.1 a real-life example of the same business as represented in three national registries (some details, irrelevant in this context, have been changed for privacy reasons).

Agency	Identifier	Name	Type of activity	Address	City
Agency 1	CNCBTB765SDV	Meat production of John Ngombo	Retail of bovine and ovine meats	35 Niagara Street	New York
Agency 2	0111232223	John Ngombo canned meat production	Grocer's shop, beverages	9 Rome Street	Albany
Agency 3	CND8TB76SSDV	Meat production in New York state of John Ngombo	Butcher	4, Garibaldi Square	Long Island

Fig. 5.1. How three agencies see the same business

The three tuples present several differences:

1. Values of the identifiers are different due to different policies of the three agencies; also, in the case in which they share a common domain and meaning (this is the case for Agencies 1 and 3), they differ due to some data entry errors.

2. Names are different, although several common or similar parts exist (also, in this case, some data entry error can be recognized).
3. Types of activity are different; this difference may be due to several reasons, such as typos, deliberately false declarations, or data updated at different times.
4. Further differences appear in remaining `Address` and `City` attributes.

Yet, the three tuples represent the same business!

We call *object identification* the data quality activity needed to identify whether data in the same source or in different ones represent the same object of the real world.

As mentioned in Chapter 1, poor data quality in a single database produces poor service quality and economic losses. Poor data quality referring to the same types of objects (e.g., persons, businesses and portion of territory) in different databases yields poor results in all applications (e.g., queries, transactions and aggregations) that access the same objects in the different databases. This type of access is typical of many Government/Business/Citizen-to-Government/Business/Citizen interactions. For example, to discover tax frauds, different agencies can cross-check their databases in order to search for contradictions or correlations among data: this is possible only if data referring to the same object can be identified.

This chapter is organized as follows. In Section 5.1 we briefly provide a historical perspective of the object identification problem. In Section 5.2, we discuss the different data typologies involved in the object identification process. In Section 5.3 we describe the general steps of the process that are detailed in Section 5.4. In Section 5.5 we introduce the specific object identification techniques that are detailed in the following sections: Section 5.6 describes probabilistic techniques, Section 5.7 illustrates the empirical ones, and, finally, Section 5.8 details the knowledge-based techniques. The chapter ends with a comparison of the techniques in Section 5.9.

5.1 Historical Perspective

The term *record linkage* is mentioned for the first time in [64]. Since computer applications have been used to automate more and more administrative activities, demographic studies, health experiments, and epidemiological analyses, it has become clear that data often result from the merging of different sources, created and updated at different times and by different organizations or persons. Moreover, merging data produces new data of potentially higher value, since properties that are merged can be related with new types of aggregations, analyses, and correlations.

In 50' and 60', data was represented in *files*, *records*, and *fields*, and terminology that justifies the original term *record linkage* as the activity that results in the integration of information from two or more independent sources.

In this chapter we will frequently use the *file/record/field* terminology, instead of the *relation/tuple/attribute* terminology, whenever the techniques apply to the more general file structure.

One of the first efforts for moving from empirical procedures to formal methods originates from the geneticist Howard Newcombe [146], who introduced frequencies of occurrences of values in strings and decision rules for matching and non-matching records. Such procedures were used in the development of health files of individuals. Fellegi and Sunter [77] provided a mature formal theory for record linkage (see Section 5.6.1). A great number of subsequent experiments and theoretical improvements originated, in addition to health applications, also in administrative and census applications, characterized by a large amount of data, from sources with various degrees of trustworthiness and accuracy. In such applications, it is crucial to produce efficient computer-assisted matching procedures that can reduce the use of clerical resources, and effective methods that can reduce errors in matching and non-matching. See [216] for a general discussion on the peculiarities of record linkage methods on administrative data.

In recent years, new techniques have been proposed that extend the linkage activity from files to more complex structures. Such techniques also try to exploit knowledge on the application domain to produce more effective decision procedures. These topics will be examined in more detail in the following sections.

5.2 Object Identification for Different Data Types

Techniques developed for dealing with the object identification problem strictly depend on the type of data used to represent objects. Refining and adapting the classifications provided in Chapter 1, we distinguish three main data types that refer to the same class of objects:

1. *Simple structured data,* that correspond to pairs of files or relational tables.
2. *Complex structured data,* i.e., groups of logically related files or relational tables.
3. *Semi-structured data,* such as pairs of XML marked documents.

In Figure 5.2, data of the three different types are shown. In Figures 5.2a and 5.2b, an object of type **Person** is represented, while a **Country** is represented in Figure 5.2c.

In order to discover matching and non-matching objects within the three structures, we need intuitively different strategies. Historically, simple structured data correspond to traditional files, which have poor mechanisms to represent the semantics of data. With the advent of database management systems (DBMSs), and, specifically, relational DBMSs, it has been possible to assign semantics to such structures, in terms of domains, keys, functional dependencies, and constraints. The advent of networks and Internet and the

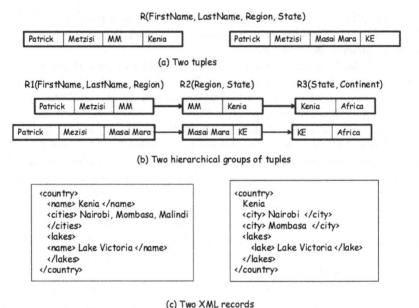

(a) Two tuples

(b) Two hierarchical groups of tuples

(c) Two XML records

Fig. 5.2. Examples of matching objects of the three data typologies

development of the XML standard have pushed the investigation of techniques for semi-structured data.

In relation to the above discussion, two different terms are widely used in the literature: *record linkage* and *object identification*. Other terms used are *record matching* and *entity resolution*. *Record linkage* is used when the matching activity is performed on simple structured data, in our terminology, files or relations. Usually, it is known a priori that the two relations model the same entity of the real world, e.g. persons, businesses, or buildings. The goal of record linkage is to produce a new file where all the tuples of the two input files referring to the same entity of the real world (e.g., the same person, the same business) are merged into a unique record; techniques may also simply produce the cluster of matching records without choosing the representative record. When a unique file is considered, the goal of record linkage is to discover and unify the records in the file that refer to the same entity of the real world; in this case, it is called *deduplication* or *duplicate identification*.

Object identification is an evolutive term for record linkage, and deals with complex structured data and XML documents where objects of the real world are represented, in general, with a wider spectrum of structures than simple structured data. For instance,

1. in data warehouses, objects used for dimensions in a star schema are represented with a group of relations related by foreign key constraints; this is the case of the tuples in Figure 5.2b;
2. in normalized relational schemas, several relations are needed to represent an object; and
3. in documents, objects are hidden in natural language descriptions, and their presence may be revealed by some schema specification (e.g., XML schemas).

These characteristics call for more sophisticated techniques when moving from simple structured data to complex structured data and semistructured data; at the same time, the semantic wealth of DBMS and XML models, in comparison to files, provides richer mechanisms (e.g., keys) to reveal structural similarities between data, resulting in more complex, but also more powerful, techniques.

5.3 The High-Level Process for Object Identification

Although inspired by different general paradigms and tailored to the different types of data introduced in the previous section, techniques for object identification have a generally common structure, described with different levels of detail in Figures 5.3 and 5.4, where we assume for simplicity we have two files as input data.

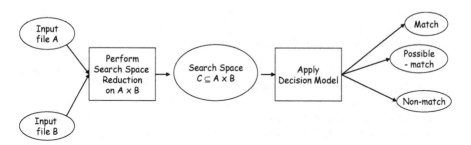

Fig. 5.3. Relevant steps of object identification techniques

In Figure 5.3, starting from the potential search space, consisting of the cartesian product of tuples in input files, a reduced search space is first constructed. The reason for this step is to reduce the complexity of the technique, which, otherwise, is $O(n^2)$, where n is the cardinality of each of the input relations. Then, a decision model is used to decide if records in the reduced search space match, i.e., correspond to the same object, do not match, or no decision can be made automatically, and a domain expert has to be involved. Minimization of *possible matches* is a typical goal of object identification techniques to reduce clerical involvement. At the same time, a further goal to be achieved is to minimize *false positives*, i.e., false assignments of pairs of tuples to the match decision, and the complementary *false negatives*.

Step 1. Preprocessing
Standardize fields to compare and correct simple errors
Step 2. Perform search space reduction
Given the search space A x B of the two files, find a new search space $C \subseteq A \times B$ to apply further steps
Step 3. Choose comparison function
Choose the function(s)/set of rules that expresses the distance between records in C
Step 4. Apply decision model
Choose the method for assigning pairs in C to M, the set of matching records, U the set of unmatching records, and P the set of possible matches
Step 5. Verification
Check the effectiveness of method if not satisfactory, go back to Step 2

Fig. 5.4. Description of relevant steps

Figure 5.4 adds three more phases to the general process, namely,

- a *prepropressing* activity that has the goal of working on data in order to standardize it and correct evident errors (see Section 5.4.1);
- the *choice of a comparison function* between tuples, to be used in the decision model activity;
- a *verification* step, during which some quality measures are performed to assess if the result is satisfactory, and, if needed, to iterate the method, such as by making a different choice (for example, adopting a new comparison function).

Three major categories of techniques for object identification can be identified on the basis of the underlying research paradigms:

1. *Probabilistic techniques*, based on the extremely relevant set of methods developed in the last two centuries in statistics and probability theory, ranging from Bayesian networks to data mining tools.
2. *Empirical techniques* that make use in the different phases of the process of algorithmic techniques such as sorting, tree traversal, neighbor comparison, and pruning.
3. *Knowledge-based techniques*, in which domain knowledge is extracted from the files involved, and reasoning strategies are applied to make the process more effective.

Both in probabilistic and in knowledge-based techniques, the steps of the general procedure, described in Figure 5.4, can be either performed independently of the domain (*domain-independent techniques*) or could be based on domain-specific information or knowledge (*domain-dependent techniques*).

Furthermore, in some applications it is useful to have a priori a sample of data for which it is known whether they match or not; such a sample is called *labeled data*, while *unlabeled data* are data for which the matching status is unknown. Labeled data can be used effectively to learn probabilities, distance functions, or knowledge used in the different techniques. Therefore, two different types of learning can be identified: *supervised learning*, when knowledge is available on matching/unmatching pairs, and *unsupervised learning*, when the source knowledge is of a different nature (e.g., integrity constraints on the domain).

Finally, in the case in which complex structured data and semistructured data are involved, further tree/graph traversal activity is needed in order to apply the strategy to all parts of the structure.

5.4 Details on the Steps for Object Identification

In this section, the first three steps described in Figure 5.4, namely, preprocessing, search space reduction, and the issues related to comparison functions, will be illustrated in detail. The next sections deal with step 4, apply decision method. In the last section of the chapter we will introduce metrics for step 5, verification.

5.4.1 Preprocessing

The preprocessing step includes the following activities:

- *Conversion of upper/lower cases*, in which data to be compared corresponding to alphabetic strings are transformed to be homogeneous in terms of upper and lower cases. So, for instance, if names of companies are stored such that the first character is upper case, then the corresponding strings are converted such that all their characters are lower cases, e.g. `Hewlett Packard` is transformed into `hewlett packard`,and `Microsoft` into `microsoft`.
- *Replacement of null strings*. Null strings must be replaced in order to allow proper comparisons. For example, `hewlett packard` must be transformed into `hewlettpackard`.
- *Standardization*, consisting of reorganization of composed fields, data type checks, replacement of alternative spellings with a single one. A typical example of *reorganization* of a composite field is given by addresses. In many applications addresses are stored as a single string; the standardization activity may consider parsing the string into substrings corresponding, for instance, to `StreetName`, `CivicNumber`, `City`, and `State`. In the context of object identification, this type of reorganization has the purpose of making comparisons easier. However, it can be performed also to facilitate accuracy checks. Indeed, for fields derived from decomposition, dictionaries may be available for the use as lookup tables for correcting the data. *Data type checks* regard the standardization of formats. For example, dates must be expressed in the same format: 1 Jan 2001, 01-1-2001, 1st January

2001 should be homogenized to a single format. *Replacement of alternative spellings* include abbreviations that can be replaced by the corresponding complete word, e.g., `rd.` by `road`.

- *Schema reconciliation* is a more complex activity that must address all conflicts that can occur when data under consideration come from disparate data sources. Examples of such conflicts are heterogeneity conflicts, semantic conflicts, description conflicts, and structural conflicts. More details on this can be found in Chapter 6.

5.4.2 Search Space Reduction

The object identification problem has a search space dimension equal to the cardinality of A × B, given two sets of records A and B to be compared. The reduction of the search space can be done by three different methods, namely, blocking, sorted neighborhood and pruning (or filtering).

Blocking implies partitioning a file into mutually exclusive blocks, and limiting comparisons to records within the same block. Blocking can be implemented by choosing a *blocking key* and grouping into a block all records that have the same values on the blocking key. Blocking can also be implemented by *hashing*. The blocking key is used for hashing records in hash blocks. If b is the number of blocks and n/b is the dimension of each block, then the total time complexity of blocking is $O(h(n) + n^2/b)$ where $h(n)=n \; logn$ if blocking is implemented by sorting, or $h(n)=n$ if blocking is implemented by hashing.

Sorted neighborhood consists of sorting a file and then moving a window of a fixed size on the file, comparing only records within the window. The number of comparisons is consequently reduced from n^2 to $O(wn)$, where w is the size of the window; considering the sorting complexity $O(nlog)$, the method requires a total time complexity of $O(nlogn + wn)$. See also Section 5.9.2 for a comparison between blocking and sorted neighborhood methods.

Pruning (or *filtering*) has the objective of first removing from the search space all records that cannot match each other, without actually comparing them. As an example, let us consider the case where two records are declared to be a match if a given comparison function $f(r_i, r_j)$ is greater than a threshold τ. If an upper bound for f is found, e.g., $f(r_i, r_j) <= \delta(r_i)$ for each j, then, if $\delta(r_i) <= \tau$, $f(r_i, r_j)$ will be lower than τ for each r_j; therefore, r_i cannot have any record to be matched with, and can be removed from the search space.

5.4.3 Comparison Functions

Comparison functions have been widely investigated, especially string comparison functions (see surveys [90] and [143]). In the rest of this section, we review some of the most important functions, and we provide examples to show similarities and differences.

Edit distance. The edit distance between two strings is the minimum cost of converting one of them to the other by a sequence of character insertions, deletions, and replacements. Each of these modifications is assigned a cost value. As an example, assuming that the insertion cost and the deletion cost are each equal to 1, the edit distance between the two strings `Smith` and `Sitch` is 2, as `Smith` is obtained by adding `m` and deleting `c` from `Sitch`.

n-grams, bi-grams, q-grams. The n-grams comparison function forms the set of all the substrings of length n for each string. The distance between the two strings is defined as: $\sqrt{\sum_{\forall x} |f_{s'} - f_{s''}|}$, where $f_{s'}$ and $f_{s''}$ are the number of occurrences of the substrings x in the strings s' and s'', respectively. Bi-grams comparison ($n = 2$) is widely used, and is effective with minor typographical errors. Positional q-grams are obtained by sliding a window of length q over the characters of a string s.

Soundex code. The purpose of the soundex code is to cluster together names that have similar sounds. For example, the soundex code of `Hilbert` and `Heilbpr` is similar. A soundex code always contains four characters. The first letter of the name becomes the first character of the soundex code. The remaining three characters are drawn from the name sequentially, by accessing a predefined table. As an example, the soundex code of `Hilbert` and `Heilbpr` is H416. Once the four-character limit has been reached, all remaining letters are ignored.

Jaro algorithm. Jaro introduced a string comparison function that accounts for insertions, deletions, and transpositions. Jaro's algorithm finds the number of common characters and the number of transposed characters in the two strings. A *common character* is a character that appears in both strings within a distance of half the length of the shorter string. A *transposed character* is a common character that appears in different positions. As an example, comparing `Smith` and `Simth`, there are five common characters, two of which are transposed. The (scaled) Jaro string comparator is given by

$$f(s_1, s_2) = \frac{\frac{N_c}{lengthS_1} + \frac{N_c}{lengthS_2} + 0.5\frac{N_t}{N_c}}{3},$$

where s_1 and s_2 are strings of lengths $lengthS_1$ and $lengthS_2$ respectively, N_c is the number of common characters between the two strings (where the distance for common characters is half the minimum length of s_1 and s_2), and N_t is the number of transpositions.

Hamming distance. The Hamming distance counts the number of mismatches between two numbers. It is used primarily for numerical fixed size fields like zip codes or social security numbers. For example, the Hamming distance between 00185 and 00155 is 1 because there is one mismatch.

Smith-Waterman. Given two sequences, the Smith-Waterman algorithm uses dynamic programming to find the lowest cost of changes that convert one string into another. Costs for individual changes, namely modifications, insertions, and deletions, are parameters of the algorithm. The algorithm performs well for many abbreviations, taking into account gaps of unmatched characters, and also when records have missing information or typographical mistakes.

TF-IDF. The Token Frequency-Inverse Document Frequency (TF-IDF) or *cosine similarity* is widely used for matching similar strings in documents. The basic idea is to assign higher weights to tokens appearing frequently in a document (TF weight) and to assign lower weights to tokens that appear frequently in the whole set of documents (IDF weight). For a term i in a document j the weight $w_{i,j}$ is

$$w_{i,j} = (tf_{i,j}) \times \log(\frac{N}{df_i})$$

where $tf_{i,j}$ is the number of occurrences of i in j, df_i is the number of documents containing i, and N is the total number of documents. The similarity between two documents is then computed as the cosine between their respective weighted term vectors. Specifically, being $V = \{w_1, \ldots, w_n\}$ and $U = \{w_1, \ldots, w_n\}$ the weighted term vectors, the cosine similarity is

$$\frac{V \cdot U}{|V| \cdot |U|}.$$

5.5 Object Identification Techniques

In Figure 5.5, the set of object identification techniques that will be detailed in the rest of this chapter is shown. Each technique is described by a name, the technical area within which the technique was proposed (probabilistic, empirical, or knowledge-based) and the type of data representing objects to be identified (pairs of files, relational hierarchies, or XML documents). Several object identification techniques are not described in the text, including [45, 62, 172] and [115]. The main criteria used to select the listed techniques are

- adoption: Fellegi and Sunter (and its extensions) is the first and by far the more established technique, and it is representative of probabilistic techniques. The sorted neighborhood method and its variants are also representative of empirical methods.
- novelty: DogmatiX is among the first techniques actually dealing with object identification in XML documents, and Delphi is among the first ones dealing with complex structured data. Cost-based techniques have the originality of dealing with costs of linkage errors. Both the knowledge-based techniques are actually novel contributions, as there are quite a few works on knowledge-based approaches to object identification.

5.6 Probabilistic Techniques

In this section we describe the probabilistic techniques based on the Fellegi and Sunter theory, providing the original model, subsequent extensions, and a cost-based technique.

Name	Technical Area	Type of data
Fellegi and Sunter and extensions	probabilistic	Two files
Cost-based	probabilistic	Two files
Sorted Neighborhood and variants	empirical	Two files
Delphi	empirical	Two relational hierarchies
DogmatiX	empirical	Two XML documents
Intelliclean	knowledge-based	Two files
Atlas	knowledge-based	Two files

Fig. 5.5. Object identification techniques

5.6.1 The Fellegi and Sunter Theory and Extensions

The record linkage theory was proposed by Fellegi and Sunter in [77]. In this section, we summarize the proposed theory and briefly describe the subsequent extensions and refinements.

Given two sets of records A and B, let us consider the cross product $A \times B$ = $\{(a,b)|a \in A \ and \ b \in B\}$. Two disjoint sets M and U can be defined starting from $A \times B$, namely, M= $\{(a,b)|a \equiv b, a \in A \ and \ b \in B\}$ and U= $\{(a,b)|a! \equiv b, a \in A \ and \ b \in B\}$, where the symbol $\equiv$ means that the records a and b represent the same real world entity (and $! \equiv$ they do not). M is named the *matched set* and U is named the *unmatched set*. The record linkage procedure attempts to classify each record pair as belonging to either M or U. A third set P can be also introduced representing possible matches.

Let us suppose that each record in A and B is composed of n fields; a *comparison vector* γ is introduced that compares field values of records a_i and b_j (see Figure 5.6), namely, $\gamma = [\gamma_1^{ij}, \ldots, \gamma_n^{ij}]$. γ is obtained by means of comparison functions, defined as $\gamma_k^{ij} = \gamma(a_i(k), b_j(k))$, denoted in the following for brevity as γ_k. Usually, only a subset of the fields of A and B is compared. γ is a function of the set of all $A \times B$ record pairs; with each couple of fields of each pair, it associates a specific level of agreement. As an example, given two files with fields Name, Surname, and Age, we may define a γ comparison function made of three predicates on each of the fields, namely **agree Name**, **agree Surname**, and **agree Age**.

The functions γ_i can compute a binary agreement on values, i.e., $\gamma(v_1, v_2) = 0$ if $v_1 = v_2$, and 1 otherwise; the functions can also compute a three-value result, i.e., $\gamma(v_1, v_2) = 0$ if $v_1 = v_2$, 1 if either v_1 or v_2 is missing, 2 otherwise. The functions can also compute continuous attribute values; relevant comparison functions are described in detail in Section 5.4.3. The set of all comparison vectors is the comparison space Γ.

Given (a_i, b_j), the following conditional probabilities can be defined:

- $m(\gamma_k) = \text{Pr}(\gamma_k | (a_i, b_j) \in M)$ and

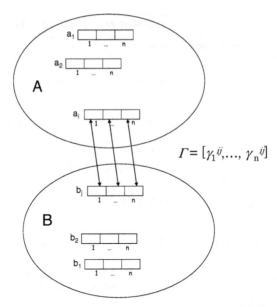

Fig. 5.6. The Fellegi and Sunter record linkage formulation

- $u(\gamma_k)=\Pr(\gamma_k|(\mathbf{a}_i,\mathbf{b}_j) \in \mathsf{U})$.

As an example, for the above files with fields `Name`, `Surname`, and `Age`, the probabilities `Pr(agree Name|M)`, `Pr(agree Surname|M)`, and `Pr(agree Age|M)` and `Pr(agree Name|U)`, `Pr(agree Surname|U)`, and `Pr(agree Age|U)` can be defined. Note that the size of Γ depends on its inner structure.

By considering all the fields, we define analogous formulas for γ:

- $m(\gamma)=\Pr(\gamma|(\mathbf{a}_i,\mathbf{b}_j) \in \mathsf{M})$ and
- $u(\gamma)=\Pr(\gamma|(\mathbf{a}_i,\mathbf{b}_j) \in \mathsf{U})$.

The above probabilities are called *m-* and *u-probabilities*, respectively. In the case in which we are able to estimate such probabilities, they become crucial in a possible assignment decision procedure. Fellegi and Sunter introduced the ratio R among such probabilities as a function of γ, namely,

$$R = m(\gamma)/u(\gamma),$$

where γ ranges in the comparison space Γ, and, we recall, is a function of the set of all $\mathsf{A} \times \mathsf{B}$ record pairs. The ratio R, or the natural logarithm of such a ratio, is called *matching weight*. By composition, R is a function of the set of all $\mathsf{A} \times \mathsf{B}$ record pairs.

Fellegi and Sunter defined the following *decision rule*, where T_μ and T_λ are two thresholds (on them we will comment in a moment):

- if $R > T_\mu$, then designate pair as a match,

- if $T_\lambda <= R <= T_\mu$ then designate pair as a possible match,
- if $R < T_\lambda$ then designate pair as a non-match.

The area $T_\lambda <= R <= T_\mu$ partitions the set of $\gamma \in \Gamma$, and corresponding record pairs, into three disjoint subareas, namely, A_1, including pairs declared as *match*, A_2, including pairs declared as *possible match*, and A_3, including pairs declared as *non-match*. Figure 5.7 shows the three areas, where record pairs in the areas (represented with pairs of white and gray circles) are ordered to be monotonically decreasing by matching weight R. The figure shows that pairs designated as matching are usually much less than pairs designated as non-matching.

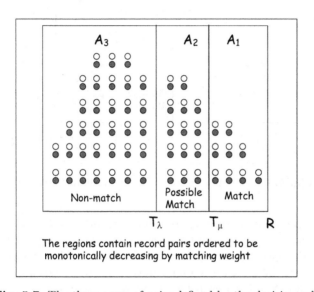

Fig. 5.7. The three areas of pairs defined by the decision rule

It is clear that the thresholds T_μ and T_λ play an essential role in the decision procedure. Therefore, an important problem is how to fix them. Observe that if γ consists mainly of agreements, then R is large; conversely if γ consists mainly of disagreements R is small. Since R is a ratio of probabilities, the assignment of pairs (a, b) for each value of R to the matching set M or to the non-matching set U may results in possible false assignments. *False matches* and *false non-matches* are the two types of errors that are possible in the model, and μ and λ represent the related error rates. High values of R (see the A_1 area in Figure 5.8) correspond to low probability of false matches assignments, with the probability of false matches increasing while values of R decrease. Similarly, for low values of R, the probability of false non-match decreases while decreasing the values of R. In Figure 5.8, the line crossing the three areas represents a possible trend of probabilities of false matches and false non-matches. So, the three areas are identified by specific values of T_λ

and T_μ, and the A_1 and A_3 regions are further divided into true/false match and true/false non-match regions, respectively.

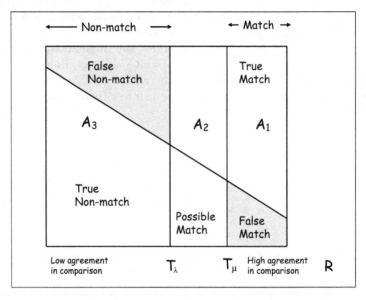

Fig. 5.8. The regions of the Fellegi and Sunter Model [88]

In order to provide criteria to fix the two thresholds T_μ and T_λ, we have to decide which are the rates of error we are willing to accept in the decision rule proposed above; such error rates correspond to the two gray areas in Figure 5.8. Once the error rates are fixed, the two thresholds are consequently fixed. Fellegi and Sunter proved that the above decision rule is optimal, where optimal means that the rule minimizes the probability of classifying pairs as belonging to the area A_2 of possible matches.

Parameters and Error Rates Estimation

The Fellegi and Sunter theory is based on the knowledge of the u- and m-probabilities. Several methods have been proposed to compute or estimate such probabilities. First, Fellegi and Sunter proposed a method to compute the u- and m-probabilities providing a closed-form solution under certain assumptions. More specifically, considering that

$$\Pr(\gamma) = \Pr(\gamma|\mathrm{M})\Pr(\mathrm{M}) + \Pr(\gamma|\mathrm{U})\Pr(\mathrm{U})$$

they observed that if the comparison vector γ regards three fields, among which a conditional independence assumption holds, then a system of seven equations and seven unknowns can be solved to find $\Pr(\gamma|\mathrm{U})$ and $\Pr(\gamma|\mathrm{M})$

(being $7 = 2^3 - 1$, where the subtracting term is due the constraint that probabilities must be equal to 1).

Several parameter estimation methods for the theory have been proposed in the literature. Basically, such methods provide an *estimation* of the u- and m-probabilities rather than a computation of such parameters in closed form. The expectation-maximization algorithm and machine learning methods are the principal methods used for the estimation.

The *expectation-maximization*(EM) algorithm is used to find maximum likelihood estimates of parameters in probabilistic models, where the model depends on unobserved latent variables. EM includes an expectation (E) step, which computes the expected values of the latent variables, and a maximization (M) step, which computes the maximum likelihood estimates of the parameters, given the data and setting the latent variables to their expectation [61].

While continuing holding the conditional independence assumption, Winkler first showed how to estimate m- and u- probabilities by means of the EM-algorithm in [211]. Jaro [105] proposed another method to compute the $m(\gamma), \gamma \in \Gamma$ with the EM algorithm, which is implemented by commercially available software. Estimation methods have focused more recently on specific domains, such as persons and businesses, and specific fields, such as first names, last names, street names (see [212] for a detailed discussion).

The conditional dependence assumption holds very rarely. Proposals for estimating m- and u-probabilities under the *conditional dependence assumption* have been made in various works that come from the areas of statistics, information retrieval, and machine learning (see [214] for a survey). Specifically, generalized EM methods can be used ([210]) for estimations of such probabilities. The methods of Larsen and Rubin [113] are based on Bayesian models. The probability estimation of such methods are not accurate enough to estimate the error rates in the record linkage. The proposal of Belin and Rubin [23] goes in the direction of addressing this limitation. Specifically, Belin and Rubin proposed a mixture model for estimating false match rates, for given threshold values. The method requires training data and works well in a few situations, i.e., when there is a good separation between weights for matching and non-matching. Also, training data are considered a problem with very large data files.

In machine learning applications, typically, labeled training data (see section 5.3) are used, for which the true classification is known, allowing *supervised learning*. In [147], it is observed that the use of Bayesian networks makes it possible to straightforwardly combine labeled and unlabeled data during training, in order to obtain suitable decision rules. If only unlabeled data are used, then the decision rules may be very poor.

5.6.2 A Cost-Based Probabilistic Technique

In this section we describe a probabilistic technique [197] for performing record matching with the aim of minimizing the cost associated with misclassification errors, corresponding to false matches and false non-matches in Figure 5.8.

As previously described, the Fellegi and Sunter model proves that the proposed decision rule is optimal with respect to the minimization of the area needing clerical review (possible matches), for any pair of fixed thresholds on the probabilities of false matches and false non-matches.

The perspective adopted in [197] is different, in that it aims to minimize the *cost* associated with the misclassification error. The cost is considered as constituted by two different components, namely, (i) the cost of the decision process, including, for instance, the number of comparisons needed for the decision, and (ii) the cost of the impact of a certain decision. The comparison vector that, as introduced, corresponds to the attribute values of two given records that need to be compared is indicated by $\bar{x}$. In the following we provide an example showing the difference between error-based models and cost models. Given a comparison vector $(1,1,0)$ with the probability of 75% of appearing among matches and 25% of appearing among non-matches, a rule based on the minimum error would assign it to M. Conversely, assuming that the cost of misclassifying a record as a match is more than three times the cost of misclassifying a record as a non-match, the comparison vector would be assigned to U.

Costs are domain dependent and are considered given in the proposed model. Moreover, the matching probabilities of the comparison records are also considered as given. Given such inputs, the model produces as outputs the decision rule on the membership to M or U and the required thresholds.

In the model, the costs c_{ij} are considered, meaning the costs of making a decision A_i when the compared pairs of records has an actual matching status j (M or U). Decisions correspond to assignments to the three areas A_1, A_2, and A_3 defined in Section 5.6.1, related, respectively, to matching, possible matching, and non-matching pairs. Therefore, a cost is assigned to each decision, as shown in the table in Figure 5.9.

Cost	Decision	Actual Matching
C_{10}	A_1	M
C_{11}	A_1	U
C_{20}	A_2	M
C_{21}	A_2	U
C_{30}	A_3	M
C_{31}	A_3	U

Fig. 5.9. Costs corresponding to various decisions

The cost that has to be minimized is given by

$$c_m = c_{10} * \mathrm{P}(d = A_1, r = \mathtt{M}) + c_{11} * \mathrm{P}(d = A_1, r = \mathtt{U})$$
$$+ c_{20} * \mathrm{P}(d = A_2, r = \mathtt{M}) + c_{21} * \mathrm{P}(d = A_2, r = \mathtt{U})$$
$$+ c_{30} * \mathrm{P}(d = A_3, r = \mathtt{M}) + c_{31} * \mathrm{P}(d = A_3, r = \mathtt{U}),$$

where d is the predicted class of a pair of records and r is the actual matching status of a pair of records. The attribution of every point in the decision space constituted by the union of A_1, A_2, and A_3 is done in order to have the cost c_m minimized. Inequalities are imposed on a particular expression of c_m obtained by applying the Bayes theorem and a few other transformations to the formulation given above. Further details can be found in [197].

5.7 Empirical Techniques

The first proposal for a record matching technique based mainly on an empirical approach can be traced to 1983, to the work by Bitton and DeWitt [28]. The idea is to detect *exact* duplicates in a table, first sorting the table and then checking the identity of neighboring tuples. This basic approach has been adapted and extended in subsequent works in order to detect *approximate* duplicates with the goal of achieving better accuracy and performance results. In this section, we will review some major empirical techniques, starting from the sorted neighborhood method (Section 5.7.1) and the related priority queue algorithm (Section 5.7.2), then describing a technique for matching complex structured data (Section 5.7.3), and concluding with a technique for matching XML data (Section 5.7.4) and some additional empirical approaches to search space reduction (Section 5.7.5).

5.7.1 Sorted Neighborhood Method and Extensions

The basic sorted neighborhood method (SNM) was proposed in [182] and [93], and is also referred to as the *merge-purge* method. Given a collection of two or more files, the sorted-neighborhood method is applied to a sequential list of records built from such files. The method can be summarized in three phases, depicted in Figure 5.10 (let x_i, y_i, and z_i denote a possible matching record i in three different sources):

- *Create keys.* Given the list of records derived from the union of available sources in a single file (see Figure 5.10, left), a key is computed by extracting a subset of relevant fields or portions of fields. Indeed, the rationale is that similar data will have closely matching keys. If N is the total number of records in the list, the complexity of this step is $O(N)$.
- *Sort data.* On the basis of the key selected in the previous phase, records are sorted in the data list (see Figure 5.10, middle). The complexity of this step is $O(N log N)$.

- *Merge.* A fixed size window is moved through the sequential list of records, limiting the comparisons for matching records to those records in the window (see Figure 5.10, right). If the size of the window is w records, then every new record entering the window is compared with the previous $w-1$ records to find matching records. The decision about matching records is made according to domain-specific rules expressed in *equational theory*. The complexity of the merging phase is $O(wN)$.

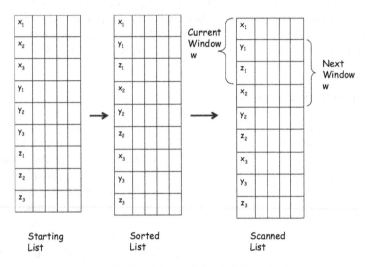

Fig. 5.10. Phases of the SNM method

When the three phases are applied serially, the total time complexity of the method is $O(NlogN)$ if $w < \lceil logN \rceil$, $O(wN)$ otherwise.

In addition to the comparison performed in the merging phase, a *transitive closure step* is performed. Specifically, if records r_1 and r_2 are found to be similar, and records r_2 and r_3 are also found to be similar, then r_1 and r_3 are marked to be similar as well. Note that while the couples (r_1, r_2) and (r_2, r_3) must be within the same window to be declared as similar, the inferred similarity between (r_1, r_3) does not require the two records to belong to the same window. This property can be exploited in order to have smaller sizes for the scanning window, with invariant accuracy of the result.

The effectiveness of the sorted neighborhood method depends highly on the key selected to sort the records, since only keys of good quality cause similar records to be close to each other in the window, after the sorting phase. As an example, the first names of person records can be selected instead of last names, since we may suppose (or know) that last names can be more frequently misspelled than first names, which are typically more familiar. The SNM assumes that a "key designer" chooses the most suitable key, based on considerations of the selectivity of the different attributes. In [26], the basic sorted neighborhood method is extended by making the choice of the key automatically. In order to choose a "good" key for matching instead of relying on "key designers", the idea is to rely on a quality characterization of records and on an identification power criterion that captures the selectivity of the different attributes. Experimental validation of the proposed method shows that whenever the quality characterization is taken into account, such automatic choice outperforms the basic SNM.

So far, the basic SNM has been described, running *once* on the list of concatenated source files. In the following, we describe two further versions: the *multi-pass approach*, which proposes several runs of the algorithm for more effectiveness, and the *incremental SNM*, which eliminates the need for the method to work on a single list of input data.

Multi-pass Approach

The multi-pass SNM is based on the consideration that running the SNM on a single sorting key does not produce the most suitable results. For example, if a highly selective key is chosen as the matching key, such as `SocialSecurityNumber`, even a single digit error can compromise the final result. Therefore, the idea is to have several runs of the method, each with a different key and very small windows. Having different keys allows to reasonably ensure that, if there are errors on some of them, the subsequent runs will compensate such errors. Also, running SNM with small windows is several less expensive steps instead of a single expensive one.

Each run of the multi-pass approach produces a set of pairs of records that can be merged. A transitive closure step is then applied to such pairs of records, and the result is the union of all pairs found in the independent runs, with the addition of pairs that can be inferred by transitive closure. The experimental evidence is that the multi-pass approach drastically improves the accuracy of the basic SNM with a single run on large varying windows, as also remarked in Section 5.9.

Incremental SNM

The incremental SNM is proposed for when it is too expensive to produce a single file of all input data. Typically, the step of producing a single file may be acceptable once; but, then, the problem occurs on how to deal with newly arrived data. The basic idea of the incremental SNM is to select a set of *prime-representatives* of records for each cluster deriving from the application of the SNM. Once new data need to be merged, they will be concatenated with the set of prime-representatives; the SNM will work on this concatenated set and new prime-representatives will be selected for subsequent incremental phases. Each cluster can have more than one eligible prime-representative, and the strategies for selecting them can be various. For example, a strategy could be to select the longest and most complete record. As another example, the prime-representative could be selected as the record representing the most general concept within the cluster.

5.7.2 The Priority Queue Algorithm

The priority queue algorithm, first proposed in [134], is based on the same ideas of sorting and scanning as in the SNM. The main distinguishing issues are

- the usage of a domain-independent strategy to perform duplicate record detection, based on the Smith-Waterman algorithm [180] (see Section 5.4.3); and
- the usage of an efficient data structure, exploiting the union-find structure [187];
- the proposal of a heuristic method based on a priority queue for improving the performance of the SNM.

The *union-find* data structure is used for detecting and maintaining the connected components of an indirect graph. The problem of detecting duplicates can be modeled in terms of determining the connected components of a graph, if considering the transitivity of equality. Specifically, each record of the file can be modeled as a node of a graph, where an undirected edge connects two nodes if they match.

The matching of a pair of records can be recursively verified by considering if they belong to the same connected component: if they do, a match is declared; if they belong to different components a non-match is declared; otherwise, they are compared to each other, and, in case of a matching, a new component is added to the graph. The two operations of the union-find structure are *union* (x,y), combining the set to which x belongs with the set to which y belongs (further, a representative for the union set is also chosen and the union set replaces the two initial sets); *find(x)*, returning the representative of the unique set containing x.

The algorithm considers a priority queue containing a fixed number of sets of records that are representatives of clusters. Only the most recently detected cluster members are stored in the queue. Given a record **a**, the algorithm first checks if it is a member of the clusters represented in the priority queue by comparing the cluster representative of **a** with the cluster representative of each set in the priority queue. This check is done by the *find* operation. If the check is successful, then **a** is already known to be a member of a cluster in the priority queue. If it is not successful, then **a** is compared with records in the priority queue by the Smith-Waterman algorithm. If a match is detected, the *union* function adds the **a**'s cluster to the cluster of the matched record; otherwise, **a** must be a member of a cluster not present in the queue, and so it is saved with the highest priority as a singleton set in the queue.

The priority queue algorithm can perform considerably better than SNM for very large files and databases. For instance, the number of record comparisons can be reduced up to five times for a database of 900,000 total records (see [134]). In Section 5.9, further details on the experimental results are provided.

5.7.3 A Technique for Complex Structured Data: Delphi

A technique for complex structured data is described in [7], where the Delphi algorithm is proposed; complex structured data considered in Delphi are called *dimensional hierarchies*; they consist of a chain of relations linked by foreign key dependencies. Given a pair of adjacent relations in the hierarchy, we call *parent* the relation on the foreign key side, and *child* the relation on the key side.

Dimensional hierarchies of relations are used typically (but not exclusively) in star schemas of data warehouses, where the chain of relations is composed of a relation representing the table of facts, and one or more relations representing the dimensions of interest for the multidimensional analysis, organized with various normalization degrees. We adopt in the following a more general term for dimensional hierarchies, namely, *relational hierarchies*.

An example of relational hierarchy is shown in Figure 5.11, where persons are represented in (i) the relation Person, (ii) their Administrative Region of residence (e.g., district or region, according to country), and (iii) Country. The relation Country is parent of the relation Administrative Region and is at the top of the hierarchy, while the relation Person is at the bottom. Note that RegId and CtryId are generated keys, used for an efficient link for pairs of tables.

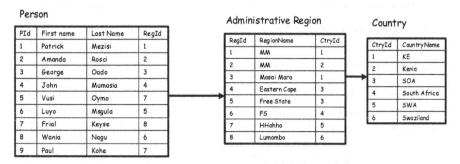

Person

PId	First name	Last Name	RegId
1	Patrick	Mezisi	1
2	Amanda	Rosci	2
3	George	Oado	3
4	John	Mumasia	4
5	Vusi	Oymo	7
6	Luyo	Msgula	5
7	Frial	Keyse	8
8	Wania	Nagu	6
9	Paul	Kohe	7

Administrative Region

RegId	RegionName	CtryId
1	MM	1
2	MM	2
3	Masai Mara	1
4	Eastern Cape	3
5	Free State	3
6	FS	4
7	HHohho	5
8	Lumombo	6

Country

CtryId	CountryName
1	KE
2	Kenia
3	SOA
4	South Africa
5	SWA
6	Swaziland

Fig. 5.11. Three hierarchical relations

In Figure 5.11, three different types of objects are represented in the schema:

1. persons, with region and country of residence;
2. regions, characterized by a set of resident persons and country;

3. countries, characterized by a set of regions and, for each region, a set of resident persons.

For each type of object, we may examine which are the duplicates in the relational hierarchy; e.g., we see that three different African countries are represented in the `Country` relation instance, with both the official name and an acronym.

The main idea of Delphi is to exploit the hierarchical structure of tuples, using both local (called *textual*) and global (called *co-occurrence*) similarity measures. Examine the tuples in the `Country` relation of Figure 5.11. If we simply adopt a similarity measure local to the relation, e.g., the edit distance between names of countries, we can falsely conclude that <SOA, SWA> are duplicates, and <KE, Kenia>, <SOA, South Africa>, <SWA, Swaziland> are not duplicates. If in addition to the edit distance we adopt a second distance that looks at how such items co-occur with linked tuples in the child `Administrative Region` relation, then we can see that (i) KE and Kenia have the MM tuple in common and (ii) for the three pairs <KE, Kenia>, <SOA, South Africa>, and <SWA, Swaziland> we can find non-overlapping groups of tuples linked with the pair.

The above example shows that in order to discover duplicates in relational hierarchies, we have to exploit the full structure of the hierarchy, or at least of adjacent relations. This strategy has two claimed advantages compared to "local" record linkage strategies:

1. it reduces the number of false matches, i.e., pairs of tuples incorrectly detected to be duplicates; this is the case with the pair <SOA, SWA>;
2. it reduces the number of false non-matches, i.e. pairs of tuples incorrectly detected as non duplicates; this is the case with the pair <KE, Kenia>.

More formally, traditional textual similarity measures are extended with a *co-occurrence similarity function* defined as follows. In a relational hierarchy, a tuple in a parent relation R_i joins with a set, which we call its children set, of tuples in the child relation; the co-occurrence between two distinct tuples is measured by the amount of overlap between the children sets of the two tuples. An unusually significant co-occurrence (more than the average overlap between pairs of tuples in R_i or above a certain threshold) is a cause for suspecting that one is a duplicate of the other. The above duplicate detection procedure can be performed for all types of objects represented in the hierarchy (in our example, persons, regions, and countries). Two objects are considered duplicates if corresponding pairs of tuples in each relation of the hierarchy either match exactly or are duplicates, according to duplicate detection functions at each level. The complete Delphi algorithm is described in Figure 5.12.

In order to make efficient the top-down traversal of the hierarchy and reduce the number of pairwise tuple comparisons, a potential duplicate identification filter is adopted to efficiently isolate a subset consisting of all potential

```
1. Process first the top most relation
2. Group relations below the top most relation into clusters of tuples
3. Prune each cluster according to properties of distance functions eliminating
tuples that cannot be duplicates.
4. Compare pairs of tuples within each group according to two comparison
functions and corresponding thresholds
        ✓ Textual similarity between two tuples
        ✓ Co-occurrence similarity between the children sets of the tuples
5. Decide for duplicates comparing a suitable combination of the two measures
against a given threshold or a set of thresholds.
6. Dynamically update thresholds
7. Move one level down in the hierarchy
```

Fig. 5.12. The Delphi algorithm

duplicates, and prune the tuples that cannot be duplicates. The pruning step corresponds to step 2, state space reduction in Figure 5.4.

The dynamic threshold update step has the goal of adapting thresholds used in step 5 to structural characteristics of different groups; the number of items of the definition domain may vary across groups, and names of regions in one country may be longer or constitute a wider set than they are in another country, thus influencing the thresholds. See Section 5.9.4 on decision methods comparison.

5.7.4 XML Duplicate Detection: DogmatiX

In this section we describe a technique for object identification for XML documents. Finding duplicates in XML data has two major additional challenges when compared to files or relational data, namely, (i) the identification of objects to compare, and (ii) the possibility that the same elements are defined with different structures due to the flexibility of XML as a semistructured data model. In [207], an algorithm called DogmatiX (Duplicates Objects Get Matched in XML) that explicitly considers these features is proposed. The algorithm has a preprocessing phase that consists of three steps:

- *Step 1: candidate query formulation and execution.* XML data are first queried to extract duplicate candidates. Duplicate candidates are considered with respect to a real-world type. For instance, `Person` and `People` can be considered as two representations of the same real-world type `Individual`. Currently, the candidate selection is not done automatically in DogmatiX.
- *Step 2: description query formulation and execution.* The descriptions of duplicate candidates are expressed by queries that select only some of the properties that are associated with objects, namely, the ones that are considered meaningful for object identification. As an example, while the `Name` and `Surname` of a `Person` can be considered as relevant for identifying it, information about the person's hobbies cannot be relevant to the scope. Two heuristics to determine the candidate's descriptions are proposed in

[207]. The heuristics are based on a locality principle: given an element e the farther some information is from e, the less related it is to it.

- *Step 3: object description (OD) generation.* A relation consisting of tuples OD(value, name) is generated, where value describes an instance of some information and name identifies the type of information by name. For instance, (Smith, Surname) is part of the object descriptor for a Person instance included in the duplicate candidates.

After such a preprocessing phase, three actual steps for duplicate detection are performed:

- *Step 4: comparison reduction.* First a filter is applied to reduce the number of duplicate candidates: the filter is defined as an upper bound to the similarity measure and does not require the computation of such a measure, but preliminarily removes objects from the set of possible duplicates. Then, a clustering phase is applied in order to compare only objects within the same cluster.
- *Step 5: comparisons.* Pairwise comparisons are performed on the basis of a similarity measure. Such a similarity measure is defined in a domain-independent way (see [207] for details). The similarity measure takes into account some important features like (i) relevance of data or their identification power, by means of the introduction of a variant of the inverse document frequency (IDF) metric; (ii) the distinction between nonspecified and contradictory data; e.g., the fact that two persons have several different preferences may be an indicator the two persons are distinct, while a missing preference should not penalize the similarity measure.
- *Step 6: duplicate clustering.* The transitivity of the relationship *is-duplicate-of* is applied to XML objects selected as duplicates in Step 5.

The algorithm is a representative example of object identification for semistructured data.

5.7.5 Other Empirical Methods

The time efficiency of the record linkage process can be improved by the reduction of the search space, which can be performed by means of blocking and windowing strategies. For instance, instead of making detailed comparisons of all 10 billion pairs from two sets of 100,000 records representing all persons in a State, it may be sufficient to consider the set of pairs that agree on LastName and ZipCode in the address. Note that there is an implicit assumption that comparisons not made due to blocking are non-match records. A good field to be chosen for blocking should contain a large number of values that are fairly uniformly distributed, and must have a low probability of inaccuracy errors; specifically, this last property is due to the fact that errors in a field used for blocking can result in failure to bring linkable record pairs together.

When specific conditions hold, further techniques can be applied to optimize record linkage. In the following, we briefly describe the 1-1 matching technique that can be used when it is known that few duplications occur. Then, we describe the bridging file technique that can be used when a third source is available that links the two sources that are going to be matched.

1-1 Matching Technique

The basic idea of the 1-1 matching technique is to force each record of the set A to be matched with at most one record of the set B. The rationale behind this technique is that if there are few duplicates, it is sufficient to stop to the *best* matching record, which is the record having the highest agreement weight with the observed one. In [105] a technique to force 1-1 matching is proposed, in which the set of matching assignments is globally optimized.

Bridging File

Given the two files A and B, the bridging file includes a set of common identifying information for them. For instance, let us suppose that both A and B store personal information of citizens, namely, Name, Surname, and Address, but A stores, in addition, tax-related information, while B stores social service-related information. The information common to A and B, can be available in a *bridging file*, as represented in Figure 5.13. Notice that a record in A can be linked to several records in B, but typically *not to all*; therefore, the idea is that when a bridging file is available, record linkage efficiency can be improved. However, it is very important to have high quality bridging files, in order to have good matching results.

A	A&B	B
$Tax_{1,1}$	$Name_1$, $Surname_1$, $Address_1$	$SocialService_{2,1}$
$Tax_{1,2}$	$Name_2$, $Surname_2$, $Address_2$	$SocialService_{2,2}$
...	...	...
...	...	...
$Tax_{1,n}$	$Name_n$, $Surname_n$, $Address_n$	$SocialService_{2,n}$

Fig. 5.13. Bridging file example

5.8 Knowledge-Based Techniques

In this section, we describe the details of two techniques that are classified as knowledge-based. Specifically, Section 5.8.1 describes the Intelliclean system and Section 5.8.2 describes the Atlas system.

5.8.1 A Rule-Based Approach: Intelliclean

The main idea of Intelliclean [124] is to exploit rules as an evolution of previously proposed distance functions; rules are extracted from domain knowledge and fed into an expert system engine, making use of an efficient method for comparing a large collection of rules to a large collection of objects. Rules are of two types, with different goals:

- *duplicate identification rules*, specifying conditions according to which two tuples can be classified as duplicates. Duplicate identification rules include text similarity functions, but go further, allowing more complex logic expressions for determining tuple equivalence. An example of a duplicate identification rule is shown in Figure 5.14, where duplicates are searched for in a **Restaurant** relation, with attributes **Id**, **Address**, and **Telephone**. For the rule in Figure 5.14 to be activated, the corresponding telephone numbers must match, and one of the identifiers must be a substring of the other; furthermore, the addresses must also be very similar (similarity of addresses using the *FieldSimilarity* function must be higher than 0.8). Records classified as duplicates by this rule have a certainty factor of 80 %. A *certainty factor* (CF) represents expert confidence in the effectiveness of the rule in discovering duplicates, where 0 < CF < 1. Specifically, we can assign a high certainty factor to a rule if we are sure that it will identify true duplicates. Analogously, we assign smaller values for rules that are less strict.
- *merge/purge rules*, specifying how duplicate records are to be handled. An example is "Only the tuple with the least number of empty fields is to be kept in a group of duplicate tuples, and the rest are to be deleted."

```
Define rule Restaurant_Rule
Input tuples: R1, R2
IF  (R1.telephone = R2.telephone)
AND  (ANY_SUBSTRING (R1.ID, R2.ID) = TRUE)
AND  (FIELDSIMILARITY (R1.address = R2.address) > 0.8)
THEN
DUPLICATES (R1,R2) CERTAINTY = 0.8
```

Fig. 5.14. An example of the duplicate identification rule in Intelliclean

The complete Intelliclean strategy is shown in Figure 5.15. The procedure can be seen as an improvement over the sorted neighborhood method presented in Section 5.7.1, where the improvement mainly regards the adoption of rules and a more effective transitive closure strategy.

From step 2.1 of Figure 5.15, we observe that rules are extracted from domain knowledge by domain experts; therefore the approach can be classified as domain dependent. The selection of precise, expressive, and efficient rules is a crucial activity to achieve effectiveness of the cleaning process, i.e., maximize recall and precision (see Section 5.9). Step 2.3 is motivated by the fact

> **1. Preprocessing**
> Perform data type checks and format standardization
> **2. Processing**
> > **2.1** The compared records are fed into an expert system engine together with a set of rules of the form IF ‹condition› THEN ‹action›.
> > **2.2** Check iteratively within a sliding window first Duplicate Identification rules and then Merge Purge rules using a basic production system to see which ones should fire based on the facts in the database, looping back to the first rule when it has finished.
> > **2.3** Perform transitive closure under uncertainty using an improved version of the multi-pass Sorted Neighborhood searching method
> **3. Human verification and validation stage**
> Human intervention to manipulate the duplicate record groups for which merge/purge rules are not defined

Fig. 5.15. The complete Intelliclean strategy

that transitive closure in the multi-pass sorted neighborhood algorithm tends to increase false matches. As we have seen in the example, in Intelliclean a *certainty factor* (CF) is applied to each duplicate identification rule. During the computation of the transitive closure, we compare the resulting certainty factor of the merged group to a user-defined threshold. This threshold represents how tight or confident we want the merges to be. Any merges that result in a certainty factor less than the threshold will not be executed.

As an example, let us assume we perform Step 2.3 on the following pairs of tuples: (A,B) with CF = 0.9; (B,C) with CF = 0.85; (C,D) with CF = 0.8; threshold = 0.5. The groups (A,B) and (B,C) will be firstly considered, as these groups have higher CFs. They will be merged to form (A,B,C) with CF = 0.9 x 0.85 = 0.765. Then, this group is merged with (C,D) to form (A,B,C,D) with CF = 0.765 x 0.8 = 0.612, still greater than the threshold; however, if the threshold were set at 0.7, (A,B,C) and (C,D) would remain separate, as the resulting CF of the merged group, equal to 0.612, would be less than the threshold.

5.8.2 Learning Methods for Decision Rules: Atlas

In Intelliclean, discussed in the previous section, rules are extracted from the domain knowledge by experts, and no specific learning process is conceived for their generation. In this section, we discuss Atlas, a technique, presented in [189], that improves the knowledge-based approach in the following directions:

1. The rules include a wide set of domain-independent transformations, as possible mappings between textual strings, such as <World Health Organization, WHO> which transforms a string of three items into the string made of the initials of the items. Examples of transformations are shown in Figure 5.16. <World Health Organization, WHO> is an example of the *Acronym* transformation.
2. Structural information on rules can be obtained first from an analysis performed on tuples in the input, in order to extract knowledge on recur-

rent similarities between the different pairs of attributes of objects to be matched.

3. Rules can be obtained through a learning process on a training set, with or without active expert user involvement.

Soundex converts an item into a Soundex code. Items that sound similar have the same code
Abbreviation replaces an item with corresponding abbreviation (e.g., third → 3rd)
Equality compares two items to determine if each item contains the same characters in the same order
Initial computes if one item is equal to the first character of the other.
Prefix computes if one item is equal to a continuous subset of the other starting at the first character
Suffix computes if one item is equal to a continuous subset of the other starting at the last character
Abbreviation computes if one item is equal to a subset of the other (e.g., Blvd, Boulevard)
Acronym computes if all characters of one item string are initial letters of all items from the other string

Fig. 5.16. Examples of transformations

In order to explain in more detail the overall strategy of Atlas, consider the pair of relations shown in Figure 5.17.

Relation1

LastName	Address	City	Region	Telephone
Ngyo	Mombsa Boulevard	Mutu	MM	350-15865

Relation2

LastName	Address	Region	Telephone
Ngoy	Mombasa Blvd.	Masai Mara	350-750123

Fig. 5.17. Two relations

In the figure, the two relations have four attributes in common, `LastName`, `Address`, `Region`, and `Telephone`. We assume that the two tuples refer to the same real-world object. The items in the two tuples have several differences, whose nature depends on the attribute. More specifically,

1. values of `LastName` differ, probably due to typing errors;
2. values of `Address` differ, both for a character in the first item and for "distance abbreviation transformation" in the second item;
3. values of `Region` differ in distance "acronym transformation"; and
4. values of `Telephone` match only in the area code, probably due to a different currency.

The four attributes show different behaviors with respect to the differences appearing in the corresponding items. In order to precompute candidate mappings between tuples *similarity scores* are computed for each couple of fields of tuples. They measure

1. local distances between each pair of attributes, based on a composition of applications of transformation and edit distance, applying the cosine similarity measure (see Section 5.4.3);
2. a global distance, where different weights are assigned to attributes in local distances; weights measure the selectivity of the attribute, to reflect the idea that we are more likely to believe matching between attributes in which values are rarer (for definitions and formulas see [189]).

At this point, mapping rules have to be constructed. An example of mapping rule, based on Figure 5.17, is

```
If Address > threshold1 ∧ Street > treshold2 Then matching
```

The *mapping rule learner* determines which attributes or combinations of attributes are most effective for mapping objects, with the final goal of determining the most accurate mapping rules, given threshold values. *Accuracy of mapping rules* is seen as their ability in dividing a given set of training examples in matched/not matched. This is performed by two methods:

1. *Decision trees* is an inductive learning technique, where attributes (and thresholds) are tested one at a time in the tree to discriminate between matching and non-matching pairs of tuples. Once an "optimal" decision tree is created, it is converted into the corresponding mapping rule. In general, this method requires a large number of training examples.
2. An *active learning procedure*, where a committee of decision tree learners that vote is created in order to choose the most informative examples for the user to classify as matching or non-matching.

Once mapping rules are chosen, they are applied to candidate mappings to determine the set of mapped objects.

5.9 Comparison of Techniques

In Section 5.3, *search space reduction*, *choice of comparison function* and *use of decision model* were identified as relevant steps in the object identification process. In this section, we first introduce metrics used to evaluate specific steps of object identification techniques (Section 5.9.1). Then, we describe a detailed comparison on two sets of techniques: (i) techniques that are mainly concerned with efficiency issues, i.e. search space reduction methods (Section 5.9.2) and comparison functions (Section 5.9.3); and (ii) techniques that are mainly focused on effectiveness, i.e. decision methods (Section 5.9.4). Finally, in Section 5.9.5, we comment on some experimental results.

5.9.1 Metrics

The decision on actual matching M or non-matching U of two records can give rise to two types of errors, *false positives* FPs (also called *false matches* in the chapter) for records declared as M while actually being U, and *false negatives* FNs (*false non-matches*) for records declared as U while actually being M. *True positives* TPs (*true matches*) are the correctly identified as M and *true negatives* TN (*true non-matches*) are the correctly identified U. Figure 5.18 summarizes such different cases. It follows from definitions that the following equalities hold:

$$M = TP + FN$$

$$U = TN + FP$$

M	Actual match w.r.t. real world
U	Actual non match w.r.t. real world
FP	Declared match while actual non match
FN	Declared non-match while actual match
TP	Declared match while actual match
TN	Declared non match while actual non match

Fig. 5.18. Notation on matching decision cases

Several metrics to evaluate effectiveness of object identification techniques have been proposed, combining such criteria. The most typical metrics are *recall* and *precision*. *Recall* measures how many true positives are identified in relation to the total number of actual matches. It is given by:

$$recall = \frac{TP}{M} = \frac{TP}{TP + FN}$$

The aim of an object identification technique is of course to have a high recall. *Precision* measures how many true matches are identified in relation to the total number of declared matches, including erroneous ones (i.e., FPs):

$$precision = \frac{TP}{TP + FP}$$

The aim is to have a high precision. Recall and precision are often conflicting goals in the sense that if one wants to have a greater number of true positives (i.e., to increase recall level), usually more false positives are also found (i.e., precision decreases). Besides recall and precision, other metrics that have been used are *false negative percentage* and *false positive percentage*. False negative percentage considers how many undetected matches are present relative to the number of actual matches:

$$false\ negative\ percentage = \frac{FN}{M} = \frac{FN}{TP + FN}$$

False positive percentage considers how many wrongly detected matches are present, relative to the number of actual matches:

$$false\ positive\ percentage = \frac{FP}{M} = \frac{FP}{TP + FN}$$

In order to combine recall and precision, *F-score* has also been proposed. It corresponds to the harmonic mean of recall and precision. More specifically, F-score is given by:

$$F - score = \frac{2RP}{P + R}.$$

Besides these specific metrics, traditional time complexity metrics are used to evaluate the efficiency of the object identification process; an example is the *number of comparisons* to be performed during the process.

5.9.2 Search Space Reduction Methods

As already described, given two sets of records A and B we want to compare for identifying the same objects belonging to both of them, the search space is the cartesian product A × B. In order to reduce such space, we have seen that three principal methods exist, blocking, sorted neighborhood, and pruning.

Typically, pruning is used in most empirical techniques, either in conjunction with blocking or in conjunction with sorted neighborhood; in the following we will examine blocking and sorted neighborhood. In [65], a comparison of blocking and sorted neighborhood is reported. The two methods are compared considering (i) the blocking method for different values of the block key length and (ii) the sorted neighborhood method for different values of the window size. Blocking and sorted neighborhood are evaluated on the basis of the effectiveness of the matching process, measured by the F-score metric. The experiments show that the F-score values for blocking and sorted neighborhood are comparable for appropriate choices of the blocking key length and the window size.

Furthermore, when comparing the time complexity of the two methods, a comparable behavior is similarly exhibited. Indeed, as already shown in Section 5.4.2, the total time complexity of blocking is $O(h(n) + n^2/b)$, where $h(n) = nlogn$ if blocking is implemented using sorting, which is comparable to the total time complexity of the sorted method, that is, $O(nlogn + wn)$.

5.9.3 Comparison Functions

Various empirical analyses have been done to discover which comparison functions perform better. In [65] a comparison is reported between 3-grams, bigrams, edit distance, and Jaro algorithm. The experiment considers the behavior of the functions on a set of name pairs, some of which are the same names, but misspelled, while others are different, or swapped. The result of the experiment is that Jaro outperforms for the same name misspelled and known to be different, while bi-gram outperforms for names swapped. In [215], Jaro is again compared with edit distance and bi-gram, and it is shown that it is superior, especially when transpositions are present.

5.9.4 Decision Methods

We now characterize the decision methods adopted by the object identification techniques described in this chapter. For each decision method, we report

- *input parameters*, required by the method. Note that some techniques also provide methods for computing such parameters;
- *output*, provided by the method;
- *objective*, that summarizes the main goal to be achieved by the decision method;
- *human interaction*, representing the steps of the object identification process that require an interaction with an expert;
- *selection/construction of a representative* for the matching records, showing which methods explicitly include the selection or construction of a record that represents a specific cluster obtained in the matching process.

The techniques are represented in Figure 5.19.

Technique	Input	Output	Objective	Human interaction	Selection/Construction of a representative for the matching records
Fellegi&Sunter	γ vector of comparison functions; Estimation of $T\mu$ and $T\lambda$; m- and u-probabilities	For each record pair, decision on match, non-match, possible match with given error rates	Low error rates (false match and false non-match); Minimization of possible matches	Clerical Review of possible matches	No
Cost Based	Matrix of costs of decision rules; m- and u-probabilities	For each record pair, decision on match, non-match, possible match with given error rates	Minimization of cost of errors (false match and false non-match)	Clerical Review of possible matches; Matrix of costs of decision rules	No
SNM	Declarative rules encoding domain knowledge (for tuple level decision); Comparison functions (for attribute value decision); Threshold (for attribute value decision)	For each record pair, decision on match or non-match	Precision/Recall tradeoff	Choice of the matching key; Threshold Specification; Decision Rules	No (only for incremental SNM)
Priority-Queue	Smith Waterman comparison function; Threshold (for tuple value decision)	For each record pair, decision on match or non-match	Precision/Recall tradeoff	Threshold Specification	No
Delphi	Textual Comparison Function; Co-occurrence metric; Set of thresholds (dynamically updated)	For each record pair, decision on match or non-match	Precision/Recall tradeoff	None	No
DogMatrix	XML Threshold similarity (object level)	For each XML element pair, decision on match or non-match	Precision/Recall tradeoff	Selection of candidates; Threshold Specification	No
IntelliClean	Duplicate Identification Rules (for tuple decision); Merge Purge Rules (for tuple decision); Set of thresholds (for attribute comparison and for tuple merging)	For each record pair, decision on match or non-match; Merged Result for matching records	Precision/Recall tradeoff; User controlled confidentiality for merging	Duplicate Identification,Merge/Purge Rules Specification; Threshold Specification; Human verification for merging duplicates when rules are not specified	Yes
Atlas	Learnt Decision rules; Set of domain independent transformations; Thresholds	For each record pair, decision on match or non-match	Precision/Recall tradeoff	Mapping rule learning	No

Fig. 5.19. Comparison of decision methods

Looking at the input column, the decision rules that are used by the method can be specified at attribute and at tuple levels for structured data types. For the techniques that consider relational hierarchies, such as Delphi or XML documents, e.g. DogmatiX, thresholds are specified according to the various elements of the adopted data model. Specifically, in Delphi, thresholds are specified by the comparison between tuples and their children sets; in DogmatiX, the objects to be compared need to be explicitly identified in the XML documents, and thresholds are defined for such objects.

In the output column, observe that the probabilistic techniques typically partition records into three sets, match, non-match, and possible match, at given error rates. Conversely, both the empirical and knowledge-based techniques are used to partition records into two sets, match and non-match. The underlying assumption of such techniques is that of completely automated decision methods, not requiring any human review on possible matches (consider also the human interaction column).

The objective column summarizes the objective of the decision method. The probabilistic techniques rely on formal models explicitly including such an objective. The Fellegi and Sunter model is formulated to minimize possible matches, while the cost-based model has the objective of minimizing the cost of errors. The empirical and knowledge-based methods instead are all validated against the precision/recall performance, namely, how effective the decision method is in detecting true positives (precision) and not detecting false positives (recall).

In the human interaction column, for all methods but Delphi, there is the need of human-defined thresholds. Indeed, Delphi introduces a technique to dynamically determine thresholds, based on standard outlier detection methods, and considering that a duplicate has an outlier-like behavior referred to given similarity metrics.

The representative of a cluster of matched records is actually constructed/ selected only by Intelliclean. The concept of cluster representative is proposed also within the sorted neighborhood method and the priority-queue method, but with a different scope, reducing the number of pairwise comparisons to detect duplicates. In contrast, Intelliclean identifies a strategy and appropriate rules for building cluster representatives.

5.9.5 Results

The table in Figure 5.20 describes the results obtained by the different decision methodologies and the features of the data sets used for the experiments. For each technique, we report the metrics addressed, the type of data used in the experiments (synthetic vs. real), and the provided results in terms of the different metrics, as claimed by the authors of each technique.

The first row of Figure 5.20 refers to the sorted neighborhood method. Results of experiments are reported for both the synthetic and the experimental data sets. Note that such results depend on a specific parameter, namely, the

Technique	Metrics	Synthetic/ Real Data	Results
SNM	Precision False Positive Percentage	Synthetic	Precision 50%-70% on independent pass Precision close to 90% with transitive closure False Positive Percentage not significant (0.05 - 0.2%)
	Precision False positive Percentage False negative Percentage	Real	Not significant False Negatives Percentage Not significant False Positive Percentage
Priority- Queue	Precision Efficiency (Number of comparisons)	Synthetic	Precision similar to SNM Efficiency : 5 times less than SNM
	Efficiency (Number of comparisons)	Real	Precision not provided as for real data difficult to identify actual duplicate s EffiNumber of reduced comparisons similar to the one for the synthetic data set
Delphi	False Positive Percentage False Negative Percentage	Real	False Positive Percentage less than 25% False Negative Percentage around 20%
DogmatiX	Precision Recall	Real	For similarity measure: Experiment 1: Precision 70-100% Experiment 1: Recall: 2%-35% Experiment 2: Precision 60-100%
IntelliClean	Precision	Real	Experiment 1: Precision 80% Experiment 1: Less than 8% Recall Experiment 2 :Precision: 100% Experiment 2 :Recall:100%
Atlas	Precision (accuracy)	Real	Experiment 1: Precision 100% Experiment 2: Precision 99%

Fig. 5.20. Metrics used by to evaluate object identification by empirical techniques and related results.

size of the sliding window: intervals of values shown in the figure correspond to different sizes of the window. For the priority queue algorithm, the result of an efficiency test is shown, measured by the number of comparisons that the algorithm performs. The results for Delphi concern the first level of the hierarchy (see Section 5.7.3). For DogmatiX the reported results concern primarily the similarity measure included in the approach. The intervals of the metrics refer to the variability of the threshold used for the measure.

The experimental data sets, as well as the experimental conditions and assumptions, are different, and therefore it is not possible to actually compare the different techniques. Nevertheless, the figure's utility is in its summarizing the features of the experimental validation and testing performed on each technique.

5.10 Summary

In this chapter we have described several techniques proposed for the most relevant data quality activity, object identification. Due to heterogeneous schemas, and to possible errors in data entry and update processes, objects happen to have different representations and values in distinct databases. As a consequence, a *loss* of a clear identity may affect objects, thus compromising the possibility of reconstructing information sparse in distinct sources. Object identification techniques aim at repairing this loss of identity using context information available on the similarity of objects' representations in terms of tuples, hierarchical relations, and XML files. The concepts of "context information available" and "similarity" are formalized in different ways in probabilistic, empirical, and knowledge-based techniques. Moreover, techniques proposed in the three areas can be differently characterized with respect to the level of adoption, their efficiency, and their effectiveness. The probabilistic techniques emerge as the most adopted ones, due to their relative maturity and the experiences gained from their application. The empirical techniques have the efficiency as a major objective, and thus are particularly suitable for time critical applications. The knowledge-based techniques have the best potential effectiveness, due to the explicit modeling of domain knowledge. Comparisons between techniques, described in Section 5.9, as well as criteria adopted by specific techniques, provide the reader elements for choosing the most effective technique according to the context. We will discuss these issues in more depth in Chapter 7.

6

Data Quality Issues in Data Integration Systems

6.1 Introduction

In distributed environments, data sources are typically characterized by various kinds of heterogeneities that can be generally classified into (i) technological heterogeneities, (ii) schema heterogeneities and (iii) instance level heterogeneities. *Technological heterogeneities* are due to the use of products by different vendors, employed at various layers of an information and communication infrastructure. An example of technological heterogeneity is the usage of two different relational database management systems like IBM's DB2 vs. Microsoft's SQLServer. *Schema heterogeneities* are principally caused by the use of (i) different data models, such as one source that adopts the relational data model and a different source that adopts the XML data model, and (ii) different data representations, such as one source that stores addresses as one single field and another source that stores addresses with separate fields for street, civic number, and city. *Instance-level heterogeneities* are caused by different, conflicting data values provided by distinct sources for the same objects. This type of heterogeneity can be caused by quality errors, such as accuracy, completeness, currency, and consistency errors; such errors may result, for instance, from independent processes that feed the different data sources.

Today, there are many examples of scenarios in which data residing at different sources must be accessed in a unified way, overcoming such heterogeneities. *Data integration* is a major research and business area that has the main purpose of allowing a user to access data stored by heterogeneous data sources through the presentation of a unified view of this data. Though data integration must face all the types of heterogeneities listed above, in this chapter we focus particularly on instance-level heterogeneities, where data quality issues become very significant. Indeed, instance-level heterogeneities can strongly affect query processing in data integration systems. Specifically, the query processing activity can be performed by considering that different data sources may exhibit different quality levels for the data. Hence, answering algorithms can be executed to provide the optimal quality results for the final user. We will describe some approaches to such *quality-driven query processing*. Furthermore, when collecting data as answers to queries, possible conflicts must be solved, by means of a specific *instance-level conflict resolution* activity; otherwise, the whole integration process cannot be correctly terminated.

Quality-driven query processing and instance-level conflict resolution can be seen as two complementary approaches that deal with instance-level heterogeneities. Specifically, it is possible to consider

1. only-quality driven query processing (without conflict resolution);
2. only conflict resolution (without quality-driven query processing);
3. both approaches used complementarily.

Quality-driven query processing modifies the query answering semantics in order to take into account varying quality of source data. It can assume (case 1) that instance-level conflicts are not solved, but metadata are available in the system to return the best quality answer (see [142]). Instance-level conflict resolution can focus on solving conflicts between sources independently of the query processing (case 2), for example by operating not at query time but at a different phase of the data integration process, such as the population of a data warehouse (see [141]). Alternatively (case 3), conflicts resolution techniques can be performed at query-time, within the quality-driven query answering process itself (see [175]).

In this chapter, first we describe some basic concepts on data integration systems (Section 6.2). Then, we provide an overview of existing proposals to deal with quality-driven query processing (Section 6.3) and instance-level conflict resolution (Section 6.4). Finally, we give some insights into theoretical proposals to address inconsistent query answering in data integration systems (Section 6.5).

6.2 Generalities on Data Integration Systems

Two main approaches to data integration can be identified, based on the actual location of data stored by sources to be integrated

- *virtual data integration*, where the unified view is virtual and data reside only at sources. A reference architecture for virtual data integration is the mediator-wrapper architecture [209]; and
- *materialized data integration*, where the (unified view of) data is materialized, for instance, in a data warehouse.

In this chapter, we will refer mainly to *virtual* data integration. When describing quality-driven query processing we will essentially focus only on virtual data integration systems. In contrast, the concepts related to instance-level conflict resolution techniques can be applied in both virtual and materialized data integration scenarios.

In the following section, we will describe the major features of a virtual data integration system. As already discussed in the introduction, data integration is the problem of combining data residing in different sources, providing the user with a unified view of this data, called *global schema*. A data integration system (DIS) is composed of three elements: (i) a *global schema*; (ii) a set of *source schemas*, including schemas of all sources; and (iii) a *mapping* between the global schema and the source schemas, which specifies the relationships between the concepts expressed in the global schema and the concepts in the source schemas.

Virtual data integration typically assumes a mediator-wrapper architecture, depicted in Figure 6.1. Wrappers have the main task of providing a uniform data model to the mediator. The mediator has the task of decomposing the global query into queries on the schemas of data sources. Furthermore, the mediator must combine and reconcile the multiple answers coming from wrappers of local data sources.

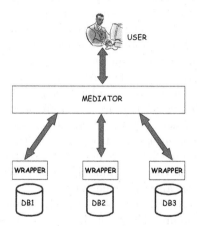

Fig. 6.1. Mediator-wrapper architecture

Two basic approaches have been proposed to specify the mapping [116]. The first approach, called *global-as-view* (GAV), requires the global schema to be expressed in terms of queries (or views) over the data sources. The second approach, called *local-as-view* (LAV), requires each data source to be expressed in terms of queries over the global schema. A third approach is called *global-local-as-view* (GLAV), and it is a mixture of the two; it combines the GAV and LAV approaches in such a way that queries over the sources are put into correspondence with queries over the global schema.

6.2.1 Query Processing

Irrespective whether the mapping is GAV or LAV (or GLAV), query processing in data integration requires a reformulation step: the query posed over the global schema has to be reformulated in terms of a set of queries over the sources. Nevertheless, the actual realization of query processing in data integration systems is strictly dependent on the method used for the specification of the mapping.

Query processing in GAV can be based on a simple *unfolding* strategy: given a query q over the alphabet of the global schema A_G, every element of A_G is substituted with the corresponding query over the sources, and the resulting query is then evaluated on data stored by local sources. Query processing in GAV is reduced to unfolding (and is therefore not complex), if there are no integrity constraints on the global schema. Conversely, if integrity constraints are present, data retrieved from the sources may or may not satisfy such constraints. If constraints are violated, the parts of data that do not violate the constraints may still be of interest, and the query answering process should allow their return as a result. Therefore, introducing integrity constraints in GAV implies dealing with issues related to query answering in the presence of incomplete information, and to query answering in the presence of inconsistent information [37]. However, typically, query answering in GAV has the advantage of leading to simpler query answering mechanisms.

Conversely, in the LAV approach it is easier to add or remove sources from the system, while generally requiring more sophisticated query answering techniques. Specifically, since in the LAV approach sources are modeled as views over the global schema, the problem of processing a query is called *view-based query processing*. There are two approaches to view-based query processing: view-based query rewriting and view-based query answering.

View-based query rewriting consists of reformulating the query into a possibly equivalent expression that refers only to the source structures. Once the rewriting of the query has been computed, it can be directly evaluated over the sources to obtain the answer to the query.

View-based query answering is more direct: besides the query and the mapping definitions, we are also given the extensions of the views over the global schema. The goal is to compute the set of tuples that is the answer set of the query in all databases consistent with the information on the views.

More details on query processing and on the definition of a formal framework for data integration are described in Section 6.5.1. In the following, we provide an example to show how the mapping can be specified and used for query processing. Let us consider a global schema consisting of the following relations:

- `Book(Title, Year, Author)`, representing books with their titles, their years of publication and their authors.
- `Award(Title, Prize)`, representing titles of and prizes won by the books.
- `NonProfessional(Author)`, storing names of authors whose main profession is not writing books.

Let us suppose there are two sources: S_1(Title, Year, Author) storing information on books since 1930 by non-professional authors, and S_2(Title,

Prize), storing information on awards won by books since 1970. A global query could ask for "title and prize of books published after 1980", corresponding to the Datalog formulation (see [190]):

$$\texttt{Book(T; 1980; A)} \wedge \texttt{Award(T; P)},$$

where, the query is expressed as the conjunction of two atomic formulas with arguments that are variables (T, A, P) and constants (1980). A GAV mapping would define the global concepts in terms of the sources by means of the following rules:

- Book(T; Y; A) ← S_1(T; Y; A)
- NonProfessional(A) ← S_1(T; Y; A)
- Award(T; P) ← S_2(T; P)

The global query Book(T; 1980; A) ∧ Award(T; P) is processed by means of unfolding, i.e., by expanding the atoms according to their definitions until we come up with source relations. Therefore, in this case, the unfolding process leads to the following query, expressed in terms of source schemas:

$$S_1(\texttt{T; 1980; A}) \wedge S_2(\texttt{T; P}).$$

Conversely, in the case of an LAV mapping, rules define the concepts in the local source schemas in terms of the global schema as follows:

- S_1(T; Y; A) ← Book(T; Y; A) ∧ NonProfessional(A) ∧ Y ≥ 1930
- S_2(T; P) ← Book(T; Y; A) ∧ Award(T, P) ∧ Y ≥ 1970

The query on the global schema is processed by means of an inference mechanism aiming to reexpress the atoms of the global view in terms of atoms at the sources. Therefore, in this case, the inference process leads to the following query, expressed in terms of source schemas:

$$S_1(\texttt{T; 1980; A}) \wedge S_2(\texttt{T; P})$$

This is the same query derived as a result of the unfolding process; but an inference procedure has been used instead.

6.3 Techniques for Quality-Driven Query Processing

In this section we provide an overview of several proposals to perform quality-driven query processing, which returns an answer to a global query, by explicitly taking into account the quality of data provided by local sources; however, several other techniques are present in the literature, e.g., [25, 24].

6.3.1 The QP-alg: Quality-Driven Query Planning

In this section, we describe the approach presented in [142], which we will refer to as QP-alg in the following. The mapping between local sources and the global schema is specified by means of *query correspondence assertions* (QCAs) that have the general form

$$MQ \leftarrow Si.vj \leftarrow WQ,$$

where (i) MQ is the mediator query and is a conjunctive query, (ii) Si.vj denotes an arbitrary view vj on the source Si, and (iii) WQ is the wrapper query. The mapping can be classified GLAV, as a query on the global schema is defined in terms of a query on the sources.

Three classes of data quality dimensions, called *information quality criteria* (IQ criteria), are defined:

- *Source-specific criteria*, defining the quality of a whole source. Examples of such criteria are *reputation* of the source, based on users' personal preferences, and *timeliness*, measured by the source update frequency.
- *QCA-specific criteria*, defining the quality of specific query correspondence assertions. An example of such criteria is *price*, i.e., the price to be paid for the query.
- *User-query specific criteria*, measuring the quality of the source with respect to the answer provided to a specific user query. An example of such criteria is *completeness*, based on the fullness of source relations.

Some IQ criteria metrics are predetermined, others are dynamically calculated, and the result is a set of IQ criteria vectors to be used to rank sources and plans. Note that, in a DBMS, given a query, query plans are constructed that are equivalent in terms of the query result provided; they are then ranked and selected on the basis of a cost model. Conversely, the plans built according to the QP-alg's approach produce different query results, though they are checked to be semantically correct. The phases of QP-alg are shown in Figure 6.2.

The first phase consists of a pruning of the source space by filtering out low quality sources on the basis of source-specific criteria. In order to classify sources on the basis of IQ criteria vectors, a multiattribute decision making method is used, namely, the data envelopment analysis [44].

The second phase creates plans by exploiting the fact that QCAs are actually views over the mediator schema, and thus basic data integration results for query answering using views can be exploited [117].

The third phase first evaluates the quality of QCAs (step 1 in plan selection in Figure 6.2). Specifically, QCA-specific criteria and user-query specific criteria are calculated for each QCA. Then, the quality of a plan is evaluated (step 2 in plan selection in Figure 6.2) by relying on a procedure similar to cost models for DBMSs. A tree is built for each plan, with QCAs as leaves and join operators as inner nodes. The IQ vector is recursively calculated for a node, starting from its children nodes. A set of "merge" functions for each quality criterion is defined in order to combine IQ vectors. As an example, the merge function for the price criterion is defined as the sum of both the right child and the left child of a given node, meaning that both queries must be made. In Figure 6.3, an example is shown, detailing how the price of a plan P_i is computed.

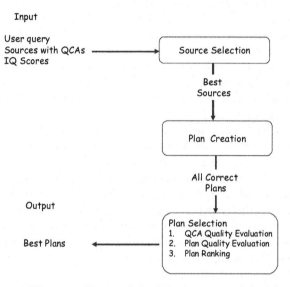

Fig. 6.2. Phases of the QP-alg approach

Then, plan ranking is performed by means of the simple additive weighting (SAW) method (step 3 in plan selection in Figure 6.2). Specifically, the final IQ score for a plan is computed as the weighted sum of scaled criteria, where weights represent the "importance" of each criterion to the user. Finally, the best plans, according to the performed ranking, are returned.

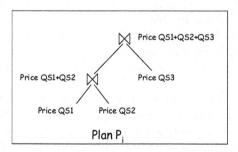

Fig. 6.3. Example of price computation for the plan P_i

6.3.2 DaQuinCIS Query Processing

The DaQuinCIS system, described in [175], is a framework for dealing with data quality in cooperative information systems. A module of the system, the *data quality broker*, is a data integration system. While the overall DaQuin-CIS system and its modules will be described in detail in Chapter 8, in this section we focus on the proposed query answering process, which is one of the functionalities of the Data Quality Broker.

The main idea of the DaQuinCIS approach is to make cooperating organizations export not only data that they intend to exchange with other organizations, but also metadata, that characterize their quality level. To this extent, a specific semistructured data model is proposed, called D^2Q. The model is extensively described in Chapter 3. On the basis of such quality characterization of exported data, user queries are processed so that the "best quality" answer is returned as a result.

Queries on the global schema are processed according to the GAV approach by unfolding, i.e., by replacing each atom of the original query with the corresponding view on local data sources. When defining the mapping between concepts of the global schema and concepts of the local schemas, while the extension of global-level concepts can be retrieved by multiple sources, the mapping is actually defined to retrieve the union of local source extensions. Such a mapping definition stems directly from the assumption that the same concept can have different extensions at a local source level due to data quality errors. Therefore, when retrieving data, they can be compared and a best quality copy can be either selected or constructed.

More specifically, query processing in DaQuinCIS is performed by the following sequence of steps:

1. *Query unfolding.* A global query Q is unfolded according to a static mapping that defines each concept of the global schema in terms of the local sources; this mapping is defined in order to retrieve all copies of the same data that are available, i.e., exported by the cooperating organizations according to the D^2Q model. Therefore, the query Q is decomposed into $Q_1, \ldots, Q_k$ queries to be posed over local sources. Such queries are then executed to return a set of results $R_1, \ldots, R_k$ (see Figure 6.4).

2. *Extensional checking.* In this step, a record matching algorithm is run on the set $R_1 \cup R_2 \cup \ldots \cup R_k$. The result of the running of the record matching algorithm is the construction of a set of clusters composed by records referring to the same real-world objects $C_1, \ldots, C_z$ (see Figure 6.4, middle).

3. *Result building.* The result to be returned is built by relying on a *best quality default semantics*. For each cluster, a best quality representative is either selected or constructed. Each record in the cluster is composed of couples in which a quality value q is associated with each field value f. The best quality record for each cluster is selected as the record having the best quality values in all fields, if such a record exists. Otherwise, a best

quality record is constructed by composing the fields that have the highest quality from records within the same cluster. Once representatives for each cluster have been selected, the result $\mathcal{R}$ is constructed as the union of all cluster representatives (see Figure 6.4, right). Each quality value q is a vector of quality values corresponding to the different quality dimensions. For instance, q can include values for accuracy, completeness, consistency, and currency. These dimensions have potentially different scales; therefore, a scaling step is needed. Once scaled, those vectors need to be ranked. Therefore a ranking method must also be applied. Both scaling and ranking problems have well-known solutions, e.g., multi-attribute decision making methods, like AHP [170].

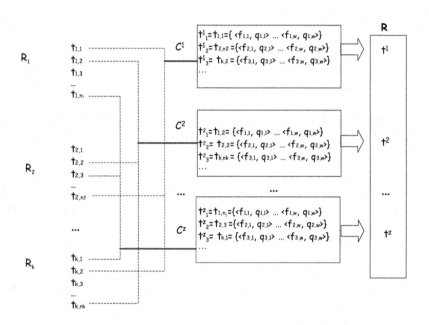

Fig. 6.4. The query result construction in DaQuinCIS

6.3.3 Fusionplex Query Processing

Fusionplex[135] models a data integration system by (i) a relational global schema D; (ii) a set of relational local sources (D_i, d_i), where d_i is the instance of the local schema D_i; and (iii) a set of schema mappings (D, D_i).

The mapping definition is GLAV, i.e., views on the global schema are put in correspondence with views on schema of the local sources. In FusionPlex, it is assumed that the *schema consistency assumption* holds, meaning that there are no modeling errors at the local sources, but only modeling differences. Instead, it is assumed that the *instance inconsistency assumption* holds, meaning that the same instance of the real world can be represented differently in the various local sources due to errors. In order to deal with such instance-level inconsistencies, Fusionplex introduces a set of metadata, called *features*, about the sources to be integrated. As better detailed in Section 6.4.2, source features include time stamp, availability, and accuracy. The data integration framework definition presented above is extended by including features into the definition of schema mappings. Specifically, the mappings are triples consisting of a global schema view D, a local schema view D_i, and, in addition the features associated with the local view. Fusionplex includes an extension of the relational algebra that takes into account the association of a set of features $F = \{F_1 \ldots F_n\}$ with source relations. For instance, the extended cartesian product concatenates the database values of the participating relations, but fuses their feature values. The fusion method depends on the particular feature. Therefore, the availability value of the new tuple is the product of the availability values of the input tuples; the time stamp is the minimum of the input time stamps; and so on. In this setting, query processing is performed in several steps:

1. Given a query Q, the set of *contributing views* is identified. First, the sets of attributes of the query and each contributing view are intersected. If the intersection is empty, the contributing view is not relevant. Next, the selection predicates of the query and the contributing view are joined. If the resulting predicate is true, then the contributing view is considered relevant to the query.

2. Once relevant contributing views are identified, *query fragments* are derived as the unit of information suitable for populating the answer to the query. A query fragment results from the removal from the contributing view of all tuples and attributes that are not requested in the query, and from the addition of null values for the query attributes that are missing from the contributing view. As an example, in Figure 6.5, two contributing views, C_1 and C_2, are shown, and the corresponding query fragments, QF_1 and QF_2.

3. From each relevant contributing view, a single query fragment is constructed, where some of these fragments may be empty. The union of all nonempty query fragments is termed a *polyinstance* of the query. Intuitively, a polyinstance includes all the information derived from the data sources in response to a user query.

In order to provide a unique answer to the query Q for the user, instance-level conflicts present in the polyinstance must be solved. Once polyinstances

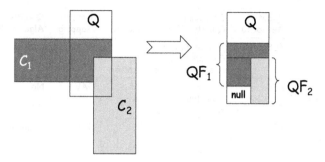

Fig. 6.5. Example of query fragment construction from contributing views

have been constructed a strategy for conflict detection and resolution is applied, as described in Section 6.4.2.

6.3.4 Comparison of Quality-Driven Query Processing Techniques

In Figure 6.6, a comparison of the query processing techniques described is shown. The techniques are compared according to the following features:

- *Quality metadata,* showing that each technique is based on a set of metadata that support the query processing activity.
- *Granularity of the quality model* that represents data elements quality metadata can be associated with. QP-alg associates quality metadata not only with sources but also with query correspondence assertions and user queries. DaQuinCIS exploits the flexibility of a semistructured data model for quality association at various granularity levels. Fusionplex allows association only at a source level.
- *Type of mapping,* showing that both QP-alg and Fusionplex have a GLAV approach to the mapping definition, while DaQuinCIS has a GAV approach.
- *Support to quality algebra,* meaning that quality values associated with local source data need to be "combined" by means of specific algebraic operators. As described in Chapter 4, Section 4.2, there are some research proposals in this direction, but it is still an open problem. Some attempts toward the algebraic manipulation of quality values are present in the merge functions of QP-alg and in the extension of the relational operators of Fusionplex.

6.4 Instance-level Conflict Resolution

Instance-level conflict resolution is a major activity in data integration systems. No data integration system can return answers to user queries if these

Techniques	Quality Metadata	Granularity of Quality Characterization	Type of Mapping	Quality Algebra Support
QP-alg	YES	Source, Query Correspondences Assertions, User Queries	GLAV	Preliminary
DaQuinCIS Query Processing	YES	Each data element of a semistructured data model	GAV	No
FusionPlex Query Processing	YES	Source	GLAV	Preliminary

Fig. 6.6. Comparison of quality-driven query processing techniques

types of conflicts are not solved. As data integration typically deals with heterogeneous and autonomous sources, instance-level conflicts are very common and frequent. Unfortunately, most of the existing data integration solutions have simplifying assumptions regarding conflicts on data values.

In this section, after a classification of these conflicts (Section 6.4.1), we describe some of the existing proposals of instance-level conflict resolution techniques (Section 6.4.2), and we conclude with a comparison between techniques (Section 6.4.3).

6.4.1 Classification of Instance-Level Conflicts

As already mentioned in Section 6.1, in order to integrate data coming from distinct data sources, problems caused by technological, schema, and instance-level heterogeneities need to solved. In the following section, we briefly describe conflict originating from schema heterogeneities, called *schema-level conflicts*, while the latter part is devoted to the description of conflicts due to instance-level heterogeneities, called *instance-level conflicts*.

Schema-level conflicts have been extensively studied (see [109]), and include

- *heterogeneity conflicts*, occurring when different data models are used;
- *semantic conflicts*, regarding the relationship between model element extensions. For instance, a `Person` entity may have different extensions in different sources that may be disjoint, partially overlapping, including one into another, or completely overlapping;
- *description conflicts*, concerning the description of concepts with different attributes. These conflicts include different formats, different attribute types, and different scaling. These conflicts are on the boundary between schema level conflicts and instance-level conflicts; for instance, in [75], such conflicts are classified as data value conflicts. We prefer to consider description conflicts at a schema-level because they are actually caused by different design choices of data schemas, though such choices certainly have an impact on values to be integrated;

- *structural conflicts*, regarding different design choices within the same model. For instance, such conflicts may occur if one source represents an Address as an entity and another source represents it as an attribute.

In contrast with schema-level conflicts, instance-level conflicts have received much less attention, and only recently has the importance of these types of conflicts increased, due to the primary role they play in the data integration processes. Instance-level conflicts are due to poor quality of data; they occur because of errors in the data collection process or the data entry process or because sources are not updated.

According to the granularity of the model element, instance-level conflicts can be distinguished into *attribute conflicts* and *key conflicts*, also called *entity* or *tuple conflicts*. Some works, e.g., [118], also consider *relationship conflicts* that are particularly meaningful at a conceptual level. In the following, we will focus on attribute and key conflicts, as they are the principal conflict types involved in data integration processes.

Let us consider two relational tables, $S_1(A_1, \ldots, A_k, A_{k+1}, \ldots, A_n)$ and $S_2(B_1, \ldots, B_k, B_{k+1}, \ldots, B_m)$, where $A_1 = B_1 \ldots A_k = B_k$. Let the same real world entity be represented by the tuple t_1 in S_1 and by the tuple t_2 in S_2, and let $A_i = B_i$; the following conflicts can be defined:

- An *attribute conflict* occurs iff

$$t_1.A_i \neq t_2.B_i.$$

- Let us further suppose that A_i is a primary key for S_1 and B_i is a primary key for S_2. A *key conflict* occurs iff

$$t_1.A_i \neq t_2.B_i \text{ and } t_1.A_j = t_2.B_j,$$

for all j ranging from 1 to k, and $i \neq j$.

In Figure 6.7, several examples of both attribute and key conflicts are shown. In the figure, two relations, EmployeeS1 and EmployeeS2, represent information about employees of a company. Notice that we assume there is no schema-level conflict, i.e., the two relations have exactly the same attributes and the same extension. Nevertheless, they present instance-level conflicts. Two attribute value conflicts are shown, concerning the Salary of the employee arpa78 and the Surname of the employee ghjk09 in the two relations. A key-level conflict is also shown between the employee Marianne Collins, as identified in the relation EmployeeS1 and as identified in relation EmployeeS2, assuming that the two tuples represent the same real-world object.

Instance-level conflicts can be present in both virtual and materialized integration. In virtual data integration, a theoretical formulation of the problem has been proposed. Specifically, the cited key and attribute conflicts have been formally specified as a violation of integrity constraints expressed over the

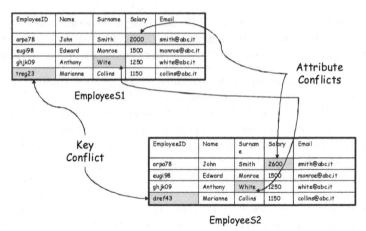

Fig. 6.7. An example of key- and attribute-level conflicts

global schema representing the integrated view. More details on the theoretical perspective on inconsistencies in data integration are provided in Section 6.5.2.

In the next section, we will describe several techniques proposed in order to solve instance-level conflicts.

6.4.2 Overview of Techniques

Techniques that deal with instance-level conflicts can be applied in two different phases of the life cycle of a data integration system, namely, at *design time* and at *query time*. In both cases, the actual conflicts occur at query time; however, the design time approaches decide the strategy to follow for fixing conflicts before queries are processed, i.e., at the design stage of the data integration system. The techniques operating at query time incorporate the specification of the strategy to follow within query formulation.

A proposal for solving conflicts at design time can be found in [55]. The main idea is to resolve attribute conflicts by means of aggregation functions to be specified for each attribute that may involve conflicts during query execution time.

Design time techniques have a major optimization problem, as outlined in [218]. Let us consider the example shown in Figure 6.7, and suppose that it is specified at design time, for the Salary attribute, that in the case of conflicts the minimum salary must be chosen. Given a global schema, Employee(EmployeeID, Name, Surname, Salary, Email), let us consider the following query:

```
SELECT EmployeeID, Email
FROM    Employee
```

```
WHERE   Salary < 2000
```

Since the `Salary` attribute is involved in the query, all employees must be retrieved in order to compute the minimum salary, not only employees with `Salary < 2000`, even if no conflicts on salary occur. Therefore, conflict resolution at design time may be very inefficient.

Query time conflict resolution techniques have been proposed to overcome such performance inefficiencies. Furthermore, query time techniques are characterized by greater flexibility, since, as we will see, they allow those who formulate the query to indicate a specific strategy to adopt for conflict resolution. Given a user query posed on the global schema, query time techniques deal with key and/or attribute conflicts that may occur on the data retrieved as results.

Key conflicts require the application of object identification techniques, described in detail in Chapter 5. With reference to the example shown in Figure 6.7, object identification techniques will match the tuple `treg23` from `EmployeeS1` with the tuple `dref43` from `EmployeeS2` by comparing the attribute values of the two tuples in order to determine whether the "Marianne Collins" represented in the two sources is the same person. After a positive matching decision, the tuples referring to "Marianne Collins" will be considered a single tuple, and a unique key will be chosen to identify the tuple, thereby solving the key conflict. If the matching decision is negative, no key conflict occurs.

With respect to attribute conflicts, several techniques for solving them have been proposed:

- SQL-based conflict resolution [141];
- Aurora [218];
- Fusionplex [135];
- DaQuinCIS [174];
- FraSQL-based conflict resolution [176]; and
- OO_{RA} [118].

In the following we describe the details of such techniques; however, several other proposals are present in the literature, including [81, 154]. Before providing the detailed description, we illustrate which are the "abstract" steps to be followed for solving attribute-level conflicts.

Let us consider again the example in Figure 6.7, and let us suppose the following query is formulated over the global schema `Employee(EmployeeID, Name, Surname, Salary, Email)`:

```
SELECT Salary
FROM    Employee
WHERE   Name = "John" AND Surname = "Smith"
```

In order to return a result to this type of query, the attribute conflict between the two values for John Smith's salary stored in the relations `EmployeeS1` and `EmployeeS2` must be solved.

A solution to this problem is to *declaratively* specify how to deal with such conflicts. A declarative specification consists of

- a set of conflict resolution functions that, on the basis of the specific attributes involved in the conflict, can select the most appropriate value;
- a set of strategies to deal with conflicts, corresponding to different tolerance degrees; and
- a query model that can take into account possible conflicts directly, i.e., with specific extensions, such as adhoc functions dealing with conflicts, or indirectly, i.e., without specific extensions.

A *resolution function* takes two (or more) conflicting values of an attribute as input and outputs a value that must be returned as the result to the posed query. Common resolution functions are MIN and MAX. To these, resolution functions that are specific to some attribute types can be added. For instance, for numerical attribute types, SUM and AVG can be used. For non numerical attributes, further resolution functions can be identified, such as CONCAT. In [141], a resolution function MAXIQ is proposed. Assuming the presence of a data quality model that associates quality values to model elements (e.g., attributes), the resolution function MAXIQ returns the value with the highest quality. In Figure 6.8, conflict resolution functions are summarized, as proposed in [141]. Some functions are the usual aggregation functions; others serve the specific purpose of resolving conflicts.

Function	Attribute Type	Description
COUNT	any	Counts number of conflicting values
MIN	any	Minimum value
MAX	any	Maximum value
RANDOM	any	Random non null value
CHOOSE(Source)	any	Chooses most reliable source for the particular attribute
MAXIQ	any	Value of highest information quality
GROUP	any	Groups all conflicting values
SUM	numerical	Sums all values
MEDIAN	numerical	Median value, namely having the same number of higher and lower values
AVG	numerical	Arithmetic mean of all values
VAR	numerical	Variance of values
STDDEV	numerical	Standard Deviation of values
SHORTEST	non-numerical	Minimum length value, ignoring spaces
LONGEST	non-numerical	Maximum length value, ignoring spaces
CONCAT	non-numerical	Concatenation of values
ANNCONCAT	non-numerical	Annotated concatenation of values, whose purpose is to specify the source, before the actual returned value

Fig. 6.8. Resolution functions as proposed in [141]

The *tolerance strategies* allow the user to define the degree of conflict permitted. For example, it is possible to specify that on a specific attribute no conflicts are admitted. This means that all values returned by the sources on that attribute must be aligned. As another example, it may be possible to specify that in the case of conflicts, a randomly chosen value among the conflicting ones be proposed as the result. As another tolerance strategy, a threshold value may be specified for distinguishing tolerable conflicts from intolerable ones. For instance, a conflict on two values for the Name attribute such as Michael and Maichael, that have a reciprocal edit distance of one character, can be tolerated since it is very easy to transform Maichael into Michael, by deleting simply one character. In contrast, for a numerical attribute like Salary, even a one digit distance may be intolerable.

With respect to the *query model*, it is possible to appropriately use SQL to specify how to solve conflicts [141], or to use adhoc extensions such as the ones proposed in [118] and [218].

The next sections will describe several techniques for conflict resolution that instantiate the abstract steps presented.

SQL-Based Conflict Resolution

The approach proposes formulating queries in SQL, exploiting the capabilities of current database systems. Three possible strategies are discussed, based on three SQL operations:

- *Group*, where by using the Group by SQL statement, a query is specified that groups tuples on the basis of one or more group attributes. Then, an aggregated function is specified to select conflicting values appropriately. For instance,

```
SELECT    EmployeeId, min(Salary)
FROM      Employee
GROUP BY EmployeeId
```

  The main disadvantage of this approach is that only the aggregation functions supported by SQL can be used.
- *Join*, which considers the union of two sources, and partitions it into three sets: the intersection of the two sources, the tuples only in the first source, and the tuples only in the second source. Then, the merging query is expressed on each of these parts, and, finally, the results are merged. The first query is expressed on the intersection:

```
SELECT EmployeeID, min(Employee1.Salary, Employee2.Salary)
FROM    Employee1, Employee2
WHERE   Employee1.EmployeeId = Employee2.EmployeeId
```

  This query has the advantage that the resolution is no longer an aggregate function, but a scalar one. This extends the possibility of using user-defined functions, thereby enlarging the spectrum of possible resolution functions while continuing to be compliant with most database systems that allow user-defined scalar functions. The following query selects the tuples of the first source that are not in the second:

```
SELECT EmployeeId, Price
FROM   Employee1
WHERE  Employee1.EmployeeId NOT IN
       (SELECT EmployeeID
        FROM Employee2)
```

The query to select the tuples of the second source that are not in the first source is similar to the above one. The query to merge is simply the combination of the results of all queries through the UNION operator. The main disadvantage of this approach is the complexity of the queries, because the number of partitions increases exponentially with the number of sources. The length and complexity of queries may become prohibitive.

- *Nested Join*, an improvement over the previous method, which can be performed when resolution functions are associative. Given N sources to be merged, the idea is to first merge two, then merge this with a third, and so on. With this approach, queries grow linearly, but still remain complex.

Aurora

Aurora is a mediation-based data integration system. The approach proposes a conflict-tolerant query model for conflict resolution at a desired degree. The conflict-tolerant query model has the following features:

- Two operators, for attribute conflict resolution, called *resolve attribute-level conflict* (RAC) and for tuple conflict resolution, called *resolve tuple-level conflict*(RTC). The operators take a resolution function as parameter. For example, consider the global population of the relation Employee, shown in Figure 6.9, which represents the global instance resulting from the integration of the two relations EmployeeS1 and EmployeeS2 shown in Figure 6.7. An example of how the operator RAC works is reported in Figure 6.10, where the specified resolution functions are MIN for Salary, LONGEST for Surname, and ANY for EmployeeID. An example for the RTC operator is shown in Figure 6.11, where the resolution function is ANY, and the tuple conflicts are solved choosing tuple dref43.
- Three strategies for conflict resolution, namely, HighConfidence, RandomEvidence, and PossibleAtAll. These strategies allow the user to define the degree of conflicts permitted, and are used in conjunction with the previously described operators when formulating queries. HighConfidence allows us to specify that no conflicts on a specific attribute are admitted. This means that all values returned by the sources on that attribute must be aligned. RandomEvidence specifies that in the

case of conflicts, a runtime function has to select a value to be returned. `PossibleAtAll` returns all values that correctly answer the query, independently of conflicts.

TupleID	EmployeeID	Name	Surname	Salary	Email
t_1	arpa78	John	Smith	2000	smith@abc.it
t_2	eugi98	Edward	Monroe	1500	monroe@abc.it
t_3	ghjk09	Anthony	Wite	1250	white@abc.it
t_4	treg23	Marianne	Collins	1150	collins@abc.it
t_5	arpa78	John	Smith	2600	smith@abc.it
t_6	eugi98	Edward	Monroe	1500	monroe@abc.it
t_7	ghjk09	Anthony	White	1250	white@abc.it
t_8	dref43	Marianne	Collins	1150	collins@abc.it

Fig. 6.9. Instance of the global relation `Employee`

TupleID	EmployeeID	Name	Surname	Salary	Email
t_1	arpa78	John	Smith	2000	smith@abc.it
t_2	eugi98	Edward	Monroe	1500	monroe@abc.it
t_3	ghjk09	Anthony	White	1250	white@abc.it
t_4	treg23	Marianne	Collins	1150	collins@abc.it

RAC(Employee,Salary(MIN), Surname(Longest), EmployeeID(Any))

Fig. 6.10. Resolution of attribute conflicts

TupleID	EmployeeID	Name	Surname	Salary	Email
t_1	arpa78	John	Smith	2600	smith@abc.it
t_2	eugi98	Edward	Monroe	1500	monroe@abc.it
t_3	ghjk09	Anthony	Wite	1250	white@abc.it
t_4	dref43	Marianne	Collins	1150	collins@abc.it

RTC(Employee,ANY)

Fig. 6.11. Resolution of tuple conflicts

The conflict-tolerant query model is built on tuple-level conflicts only, but the user is allowed to specify attribute-level conflict resolution. Some examples of conflict-tolerant queries are as follows:

- Q1: SELECT EmployeeID, Name (ANY), Salary[MIN]
     FROM   Employee
     WHERE   Salary>1800
     WITH   HighConfidence

- Q2: SELECT [ANY]EmployeeID, Name, Salary
      FROM   Employee
      WHERE   Salary>1800
      WITH   RandomEvidence

Both queries select employees with Salary greater than 1800 euros. If there is a conflict, Q1 selects employees whose Salary value is greater than 1800 in all sources. Therefore, based on Figure 6.9, the tuples t_1 and t_5 are selected. Then, applying the resolution function MIN on Salary, the returned tuple will have the Salary value of t_1, namely, 2000. Q2 selects a random Salary value, and, if it is greater than 1800, it is returned as a result. Then, the ANY tuple resolution function is applied as specified in the selection clause. Based on Figure 6.9, a random value between the Salary value of t_1 and t_5 is returned.

Fusionplex and DaQuinCIS

The two approaches to conflict resolution adopted in the Fusionplex and DaQuinCIS systems are similar. They both resolve attribute conflicts on the basis of metadata associated with data of local sources.

Fusionplex proposes the following metadata, called *features* :

- *time stamp*, representing the time the source was validated in the system;
- *cost*, which can be transmission time over the network, or money to be paid for information or both;
- *accuracy*, evaluated according to a probabilistic approach;
- *availability*, probability that the information is randomly available; and
- *clearance*, corresponding to the clearance level needed to access the information.

In Fusionplex, the features are associated with sources as a whole, with the restrictive assumption that data in sources are homogeneous with respect to a specific feature.

DaQuinCIS proposes the following metadata, referred to as *dimensions*:

- *accuracy*, concerning the syntactical accuracy of data values;
- *currency*, considering the degree of up-to-dateness of values;
- *consistency*, measuring intrasource integrity constraints; and
- *completeness*, counting the number of null values.

The D^2Q data model, described in detail in Chapter 3, is semistructured, and permits the association of metadata with data elements of different granularity, and therefore, with single values, as well as with attributes and all other model elements.

An example of the extended SQL statements that can be defined in Fusionplex is

```
SELECT  EmployeeID, Salary
FROM    EmployeeS1, EmployeeS2
WHERE   EmployeeS1.EmployeeID=EmployeeS2.EmployeeID
USING   cost>0.6
WITH    timestamp as 0.5
```

Considering an XML-based representation of the two relations `EmployeeS1` and `EmployeeS2`, an example of a DaQuinCIS query, expressed in XQuery [29], is

```
FOR     $i in input()//EmployeeS1
FOR     $j in input()//EmployeeS2
WHERE   ($i/EmployeeID=$j/EmployeeID) and
        quality($i/Salary)>0.7 and quality($j/salary)>0.7
RETURN  ($i/Name,$i/Salary)
```

As described, attribute conflict resolution is based on metadata in both Fusionplex and DaQuinCIS. Also, both systems have a step in which, upon issuing a user query, all the significant instances answering the query are collected and grouped into clusters of different copies of the same objects. Then, in both systems, a resolution policy is applied in order to produce selected tuples to be included in the result.

The two systems differ in the process for building the final result. In Fusionplex, as described in Section 6.3.3, the phase in which results are collected from local sources terminates with the construction of a polyinstance, upon which a conflict resolution strategy is applied. Conflict resolution is performed in two phases: in the first phase a utility function is used to take user preferences into account, while in the second phase the actual fusion is performed.

With reference to the first phase, users can specify the importance they assign to each feature. Then, an overall utility function consisting of the weighted sum of the feature values of a source is calculated, and a first pruning of sources is done on the basis of a fixed utility threshold.

With respect to the second phase, resolution of inconsistencies can be done either on the basis of their features, called *feature-based resolution*, or on the basis of the data, called *content-based resolution*.

A resolution policy consists of the sequential selection of

- *elimination functions*, which can be feature-based or selection-based. Examples of elimination functions are MIN and MAX; MAX(timestamp) and MIN(cost) are examples of feature-based elimination functions, while MAX(Salary) is an example of a content-based elimination function.
- *fusion functions*. Fusion functions are always content-based; examples are ANY and AVERAGE.

Note that the resolution policy is completely specified by users according to their specific requirements. Moreover, Fusionplex admits three tolerance levels: no resolution, pruning of polytuples, and selective attribute resolution. The no resolution policy aloows an answer with conflicts to be returned to the user. The pruning of polytuple policy removes tuples that either do not satisfy the feature selection predicate or are below the utility threshold. The selective attribute resolution forces resolution on some attributes only.

In the DaQuinCIS system, the reconciled result is produced according to the process described in Section 6.3.2, and it is completely based on quality values associated with data on the basis of the D^2Q model.

FraSQL-Based Conflict Resolution

The approach proposes an extension of a multidatabase query language, called *FraSQL*, which provides operations for transformation and integration of heterogeneous data. The main idea is to use grouping for duplicate elimination and aggregation for conflict resolution. For conflict resolution, FraSQL provides both *user-defined aggregation* and *user-defined grouping*. User defined aggregation is useful for conflict resolution, allowing for the selection of a representative value from a group of values corresponding to the same real-world object. The grouping of values is performed by means of user-defined grouping. User defined grouping can be of two types: (i) *context free* and (ii) *context aware*. Context free grouping is the usual approach, as in SQL standards, with, in addition, the possibility of using external functions. The following query shows the usage of a context free user-defined grouping [176]:

```
SELECT   avg (Temperature),rc
FROM     Weather
GROUP BY regionCode(Longitude,Latitude) AS rc
```

where `regionCode` is an external function that computes the region from its geographical position.

Context-aware grouping is proposed in order to overcome some limitations of the current SQL standardized group by operator. Indeed, SQL standardized group by operator works one tuple at a time, not considering possible relationships between grouping tuples. Therefore, in order to have a more flexible grouping, similarity criteria can be introduced that split or merge the group conveniently. As an example, consider the query:

```
SELECT EmployeeID,Salary
FROM    EmployeeS1
GROUP   maximumDifference(Salary,diff=150)
BY CONTEXT
```

The query considers the relation EmployeeS1 shown in Figure 6.7 and groups the tuples as shown in Figure 6.12, generating three sets corresponding to tuples for which the `Salary` values differ by at most 150.

EmployeeID	Salary
arpa78	2000

EmployeeID	Salary
eugi98	1500

EmployeeID	Salary
ghjk09	1250
treg23	1150

Fig. 6.12. Result of the context-aware query as applied to the table EmployeeS1 of Figure 6.7

OO_{RA}

Though in the following we focus only on attribute-level conflicts, the model also considers key conflicts and relationship conflicts (see [118] for more details on these two conflict types). The approach distinguishes two types of attribute conflicts, namely, *tolerable conflicts* which can be automatically solved, and *intolerable conflicts*, which have to be solved with human intervention. The two types of conflicts are separated by means of a threshold. An extended object-oriented data model, called OO_{RA}, is proposed to handle attribute-level conflicts. The main features of the model with respect to attribute conflict resolution are

- the possibility of specifying thresholds and resolution functions for attribute-level conflict resolution; and
- the representation of original and resolved attribute values.

With respect to the threshold specification and resolution functions, the following three different combinations are considered for a given attribute: (i) threshold predicate and resolution function both unspecified; (ii) specified threshold predicate and unspecified resolution function; and (iii) threshold predicate and resolution function both specified. In case (i), no conflict is tolerated, so if a conflict arises, the resolved attribute value is null. In case (ii), a conflict can arise and can be acceptable, but if it arises, the returned value is NULL. In case (iii), there can be tolerable conflicts, and the returned value is computed by the resolution function.

With respect to conflicting values representation, the OO_{RA} approach for every non-identifier attribute represents a triple: original value, resolved value, and conflict type. Conflict type is NULL if there is no conflict, RESOLVABLE if there is an intolerable conflict, and ACCEPTABLE if there is a tolerable conflict. For example, let us consider the following threshold predicate and resolution function applied to the global relation described in Figure 6.9:

```
DEFINE Salary.threshold@EMPLOYEE(s1,s2) = (abs(s1-s2)<=1000)
```

```
DEFINE Salary.resolution@EMPLOYEE(s1,s2) = MIN(s1,s2)
```

In this case, the conflict between t_1 and t_5 is tolerable, as the differences between the two values for salary are within the specified threshold. The conflict is solved by choosing the value for salary present in tuple t_1.

As another example, let us consider the following threshold predicate and resolution function, also applied to the relation in Figure 6.9:

```
DEFINE Surname.threshold@EMPLOYEE(s1,s2) = (editDistance(s1,s2)<=1)
DEFINE Surname.resolution@EMPLOYEE(s1,s2) = LONGEST(s1,s2)
```

Still, the conflict between t_3 and t_7 is tolerable, and the value for Surname stored by tuple t_7 is returned as a result. In contrast, supposing that the Surname value for t_3 were Wie, and the edit distance between t_3.Salary and t_7.Salary greater than 1, an intolerable conflict would have occurred.

6.4.3 Comparison of Instance-level Conflict Resolution Techniques

In Figure 6.13, the different declarative techniques for the resolution of inconsistencies are compared with respect to permitted tolerance strategies and query models. Reviewing the tolerance strategies column, Aurora, Fusionplex, and OO_{RA} propose a degree of flexibility that can be selected once conflicts occur. We recall that the three degrees of flexibility proposed by Aurora are (i) high confidence, meaning that no conflict is tolerated, (ii) random evidence meaning that in the case of conflicts a runtime function will select the value to be returned, and (iii) possible at all, meaning that all values that correctly answer the query must be returned. Similarly to Aurora, Fusionplex admits three tolerance levels: no resolution, pruning of polytuples, and selective attribute resolution. The no resolution policy corresponds to PossibleAtAll; in both approaches, the answer with conflicts is returned to the user. The pruning of polytuple policy, which removes tuples not satisfying the feature selection predicate or the utility threshold, is a more specific case of the RandomEvidence policy and it shares the threshold concept with OO_{RA}. The selective attribute resolution involves leaving some (or all) attributes unresolved; it is a specific case of the no resolution policy with higher granularity.

Reviewing the query model column, we see that the SQL-based conflict resolution can rely on SQL. However, it has inefficiencies due to the fact that resolution functions were not considered for the native SQL. Therefore, computing aggregation and expressing SQL statements for them can become very onerous. Both DaQuinCIS and OO_{RA} deal with models that are different from the relational model, namely, with the XML data model and the object-oriented data model, respectively.

Techniques	Tolerance Strategies	Query Model
SQL-Based Conflict Resolution	NO	SQL
Aurora	High Confidence, RandomEvidence, PossibleAtAll	Ad-hoc Conflict Tolerant Query Model
Fusionplex	No resolution strategy, selective attribute resolution	Extended SQL
DaQuinCIS	NO	Extended XML
FraQL-Based Conflict Resolution	NO	Ad-hoc FraQL
OO_{RA}	Thresholds for tolerable and intolerable conflicts	Ad hoc Object Oriented Extension (OO_{RA})

Fig. 6.13. Conflict resolution techniques

6.5 Inconsistencies in Data Integration: a Theoretical Perspective

In this section, we first provide first several basic definitions that formally specify a data integration system (Section 6.5.1). Then, we discuss an example of what inconsistency means on the basis of such formal specifications, and give some hints on specific semantics that have been defined for dealing with inconsistencies (Section 6.5.2).

6.5.1 A Formal Framework for Data Integration

A *data integration system* (*DIS*) [116] can be formally defined as a triple (G, S, M) where

- G is the global schema, expressed in a language L_G over an alphabet A_G.
- S is the source schema[1], expressed in a language L_S over an alphabet A_S.
- M is the mapping between G and S, constituted by a set of assertions of the forms

$$q_S \rightsquigarrow q_G \text{ and}$$

$$q_G \rightsquigarrow q_S,$$

where q_G and q_S are two queries of the same arity, respectively over the global schema G and the source schema S. Queries q_S are expressed in a query language $L_{M,S}$ over the alphabet A_S, and queries q_G are expressed in a query language $L_{M,G}$ over the alphabet A_G.

---

[1] The source schema in [116] is a collective name that indicates the *set* of source schemas, as introduced in Section 6.2.

In Section 6.2, we provided some examples on how mapping assertions can be specified.

Given a data integration system $I = (G, S, M)$, a *semantics* to it can be assigned by specifying the information content of the global schema G. Let D be a source database for I, i.e., a (set of) database that conforms to the source schema S and satisfies all constraints in S. On the basis of D, we can define the information content of the global schema G. We call *global database* for I any database for G. A global database B is said to be *legal with respect to* D if:

- B is legal with respect to G, i.e., B satisfies all the constraints of G; and
- B satisfies the mapping M with respect to D.

An important notion to be introduced is that of *certain answers*. Given a source database D for I, the answer $q_{I,D}$ to a query q in I with respect to D is the set of tuples t of objects such that $t \in q_B$ for every global database B that is legal for I with respect to D.

The meaning of the sentence "B satisfies the mapping M with respect to D" depends on how to interpret the assertions.

In the LAV case, where mapping assertions have the form $s \rightsquigarrow q_G$, the following cases have been identified:

- *Sound views.* When a source s is *sound*, its extension provides any subset of the tuples satisfying the corresponding view q_G.
- *Complete views.* When a source s is *complete*, its extension provides any superset of the tuples satisfying the corresponding view.
- *Exact Views.* When a source s is *exact*, its extension is exactly the set of tuples of objects satisfying the corresponding view.

In the GAV case, a similar interpretation of mapping assertions can be given, and hence, sound, complete, and exact views can correspondingly be defined. In the following section, we see the role that sound, complete, and exact views can play when dealing with inconsistent answers.

6.5.2 The Problem of Inconsistency

In a data integration system (DIS), beyond the inconsistency problems that are local to sources, inconsistency may arise due to integrity constraints that are specified on the global schema.

Integrity constraints on the global schema represent a fundamental knowledge, as they actually allow one to capture the semantics of the reality. Sources in a DIS are autonomous and independent; indeed, DISs can be seen as a particular case of cooperative information systems, where the cooperation is actually realized by means of data sharing among the distinct sources (see Chapter 1, Section 1.4). Each source in a DIS locally checks for the satisfaction of its own integrity constraints. As a component of a data integration system, each source has to check further if it violates the integrity constraints specified over the global schema. If this happens, it is necessary to set how to deal with such inconsistencies. More specifically, it is not admissible that the whole DIS not provide any answer to a user query if consistency violation occurs. Instead, specific techniques need to be introduced in order to deal with such inconsistencies. In the following, an example of integrity constraint violation is described, and different problems that arise are introduced.

Let us consider a global schema consisting of two relations, representing movies and the actors who have acted in these movies: Movie(Title, Director) and Actor(Name,Surname,Movie). Let us assume that a foreign key constraint exists between the attribute Movie of Actor and the attribute Title of Movie. Let us further assume that a GAV mapping is defined.

We first consider the case in which both the relations are defined by exact views on the sources, i.e., all and only all the data retrieved from the sources satisfy the global schema. Let us assume we retrieve the following instances:

1 <actor(Audrey, Hepburn, Roman Holidays)>
2 <movie(Roman Holidays, Wyler)>
3 <actor(Russel, Crowe, The Gladiator)>

Tuple 3 violates the foreign key constraint; therefore, a query asking for all movies would provide no answer, though tuple 2 could be provided as an answer.

If we do not consider exact views but instead consider sound or complete views, it is possible to provide answers. Recall that a view is sound in a GAV mapping if the provided data are a subset of the data satisfying the global schema. A view is complete if it provides a superset of the data satisfying the global schema.

As a second case, we consider the relation Actor defined as a complete view and Movie as a sound view. In this case, a query asking for all movies would have tuple 2 as an answer, because it is possible to delete some tuples of actors due to soundness, and it is possible to add a tuple <movie(The Gladiator, α)>, where α is a placeholder for the director's value.

Also in the case of sound or complete views, there are cases in which no answer can be provided. Indeed, if Actor were defined by a complete view and Movie by a sound view, the foreign key constraint could not be satisfied.

In order to provide consistent answers, when inconsistent databases are retrieved, it is necessary to introduce different semantics for the data integration systems that take into account the possibility of adding or deleting tuples to reinstate consistency. Some works in the direction of defining a semantics for DISs in presence of inconsistencies have been proposed in the literature. All such works are based on the notion of repair, introduced in the setting of inconsistent databases in [9]. Given an inconsistent database, a repair is a database consistent with the integrity constraint which "minimally" differs from the original database, where minimality depends on the semantic criteria adopted to define an ordering among consistent databases (e.g, based on set-containment [9, 86, 38], or cardinality [119]). Other works (see e.g., [32, 39]) generalized this notion to the context of data integration systems, properly taking into account the role of the mapping. Finally, some works have considered the problem for DISs in the presence of preferences specified on the data sources In [57], there is the proposal of a semantics for taking preference criteria into account when trying to solve inconsistencies between data sources in an LAV setting. *Preference criteria* are actually quality criteria specified on data sources. First, a maximally sound semantics is introduced. Given a data integration system I = (G, S, M), the defined semantics considers those interpretations that satisfy G and satisfy the mapping assertion in M *as much as possible* with respect to a source model D for I. Then, the concept of source preference is added, so that among maximally-sound models, only those that refer to sources that are *best* with respect to quality preferences are selected. In [87], a different semantics is introduced, based on the repair of data stored at sources in the presence of a global inconsistency. This choice is an alternative to the choice of repairing global database instances constructed on the basis of the mapping. The semantics introduced in [87] refers to the GAV mapping.

6.6 Summary

Data integration and data quality are two interrelated concepts. On the one hand, data integration can benefit from data quality. Quality-driven query processing techniques have the purpose of selecting and accessing data of the highest quality, thus deriving the maximum benefits from a context with multiple sources with varying quality of their data assets. In open contexts, such as P2P systems, these techniques are becoming increasingly more important, as discussed in Chapter 9 on open problems.

On the other hand, it is intuitive that most data quality problems become evident when data in one source are compared with similar data stored in a different source. Once they are detected, there is the need for appropriate mechanisms that allow a data integration system to perform the query processing function. These techniques are the conflict resolution techniques, which play the significant role of supporting query processing in virtual data integration systems. Note that the choice of solving conflicts at query time is an alternative to the more expensive choice of cleaning data sources *before* they are actually integrated. This would indeed require a data quality improvement activity performed independently by each source, and hence the complexity and the cost would grow.

In materialized data integration, e.g., in data warehouses, a cleaning activity is performed when populating the global schema. As instances gathered by disparate sources typically present instance-level conflicts, conflict resolution techniques can be also effectively applied for the purpose of producing a consistent materialized global instance.

7

Methodologies for Data Quality Measurement and Improvement

Measuring and improving data quality in a single organization or in a set of cooperating organizations is a complex task. In previous chapters we discussed relevant activities for improving data quality (Chapter 4) and corresponding techniques (Chapters 4, 5, and 6). Several methodologies have been developed in the last few years that provide a rationale for the optimal choice of such activities and techniques. In this chapter we discuss methodologies for data quality (DQ) measurement and improvement from multiple perspectives. Section 7.1 provides basic material, in terms of typical inputs and outputs of methodologies, classifications, finally focusing on the comparison of data and process-driven strategies adopted in methodologies. Section 7.2 deals with assessment methodologies, while Section 7.3 first focuses on the definition of common methodological phases, then describes and compares in terms of the common phases three of the most relevant general purpose methodologies. In Section 7.4 we propose CDQM, an original methodology that at the same time is complete, flexible, and simple to apply; in Section 7.5 CDQM is applied to a case study.

7.1 Basics on Data Quality Methodologies

We define a DQ methodology as a set of guidelines and techniques that, starting from the input information concerning a given reality of interest, defines a rational process for using the information to measure and improve the quality of data of an organization through given phases and decision points. In the rest of the section we focus on inputs and outputs, classifications, and typical strategies adopted in DQ methodologies.

7.1.1 Inputs and Outputs

The different types of input knowledge to a DQ methodology in the most general case are shown in Figure 7.1, where arrows represent generalization hierarchies among concepts; e.g., *Collections of data* can be *Internal groups* or *External sources*, and Internal groups can be *Data flows* or *Databases*.

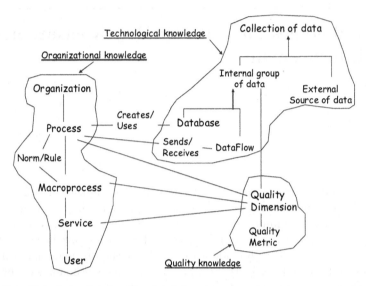

Fig. 7.1. Knowledge involved in the DQ measurement and improvement process

The main types of knowledge are

1. The *organization* or the set of organizations involved in the processes, with related organizational structures, functions, norms, and rules.
2. The business *processes* performed in the organization, and the *macroprocesses*, i.e. the groups of processes that executed together produce services or goods for users, customers and businesses.
3. The *services* delivered by processes, and the *users* requesting services.
4. The *norms/rules* that discipline the execution of processes and macroprocesses.
5. The *quality of processes, macroprocesses and services*, e.g. the execution time of a process, the usability of a service, and the accuracy of information provided by a data service.
6. The *collections of data*, corresponding to all databases and data flows which are of some interest to the organization. We distinguish among groups of data internal to the organization and external sources of data. To execute processes, organizations have to permanently store data in databases, and in order to cooperate, they have to exchange data through data flows. Both types of data, "motionless" data and "moving" data, have to be considered, since

   • errors can affect and be propagated by both; and

- depending on their quality, they can positively or negatively influence the quality of processes.

7. The *external sources of data*, often more critical than internal data for their data quality, since there is little or no control over their production process and previous origin.

8. The *data quality dimensions* and corresponding *metrics* defined in Chapter 2, a large set is concerned with the improvement process.

Besides the types of knowledge described, other relevant elements involved in a DQ methodology are

- The *data quality activities*, which is the whole set of activities introduced in Chapter 4 that can be performed to improve the quality of data.
- *Costs and benefits* of data and of processes, regarding three different cost categories: (i) costs associated with processes due to poor data quality, (ii) costs of the improvement process, (iii) and benefits (savings and/or increased revenues) resulting from the use of better quality data. Costs and benefits have been classified in Chapter 4.

Based on the knowledge involved in the DQ measurement and improvement process, the input/output structure of a general-purpose methodology for DQ is shown in Figure 7.2.

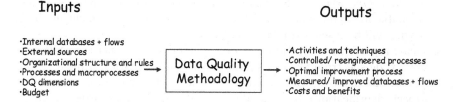

Fig. 7.2. Inputs and outputs of a DQ measurement and improvement methodology

Inputs refer to all types of knowledge described in Figure 7.1, plus the available budget, if known. The outputs concern (i) the data activities to be performed and the techniques to be applied; (ii) the business processes that have to be controlled and/or reengineered; (iii) the optimal improvement process, i.e., the sequence of activities that achieves the target quality dimensions with the minimum cost; (iv) the databases and data flows respecting new target quality dimensions; and (v) costs and benefits.

7.1.2 Classification of Methodologies

Data quality methodologies may be classified according to several criteria:

1. *Data-driven vs. process-driven.* This classification is related to the general strategy chosen for the improvement process. *Data-driven* strategies are based on using data sources exclusively to improve the quality of data; they make use of the data quality activities introduced in Chapter 4. In *process-driven* strategies, the data production process is analyzed and possibly modified to identify and remove the root causes of quality problems. We analyze this classification in more detail in Section 7.1.3. As we will see in Section 7.3, general purpose methodologies may adopt both data-driven and process-driven strategies, with different depth according to the specific methodology.

2. *Measurement* vs. *improvement.* Methodologies are needed for measuring/assessing the quality of data, or to improve their quality. Measurement and improvement activities are closely interrelated, since only when DQ measurements are available, is it possible to conceive techniques to be applied and priorities to be established. As a consequence, the boundary between the methodologies for measurement and improvement is sometimes vague. In the following, we will use the term *measurement* when we address the issue of measuring the values of a set of data quality dimensions in a database (or a set of databases). We use the term *assessment* or *benchmarking* when such measurements are compared to reference values, to enable a diagnosis of the quality of the database. Assessment methodologies will be discussed in Section 7.2.

3. *General-purpose vs. special-purpose.* A *general-purpose* methodology covers a wide spectrum of phases, dimensions, and activities, while a *special purpose* methodology is focused on a specific activity (e.g., measurement, object identification), on a specific data domain (e.g., a census, a registry of addresses of persons), or specific application domains (e.g., biology). Three of the most relevant general-purpose methodologies will be discussed in Section 7.4.

4. *Intraorganizational vs. interorganizational.* The measurement and improvement activity concerns a specific organization, or a specific sector of the organization, or even a specific process or database. Otherwise, it concerns a group of organizations (e.g., a group of public agencies) cooperating for a common goal (e.g., in the case of public agencies, providing better services to citizens and businesses).

7.1.3 Comparison among Data-driven and Process-driven Strategies

In this section we compare data-driven and process-driven strategies. We distinguish for simplicity three major strategies, using three distinct data quality activities:

1. New data acquisition from the real world. When data representing a certain reality of interest are inaccurate, incomplete or out-of-date, a possible way for improving their quality may be to again observing the reality of interest, and performing the activity called in Chapter 4 *new data acquisition*. E.g., if in a registry of employees the `DateOfBirth` is known only in 30% of the cases, we may request employees missing data. Intuitively, if the data acquisition campaign is performed effectively, this strategy immediately improves certain quality dimensions such as completeness, accuracy, and currency, since the data exactly represent the most recent reality of interest; we however note, that errors can be introduced by the measurement activity.

2. Record matching or more generally, the comparison of data whose quality dimensions have to be improved with other data in which the quality is known to be good. As an example, let us consider a database of addresses of clients that have been collected for a long period of time in a supermarket through forms, in order to provide clients with a fidelity card. After a while, certain quality dimensions, such as accuracy of residence addresses, tend to worsen. We may decide to perform a record matching activity to compare client records with an administrative database, known to be updated with the most recent data.

3. Use of data edits/integrity constraints, in which: (i) we define a set of integrity constraints against which data have to be checked, (ii) we discover inconsistencies among data, and (iii) we correct the inconsistent data by means of error localization and correction activities.

Process-driven strategies focus on processes. Consequently, they need to acquire knowledge from databases and data flows in inputs only to a limited extent. Conversely, they focus mainly on measuring the quality of processes and formulating proposals for process improvement. Two main phases characterize process-driven strategies:

- *Process control*, which inserts checks and control procedures into the data production process when (i) new data is inserted from internal or external sources, (ii) data sources accessed by the process are updated, or (iii) new data sources are involved in the process. In this way, a reactive strategy is applied to data modification events, to avoid data degradation and error propagation.

- *Process re-design*, where we avoid improving the actual process. We redesign the production processes in order to remove the causes of bad quality and introduce new activities that produce data of better quality. In the case in which the change in the process is radical, this strategy corresponds to the activity called *business process reengineering* (see [91] and [181] for a comprehensive introduction to this issue).

We compare now data- and process-driven strategies according to two coordinates of analysis: (i) the improvement the strategy is potentially able to produce on quality dimensions and (ii) the cost of its implementation. This comparison can be performed both in the short term and in the long term. In the following (see Figure 7.3), we compare improvement and costs in the long term; optimal target objectives are high improvement and low cost.

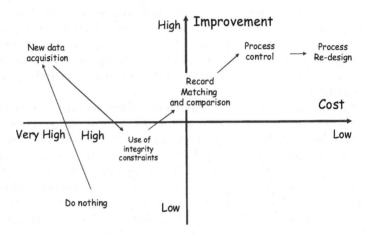

Fig. 7.3. Improvement and cost of data/process-driven strategies: comparison in the long term

The simplest and most trivial strategy is to *do nothing*. In this case, data are neglected and abandoned; certain quality dimensions, such as completeness and currency, tend to worsen in the long term. The consequence is that data progressively deteriorate the quality of business processes and the cost of lost quality increases over time.

A better strategy is *new data acquisition*; in the short term, the improvement is relevant, since data is current, complete, and accurate. However, as time goes by we are obliged to periodically repeat the process, and the cost becomes intolerable.

The strategy that uses integrity constraints leads to much lower costs, but at the same time it is less effective, since only the errors related to constraints can be checked. The errors can be corrected only to a certain extent, as we have seen in Chapter 4.

The strategy performing *record matching* has even lower costs and even more improvements, since many techniques have been developed and implemented, as we saw in Chapter 5. A relevant part of the work can be done automatically. Furthermore, once the records corresponding to the same object have been identified, high quality values can be chosen for the different attributes from the higher quality source.

In order to be effective, previous strategies that belong to the class of data driven strategies have to be repeated, leading to costs that increase in the long term. Only when we move to process-driven methods, can we optimize at the same time effectiveness and costs: *process control* activities and, above all, *process re-design* activities can get to the root of the problem and solve the problem once for all. Their costs are mainly the fixed costs related to the one shot control or re-design activity, plus variable process maintenance costs distributed over a time period.

The above considerations are valid for the long term. For the short term it is well known that process re-design can be very costly. As a consequence, data-driven strategies become more competitive. We refer the reader to [167] for a complete discussion on these issues.

7.2 Assessment Methodologies

The goal of assessment methodologies is to provide a precise evaluation and diagnosis of the state of the information system with regard to DQ issues. Therefore, the principal outputs of assessment methodologies are (i) measurements of the quality of data bases and data flows, (ii) costs to the organization due to the present low quality, and (iii) a comparison with DQ levels considered acceptable from experience, or else a benchmarking with best practices, together with suggestions for improvements. The usual process followed in assessment methodologies has three main activities:

1. relevant dimensions and metrics are initially chosen, classified, and measured;
2. subjective judgments of experts are performed; and
3. objective measurements and subjective judgements are compared.

Some examples of methodologies for the choice of dimensions and measures and for the objective vs subjective evaluation are given by Lee et al. [114], Kahn et al. in [107] Pipino et al. [161], Su et al. [185], and De Amicis et al. [56]. With regard to dimension classification, dimensions are classified in [114] (see Figure 7.4) into *sound, useful, dependable,* and *usable,* according to their positioning in quadrants related to "product quality/service quality" and "conforms to specifications/meets or exceeds consumer expectations" coordinates. The goal of the classification is to provide a context for each individual DQ dimension and metric, and for consequent evaluation. In the following we describe the methodology proposed in [56] in detail, which was tailored for the financial domain (see the main phases in Figure 7.5). For an example of benchmarking in the financial domain, see [127]. Here, we adopt the statistical term *variable* for attributes whose quality is to be measured.

Phase 1, *variables selection,* concerns the identification, description and classification of primary variables of financial registries, which correspond to the main data attributes to be assessed. The most relevant variables in financial databases are identified. Then, they are characterized, according to their meaning and role. The possible characterizations are *qualitative/categorical, quantitative/numerical,* and *date/time.*

	Conforms to specifications	Meets or exceeds consumer expectations

Product quality	Sound
	
	Dimensions:
	  Free of error
	  Coincise representation
	  Completeness
	  Consistent representation
		Useful
		
		Dimensions:
		  Appropriate amount
		  Relevancy
		  Understandability
		  Interpretability
		  Objectivity

Service quality	Dependable
	
	Dimensions:
	  Timeliness
	  Security
		Usable
		
		Dimensions:
		  Believability
		  Accessibility
		  Ease of operation
		  Reputation

Fig. 7.4. Classification of dimensions in [114] for assessment purposes

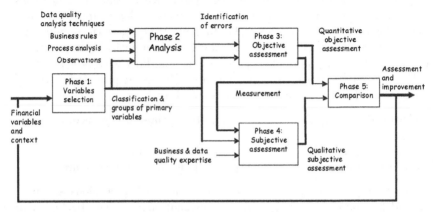

Fig. 7.5. The main phases of the assessment methodology described in [56]

In phase 2, *analysis*, data dimensions and integrity constraints to be measured are identified. Simple statistical techniques are used for the inspection of financial data. Selection and inspection of dimensions is related to process analysis. It has the final goal of discovering the main causes of erroneous data, such as unstructured and uncontrolled data loading and data updating processes. The result of the analysis on selected dimensions leads to a report with the identification of the errors.

In phase 3, *objective/quantitative assessment*, appropriate indices are defined for the evaluation and quantification of the global data quality level. The number of erroneous observations for the different dimensions and the different data attributes is first evaluated with statistical and/or empirical methods, and, subsequently, normalized and summarized. An example of quantitative assessment is shown in Figure 7.6, where the three variables considered, typical of the financial domain are

1. Moody's rating. Moody's Investors Service is a leading provider of risk analysis, offering a system of ratings of the relative creditworthiness of securities.
2. Standard and Poor's rating, from another leading provider.
3. Market currency code, e.g. EUR.

The values associated with quality dimensions represent the percentages of erroneous data by data quality dimension. Internal consistency refers to the consistency of a data value item within the same set of financial data; external consistency refers to the consistency of a data value item in different data sets.

Quality dimensions	Variables		
	Moody's Rating	Standard's & Poor Rating	Market Currency Code
Syntactic Accuracy	1.7	1.5	2.1
Semantic Accuracy	0	0.1	1.4
Internal Consistency	2.7	3.2	1.3
External Consistency	1.6	1.1	0.1
Incompleteness	3.5	5.5	8.1
Currency	0	0	0
Timeliness	8.6	9.2	2
Uniqueness	4.9	4.9	9.3
Total (average)	3.6	3.2	3.0

Fig. 7.6. Example of objective quantitative assessment

Phase 4 deals with *subjective/qualitative assessment*. The qualitative assessment is obtained by merging three independent evaluations from (i) a business expert, who analyzes data from a business process point of view; (ii) a financial operator (e.g., a trader), who uses daily financial data; and (iii) a data quality expert, who has the role of analyzing data and examining its quality. See Figure 7.7 for a possible result of this phase, where domain values are High, Medium, and Low.

	Rating Moody's	Rating S&P	Market Currency Code
Syntactic Accuracy	H	H	H
Semantic Accuracy	H	H	M
Internal Consistency	H	H	H
External Consistency	H	H	M
Incompleteness	L	L	L
Currency	H	H	H
Timeliness	M	M	H
Uniqueness	H	H	H
Total	H	H	H

Fig. 7.7. Example of subjective quantitative assessment

Finally, a comparison between objective and subjective assessment is performed. For each variable and quality dimension, we calculate the distance between the percentages of erroneous observations obtained from quantitative analysis, mapped in the discrete domain [High, Medium, Low], and the quality level defined by the judgment of the three experts. Discrepancies are analyzed by the data quality expert, to detect causes of errors and to find alternative solutions to correct them.

7.3 Comparative Analysis of General-purpose Methodologies

In this section we illustrate three of the most important general purpose methodologies for DQ measurement and improvement proposed in the literature and used in practice. The three methodologies are described in the literature with very heterogeneous styles and detail levels. We first describe in Section 7.3.1 using a common reference terminology the whole set of measurement and improvement steps of methodologies. Then we discuss the methodologies using such common reference terminology. The methodologies are

1. The Total Data Quality Methodology (TDQM) (see [177]), initially conceived as a research activity and subsequently widely used in several application domains.
2. The Total Quality data Methodology (TQdM), described in [68], was devised for consultancy purposes and is particularly suited for managers. The TQdM methodology has subsequently been renamed Total Information Quality Methodology (TIQM).
3. A methodology developed in the context of an Italian project, conceived by the Italian National Bureau of Census (Istituto Nazionale di Statistica, whose acronym is Istat) and the Authority for Information Technologies in Public Administration. The methodology, called in the following Istat methodology, concerns inter-organizational information systems; it was conceived for the public administration domain, and was first specialized for address data (see [74]).

Other methodologies have been proposed and are currently used. [167] describes a significant number of guidelines and experiences to be applied in DQ projects; they will not be discussed as a distinct methodology. [122] presents a methodology implemented at the Canadian Institute for Health Information (CIHI) to evaluate and improve the data quality of its administrative databases. Each database is evaluated annually against more than 80 measurable metrics within a hierarchical framework. For instance, accuracy is evaluated against 11 characteristics and 41 corresponding metrics. [103] is worth to be mentioned as a methodology for building data warehouses considering data quality aspects; the methodology adapts the Goal-Question-Metric approach from software quality management to a data management environment.

7.3.1 Basic Common Phases Among Methodologies

Basic common *phases* can be obtained by abstracting from specific notations adopted in the approaches. We distinguish between assessment and improvement processes. Common phases for the assessment process are

- *Data analysis*, which collects knowledge on data, their architecture, data flows, and data management rules. This may be achieved examining available documentation on data and logical schemas or through interviews.
- *DQ requirements analysis*, which collects general suggestions on possible causes of errors from users and data managers, and determines future targets to be achieved for data quality.
- *Find critical areas*, which chooses the most relevant databases and data flows, or their parts, to be analyzed in detail.
- *Model the process*, describes the process (or processes) according to a formal or semiformal model.
- *Perform measurement*, which establishes quality dimensions and perform measurements on the whole database or, if unfeasible or too expensive, on a sample.
- *Non-quality cost evaluation*, which estimates costs of processes due to poor data quality.
- *Benefits evaluation*, which estimates savings, increased revenues, and/or new intangible benefits deriving from the possible increase of data quality.
- *Assign responsibilities on processes*, which finds process owners for each process, and assigns them responsibilities for data production activities.
- *Assign responsibilities on data*, which finds data owners for each type of data, and assigns them responsibilities on data control.
- *Choose tools and techniques*, which chooses the most suitable tools and techniques from among available ones for the given organizational context, the domain knowledge available, and the budget.

Each of the above activities can be performed as a global step on the whole set of organizational units of an interorganizational information system, and as a specific step performed autonomously by a local organizational unit in an intraorganizational information system.

Common phases for the improvement process are:

- *Find causes of errors*, which analyzes possible causes of the deviation for each relevant deviation of quality dimensions from target values.
- *Design improvement solutions on data*, which chooses, among the DQ activities and techniques the most effective ones to be performed to achieve the targets.

- *Establish process control,* which defines checkpoints in the data production process, that allow for the monitoring and restoring of the desired quality dimensions during process execution.
- *Design improvement solutions on processes,* which besides controlling activities devised in the previous phase, finds further improvements for the steps of the actual process that produce corresponding DQ improvements.
- *Re-design processes,* finds radical changes to processes that correspondingly lead to significant data quality improvement.
- *Manage improvement solutions.* Under an organizational perspective, managers have to find new organizational rules for data quality. Such rules extend well-known quality principles for manufacturing products to data quality.
- *Check effectiveness of improvements,* which establishes periodical measurement and monitoring activities that provide feedback on the effectiveness of the process and enable its dynamic tuning.

Also in the case of improvement activities, methodological phases can involve a whole organization, or a group of organizations, or a specific organizational unit.

We detail here the three selected methodologies, highlighting specific peculiarities and proposals for organizing previous phases in a coherent process. To do so, we summarize the detailed process for each of the methodologies in a table, where a two/three level itemization is used. Names adopted in the first levels are in general coherent with the terminology introduced so far, while for subtasks we adopt the specific terminologies provided in the references cited.

7.3.2 The TDQM Methodology

The TDQM methodology proposed in [177] can be seen as an extension of total quality management to data, which was originally proposed for manufacturing products. Several enrichments of TDQM have been proposed, including the languages IP-MAP and IP-UML described in Chapter 3, leading, in this second case, to a new methodology. We describe the organization in phases of the original TDQM methodology and the IP-UML methodological extension in Figure 7.8, within the common definition framework proposed in the previous section. Terminological differences for the IP-UML extension are highlighted.

The process underlying TDQM considers four phases as necessary for managing the information products: definition, measurement, analysis, and improvement. These phases are iteratively executed, thus constituting a cycle. The *definition* phase includes the identification of data quality dimensions and related requirements. The *measurement* phase produces quality metrics that provide feedback to data quality management and allow for the comparison of the effective quality with predefined quality requirements. The *analysis* phase

> 1. Definition
>   Data quality requirements analysis (named Quality Analysis in the IP-UML extension)
> 2. Measurement
>   Perform measurement (part of Quality Analysis in IP-UML)
> 3. Analysis
>   Data Analysis (the same name in IP-UML)
>   Model the processes (less relevant in IP-UML)
> 4. Improvement (Quality improvement in IP-UML)
>   Design improvement solutions on data and processes (Quality verification in IP-UML)
>   Re-design processes (only in IP-UML, named Quality improvement)

Fig. 7.8. TDQM description

identifies the roots of quality problems and studies their relationships. The *improvement* phase devises quality improvement activities.

Phases defined in IP-UML are data analysis, quality analysis, and quality improvement design. Quality improvement design is composed of quality verification and quality improvement. In the *data analysis* phase, information products are identified and modeled. As a second step, in the *quality analysis* phase, the quality dimensions are defined, along with the requirements on the information product and on its constituents. It distinguishes between the requirements for raw data and component data. In Figure 7.9, an example of a quality analysis model is shown, referring to quality requirements of location data of citizens. A timeliness constraint is expressed on the information product PureLocationData, and completeness constraints are expressed on attributes Municipality, Region, and Area.

The *quality verification* phase focuses on the identification of areas that are critical, and on the quality checks to be introduced in the data flows of the information production process. Finally, the *quality improvement* phase investigates a reengineering of processes aimed at improving the quality of data. An example of a quality improvement model is shown in Figure 7.10, where the process of transfer of a citizen from one to another municipality is considered. Municipality A, where the citizen transfers from, notifies the transfer event to Municipality B, where the citizen transfers to, and to all other organizations involved in such an event. In this way, location data are kept current and accurate in all databases.

The quality requirements specified in the quality analysis model are the drivers of the re-design performed in this phase. The concept of *data steward*, i.e. person, role, or organization that is responsible for data involved in the process, is introduced. In our example of Figure 7.9, the data steward of the raw data PureLocationData is assumed to be the Municipality A the citizen has transferred from, and therefore Municipality A is in charge of starting the event notification.

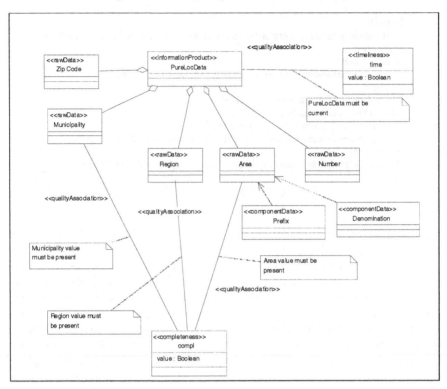

Fig. 7.9. An example of quality analysis model in IP-UML

7.3.3 The TQdM Methodology

The TQdM methodology (see [68]) was initially designed for data warehouse projects, but its broad scope and its level of detail characterize it as a general-purpose DQ methodology. In a data warehouse project, one of the most critical phases concerns the activity of off-line consolidation of operational data sources into a unique, integrated database, used in all types of aggregations to be performed. In the consolidation phase, errors and heterogeneities present in sources have to be discovered and solved, or suffer of data warehouse corruption and failure.

The orientation of TQdM toward data warehouses results in a prevalent data-driven character of the methodology. The general strategy of TQdM is synthesized in Figure 7.11. The areas in which TQdM is original and more comprehensive when compared to other methodologies are cost-benefit analysis and managerial perspective. We have discussed the cost-benefit analysis classification model of TQdM in Chapter 4. TQdM provides extensive guidelines for evaluating costs of loss of quality, costs of the process of data improvement, and benefits and savings resulting from data quality improvement. We notice here that another methodology, specifically focused on costs and

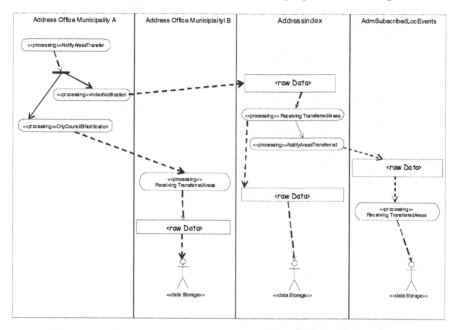

Fig. 7.10. An example of a quality improvement model in IP-UML

savings, is described in [123], while [16] describes an integer linear programming formulation of a quality improvement process that optimizes costs. We focus now on the managerial issues of TQdM.

Management of Improvement Solutions

The main aspect discussed in TQdM concerns the managerial perspective, i.e., the strategy that has to be followed in an organization in order to make effective technical choices. The choices are in terms of DQ activities to be performed, databases and flows to be considered, and techniques adopted. So, in the final stage of TQdM, the focus is moved from technical to managerial aspects. The extent of the steps, shown in Figure 7.11, provides evidence of the attention devoted to this issue. Some steps are also present in preceding phases, which we do not comment on. Specific tasks of the managerial perspective concern:

1. Assessment of organization readiness in pursuing DQ processes.
2. Survey of customer satisfaction, in order to discover problems at the source, i.e., directly from service users.
3. Initial focus on a pilot project, in order to experiment with and tune the approach and avoid the risk of failure in the initial phase, which is typical of large-scale projects performed in one single phase. This principle is inspired by the well-known motto "think big, start small, scale fast."

1. Assessment
   Data analysis
      Identify information groups and stakeholders
      Assess consumer satisfaction
   DQ requirements analysis
   Measurement
      Identify data validation sources
      Extract random samples of data
      Measure and intepret data quality
   Non quality evaluation
      Identify business performance measures
      Calculate non quality costs
   Benefit evaluation
      Calculate information value
2. Improvement
   Design solution improvement
      On data
         Analyse data defect types
         Standardize data
         Correct and complete data
         Match, transform and consolidate data
      On processes
         Check effectiveness of improvement
3. Management of improvement solutions – organizational perspective
   Assess the organization's readiness
   Create a vision for information quality improvement
   Conduct a customer satisfaction survey of the information stakeholders
   Select a small and payoff area to conduct a pilot project
   Define the business problem to be solved
   Define the information value chain
   Perform a baseline assessment
   Analyze customer complaints
   Quantify costs due to quality problems
   Define information stewardship
   Analyze the systematic barriers to DQ and recommend changes
   Establish a regular mechanism of communication and education with senior managers

Fig. 7.11. TQdM description

4. Definition of information stewardship, i.e., the organizational units and their managers who, with respect to the laws (in public administrations) and rules (in private organizations) that govern business processes, have specific authority on data production and exchange.

5. Following the results of the readiness assessment, analysis of the main barriers in the organization to the DQ management perspective in terms of resistance to change processes, control establishment, information sharing, and quality certification. In principle, every manager thinks that her or his data is of very high quality, and he or she is reluctant to accept controls, respect standards and methods, and share information with other managers. This step concerns a well-known habit of managers to consider data as a type of power.

6. Establishmnet of a specific relationship with senior managers, in order to get their consensus and active participation in the process.

Before concluding this section on TQdM, we mention a second set of major managerial principles inspired by [50].

- Principle 1. Since data are never what they are supposed to be, check and recheck schema constraints and business rules every time fresh data arrive. Immediately identify and send discrepancies to responsible parties.
- Principle 2. Maintain a good and strict relationship with the data owners and data creators, to keep up with changes and to ensure a quick response to problems.
- Principle 3. Involve senior management willing to intervene in the case of uncooperative partners.
- Principle 4. Data entry, as well as other data processes, should be fully automated in such a way that data be entered only once. Furthermore, data should only be entered and processed as per schema and business specifications.
- Principle 5. Perform continuous and end-to-end audits to immediately identify discrepancies; the audits should be a routine part of data processing.
- Principle 6. Maintain an updated and accurate view of the schema and business rules; use proper software and tools to enable this.
- Principle 7. Appoint a data steward who owns the entire process and is accountable for the quality of data.
- Principle 8. Publish the data where it can be seen and used by as many users as possible, so that discrepancies are more likely to be reported.

7.3.4 The Istat Methodology

The Istat methodology (see [74] and [73]) has been designed for Italian public administration. Specifically, it concerns address data of citizens and businesses. Notwithstanding these limitations, it is characterized by a rich spectrum of strategies and techniques that allow for its adaptation to many other domains. The principal reason for this is the complexity of the structure of the Italian public administration, as of many others, characterized typically by at least three tiers of agencies:

1. *central agencies*, located close to each other, usually in the capital city of a country;
2. *peripheral agencies*, corresponding to organizational structures distributed thorough the territory, hierarchically dependant on central agencies;
3. *local agencies*, that are usually autonomous from central agencies, and correspond to districts, regions, provinces, municipalities, and other smaller administrative units. Sometimes they are functionally specialized, e.g., hospitals.

The above is an example of the organizational structure of public administration; it has many variants in different countries. The common aspects to many administrative, organizational, and technological models concern

- their complexity, in terms of interrelations, processes, and services in which they are involved, due to the fragmentation of competencies among agencies. This frequently involves information flows exchanged between several agencies at the central and local level;
- their autonomy, which makes it difficult to enforce common rules; and
- the high heterogeneity of meanings and representations that characterize databases and data flows, and the high overlapping of usually heterogeneous records and objects.

Improving DQ in such a complex structure is usually a very large and costly project, needing an activity that may last several years. In order to solve the most relevant issues related to data quality, in the Istat methodology attention is primarily focused on the most common type of data exchanged between agencies, namely, address data. When compared to previously examined methodologies, this methodology is innovative since it addresses all the coordinates introduced in Section 7.1.2, specifically, data vs process-driven, and intraorganizational vs interorganizational. A synthetic description of the Istat methodology is shown in Figure 7.12, where the three main phases are represented, together with the information flows between them.

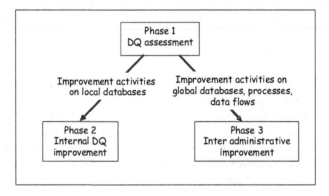

Fig. 7.12. General view of the Istat methodology

The assessment made in Phase 1 identifies the most relevant activities to be performed in the improvement process. These activities are:

1. Phase 2, activities on databases locally owned by agencies under their responsibility. Tools are distributed for performing these types of activities autonomously, and courses are offered for learning more on DQ issues.
2. Phase 3, activities that concern the overall cooperative information systems of administrations, in terms of exchanged data flows, and central databases set up for possible coordination purposes. These activities are centrally planned and coordinated.

```
1. Global assessment and improvemement
1.1 Global assessment
      DQ Requirements analysis – Isolate from a general process analysis relevant qualities
      for address data: accuracy, completeness.
      Find critical areas, using statistical techniques
            Choose a national database
            Choose a representative sample
            Find critical areas
            Find potential causes of errors
      Communicate results of assessment to single agencies
1.2 Global improvement
      Design improvement solutions on data
            Perform record linkage between relevant national databases
            Establish a national data owner for specific fields
      Design improvement solutions on processes – Use the results of the global assessment
      to decide specific interventions on processes
      Choose tools and techniques – Make or buy, and adapt, tools for most relevant
      DQ activities to deliver to agencies
2. Internal DQ improvement (for each agency, autonomous initiative)
      Design improvement solutions on processes
            Standardize acquisition format
            Standardize internal exchange format using XML
      Perform specific local assessments
      Design improvement solutions on data and processes in critical areas
            Use the results of the global assessment and local assessment to decide specific
            interventions on internal processes
            Use the results of the global assessment and the acquired tools to decide specific
            interventions on data, e.g. perform record linkage between internal databases
3. DQ improvement of inter administrative flows
            Standardize inter administrative flows format using XML
            Redesign exchange flows, using a public and subscribe event-driven architecture
```

Fig. 7.13. Detailed description of the Istat methodology

A more detailed description of the methodology is shown in Figure 7.13; the innovative aspects concern

- the assessment phase, initially performed on central databases, with the goal of detecting a priori critical areas. For example, within addresses of some regions, such as New Mexico in the US or Alto Adige in Italy, the names of streets are bilingual or they have a different spellings in their original and official languages, leading to errors. In our example, the original languages are, respectively, Spanish and German, and the official languages are English and Italian. New Mexico and Alto Adige are potentially critical areas for the assessment phase;
- the application of a variety of simple but effective statistical techniques in quality measurement steps;
- the definition of data owners at a very detailed granularity level, corresponding to single attributes, such as MunicipalityCode and SocialSecurityNumber;
- the arrangement of tools and techniques for the most relevant cleaning activities produced and distributed to single agencies, assisting them in tailoring the activities to specific territorial or functional issues;
- the standardization of address data formats and their expression in a common XML schema, implemented to minimize internal changes to agencies and to allow interoperability in flows between agencies;

- the redesign of exchanged data flows, using a publish and subscribe event-driven technological architecture, an example of which we will see in the case study at the end of the chapter.

7.3.5 Comparisons of Methodologies

In Figure 7.14, we compare the three previously described methodologies by showing the degree of coverage of improvement phases introduced in Section 7.3.1. A cross in a cell means that the phase is adequately covered in the methodology, with original strategies, techniques, and suggestions; its absence means that the phase is absent or poorly covered. A criterion based on prevalence is adopted.

Phase	TDQM	TQDM	Istat
Presence of an interorganizational phase			X
Find causes of errors	X	X	X
Design improvement solutions – on data		X	X
Establish process control	X		
Design improvement solutions – on processes (Process redesign)	X		X
Business process reengineering			X
Manage improvement solutions – organizational perspective		X	
Check effectiveness of improvements		X	

Fig. 7.14. Comparison of improvement steps mainly covered in methodologies

First of all, only the Istat methodology provides for an interorganizational approach, while TDQM and TQdM are suitable for specific organizations or information products. All three methodologies provide guidelines for finding the causes of errors. Concerning their attitude with respect to data-driven vs process-driven strategies, TDQM has a clear approach oriented to process driven guidelines, while TQdM and Istat cover both data-driven and process-driven activities, though TQdM does so to a limited extent. With regard to the type of process improvement suggested, no methodology covers the three types, namely process control, process redesign, and business process reengineering, while only Istat addresses the strategy of radically changing the processes, through process reengineering activities.

As we have already seen, TQdM is the methodology most suited to managers. It provides a large number of indications for applying and generating a consensus for the methodology in an organization. TQdM is also unique in establishing detailed guidelines for checking the effectiveness of improvements.

We compare the methodologies also with regard to the level of formalism used and the consolidation. TDQM is very rich, as we have seen in Chapter

3, in the model proposed to describe the data production process. TQdM typically uses very simple formalisms, e.g., charts. The Istat methodology provides a significant number of statistical techniques. With regard to the consolidation, TDQM and TQdM have been widely applied since the 1990s in U.S. and, to some extent, in other countries, while the Istat methodology is very recent, with a limited number case studies documented.

7.4 The CDQM methodology

Now we discuss an original methodology, characterized by a reasonable balance between completeness and the practical feasibility of the data quality improvement process. The methodology deals with all types of knowledge described in Figure 7.1; for this reason, we will call it *Complete Data Quality Methodology* (*CDQM*) methodology. The phases and steps of CDQM are shown in Figure 7.15.

Phase 1: State reconstruction

1. Reconstruct the state and meaning of most relevant databases and data flows exchanged between organizations, and build the *database + dataflow/organization matrixes*.

2. Reconstruct most relevant business processes performed by organizations, and build the *processes /organizations matrix*.

3. For each process or group of processes related in a macroprocess, reconstruct the norms and organizational rules that discipline the macroprocess and the service provided.

Phase 2: Assessment

4. Check the major problems related with the services provided with the internal and final users. Fix these drawbacks in terms of process and service qualities, and identify the causes of the drawbacks due to low data quality.

5. Identify relevant DQ dimensions and metrics, measure data quality of databases and data flows, and identify their critical areas.

Phase 3: Choice of the optimal improvement process

6. For each database and data flow, fix the new DQ levels that improve process quality and reduce costs under a required threshold.

7. Conceive process re-engineering activities and choose DQ activities, that may lead to DQ improvement targets set in step 6, relating them in the *data/activity matrix* to clusters of databases and data flows involved in DQ improvement targets.

8. Choose optimal techniques for the DQ activities.

9. Connect crossings in the *data/activity matrix* in reasonable candidate improvement processes

10. For each improvement process defined in the previous step, compute approximate costs and benefits, and choose the optimal one, checking that the overall cost-benefit balance meets the targets of step 6.

Fig. 7.15. Phases and steps of CDQM

The overall strategy of CDQM sees the measurement and improvement activities as being deeply related to the business processes and to the costs of the organization. In phase 1 all the most important relationships between organization units, processes, services, and data, if not known are reconstructed. Phase 2 sets new target quality dimensions which are needed to improve process qualities, and evaluates reduced costs and new benefits. Phase 3 finds the optimal improvement process, i.e., the sequence of activities that has the optimal cost-effectiveness. In this section we examine the specific steps. The next section will provide a detailed case study.

7.4.1 Reconstruct the State of Data

Similarly to what happens in information system planning methodologies, at the beginning of the DQ process we reconstruct a model of the most relevant relationships between organizations or organizational units and data used and exchanged. This information is important, since it provides a picture of the main uses of data, of providers, and of consumers of data flows. We can represent these relationships with two matrixes:

1. the *database/organization matrix* (see Figure 7.16), where, for the most relevant databases, we represent organizations that create data and organizations that use data. This matrix could be refined, representing single entities (or tables), but in order to make its size reasonable, we set the granularity at the database level; and

Database/ Organization	Database 1	Database 2	....	Database n
Organization 1	Creates	Uses		Uses
Organization 2		Uses		
....				
Organziation m		Creates		Creates

Fig. 7.16. The database/organization matrix

2. the *dataflow/organization matrix* (see Figure 7.17), similar to the previous one, in which we represent the provider and consumer organizations of the most relevant data flows.

Dataflow/ Organization	Dataflow 1	Dataflow 2	....	Dataflow n
Organization 1	Provider	Consumer		Consumer
Organization 2		Consumer		Provider
....				
Organziation m	Consumer	Provider		Consumer

Fig. 7.17. The dataflow/organization matrix

7.4.2 Reconstruct Business Processes

In this step we focus on processes and their relationships with organizational units. *Processes* are units of work performed in the organization and related to the production of goods or services. For every process we have to find the organizational unit that is its owner, and the units that participate in the execution of the process: the whole set of cross-relationships is represented in the *process/organization matrix*, an example of which is given in Figure 7.18. Distinguishing the owner of the process is important in DQ issues, since we can assign precise responsibilities in data-driven and process-driven improvement activities.

Process/ Organization	Process 1	Process 2	....	Process n
Organization 1	Owner	Participates		
Organization 2		Participates		Owner
....				
Organziation m	Participates	Owner		Participates

Fig. 7.18. The process/organization matrix

7.4.3 Reconstruct Macroprocesses and Rules

In this step we analyze two aspects in depth: the structure and the final objectives of the processes in the organization, i.e., how they are related and linked in the production of goods/services (denoted in the following for simplicity as services), and the legal and organizational rules that discipline and specify this structure. The relevant characteristics of processes are described in the *macroprocess/norm-service-process matrix* (see Figure 7.19), where the following aspects are represented:

- the *macroprocess*, i.e., the set of processes that are all together involved in service provision;
- *services* provided, identified by a name and, possibly, by the class of users of the service, their characteristics, and the organization responsible for service provision;
- *norms* that discipline the high-level specification of the process.

Reconstructing the macroprocesses is an important activity, since modeling processes independently provides only a fragmented view of the activities of the organization. On the contrary, we need an integrated view to make decisions related to the possible restructuring of processes and information flows. At the same time, especially in public organizations, the knowledge of norms related to the macroprocesses is relevant to precisely understand (i) the area at our disposal for "maneuvers" in process-driven activities, (ii) the extent to which we are free to restructure processes, and (iii) the norms or organizational rules to be repealed, changed, or modified.

Notice in Figure 7.19 that macroprocesses are represented as a set of processes. This model is very simple, and could be enriched using a process specification language (see example in [193]).

Macroprocess	Macroprocess1	Macroprocess2	....	Macroprocess m
Norm/organiza-tional rule	Norm 1	Norm 2		Norm3 and Norm4
Service(s)	S1 and S5	S2 and S5		S3 and S4
Process 1	X			
Process 2		X		
Process 3	X			
Process 4	X			
...				
Process n				X

Fig. 7.19. The macroprocess/norm-service-process matrix

7.4.4 Check Problems with Users

The goal of this step is to identify the most relevant problems, in terms of causes of poor data quality. Focusing initially on services, they can be identified by interviewing internal and final users, and by understanding the major burdens and negative effects of poor data quality on the activities of internal users and on the satisfaction of final users. Then, the analysis goes back to processes to find the causes, in terms of quality and the nature of processes, that produce such burdens and negative effects. As an example, taxpayers of a district are bothered, if they receive erroneous notices of assessment from the revenue agency. It may be discovered that tax files for that district are not accurate, due to delayed or incorrect updates.

7.4.5 Measure Data Quality

In previous steps we have identified main problems that lead to poor data quality; here, we have to select, among the set of dimensions and metrics discussed in Chapter 2, the most relevant ones for our problem; for such dimensions, we have to choose metrics to provide a quantitative evaluation of the state of the system. For example, if the major burden perceived by final users is the time delay between an information service request and service provision, we have to focus on the currency dimension, and organize a process to measure it.

Another relevant aspect of this step is locating critical areas, mentioned in the discussion on the Istat methodology. Since the improvement activities are complex and costly, it is advisable to focus on the parts of databases and data flows that reveal major problems. This activity can be performed in two ways:

- Analyzing problems and causes, and trying to identify the data whose poor quality is more negatively influenced by them. In the taxpayer example, we focus on one specific district, since complaints come prevalently from that area.
- Analyzing statistics on data quality metrics selected according to different properties of data, and determining where poor quality is located. We have seen this case in the example on names of streets discussed in Section 7.3.4.

7.4.6 Set New Target DQ Levels

In this step we set new target DQ levels, evaluating the economic impact of the improvement in terms of (hopefully) reduced costs and improved benefits. We have discussed in Chapter 4 some classifications of costs and benefits, and proposed a new one. The idea in this step is to use such classifications as a checklist; for each item in the classification, or in a subset of it, we collect data that allow some approximate estimate of the costs, savings, and other benefits associated with the item. Some items are easily calculated, such as, e.g., the cost of equipment involved in data cleaning activities. Other items need an estimate. For example, we may have perceived that a significant cost item is related to the time spent by clerks in looking for unmatched citizens, or for missing businesses in a registry. In the former case, we (i) estimate the number of clerks involved in the activity in terms of person-months a year; (ii) multiply this number by the average of the gross salary. Some cost items are difficult or even impossible to estimate. In this case, we identify a proxy cost item that provides an indirect valuation of the item that cannot be estimated.

Other aspects to be addressed concern the so called *intangible benefits*, which are difficult to express in monetary terms, and have to be eventually considered on a qualitative basis. Finally, the calculation of return on investment is useful to help senior management make a decision about the level of commitment to the data quality program.

The last issue to be dealt with in this step is the establishment of a relationship between costs, benefits, and quality levels. For instance, we assume that presently 10% of customer addresses are not correct, and such poor quality reduces potential revenues of sales campaigns by 5%. We have to identify, at least qualitatively, the functions that relate(i) costs of processes, (ii) savings, and (iii) the cost of the improvement program for accurate addresses. Then, we have to superimpose the three functions, to find the optimal balance between cost and savings and the corresponding target quality level to be achieved.

7.4.7 Choose Improvement Activities

This step is perhaps the most critical one for the success of the methodology. The goal here is to understand which process-driven activities and which data-driven activities lead to the most effective results for quality improvement of databases and data flows. In this choice we may group databases and data flows or split them, in order to examine only critical areas or specific parts that are relevant in an activity.

With regard to process-driven activities, business process reengineering activity (see [91], [181], and [137] for a comprehensive discussion) is composed of the following steps:

- Map and analyze the *as-is process*, in which the objective is typically to describe the actual process.
- Design the *to-be process*, producing one or more alternatives to the current process.
- Implement a reengineered process and improve continuously.

Data-driven activities have been described in great detail in previous chapters. To choose from them, we have to start the analysis from causes and problems, discovered in step 4. We discuss a few cases.

1. If a relational table has low accuracy, and another source represents the same objects and common attributes with higher accuracy, we perform an *object identification* activity on the table and the source. Then, we select the second source for values of common attributes.
2. Assume that a table exists used mainly for statistical applications, and characterized by low completeness. We perform an *error correction* activity that changes null values to valid values, keeping the statistical distribution of values unchanged.
3. Assume that a certain data flow is of very poor quality; in this case, we perform a source selection activity on data conveyed by the data flow. The goal of a *source selection* activity is to change the actual source, selecting one or more data sources that together provide the requested data with better quality. Source selection can be seen as a particular case of quality-driven query processing, discussed in Chapter 6.

At the end of the step, we should be able to produce a *data/activity matrix* like the one shown in Figure 7.20, where we put a cross for every pair of (i) activity and (ii) groups of databases or data flows to which it applies.

Data/Activity	DB1+DB2	DB1+DB3	DB4	DB5	DF1+DF2	DF3
DQ Activity 1	X		X			
DQ Activity 2		X				X
DQ Activity 3		X		X	X	
Process Re-design Activity 1	X		X			X
Process Re-design Activity 2		X	X		X	
Process Control Activity 1	X	X		X	X	

Fig. 7.20. The data/activity matrix

7.4.8 Choose Techniques for Data Activities

In this step we have to choose the best technique and tool for each data activity in the *data/activity matrix*. To choose the technique, starting from the available knowledge domain, we use all the arguments and comparative analysis dealt with in Chapters 4, 5, and 6. Here, we need to look at the market to check which techniques, among the chosen ones, are implemented in commercial DQ tools. We have to compare their costs and technical characteristics; therefore, the choice of the technique is influenced by the market availability of the tools. With reference to the object identification activity, many commercial tools or open source tools include probabilistic techniques, while tools adopting empirical and knowledge-based techniques are less widespread. If the tool is extendible, it can be chosen and then adapted to specific requirements. For instance, assume that we have performed in the past a deduplication activity on citizens of a country, in which last names are typically very long; now we have to perform the same activity on citizens of another country where last names are shorter. If in the past we have used a probabilistic technique with given distance functions for the attributes Name, LastName, and Address, we could modify the technique, adapting the decision procedure to the changed context, by changing, for instance, for the attribute LastName the distance function and weights as discussed in Chapter 5.

7.4.9 Find Improvement Processes

We now have to link crosses in the data/activity matrix in order to produce possible candidate improvement processes, with the objective of achieving completeness, i.e., all databases and data flows involved in the improvement program are covered. Linking of crossings in the data/activity matrix can be performed in several ways, and gives rise to several candidate processes, two or three of them usually sufficient to cover all possible relevant choices. In Figure 7.21 we see one of them, in a context in which we have chosen object identification, error correction, and data integration as data-driven activities, and business process reengineering as process-driven.

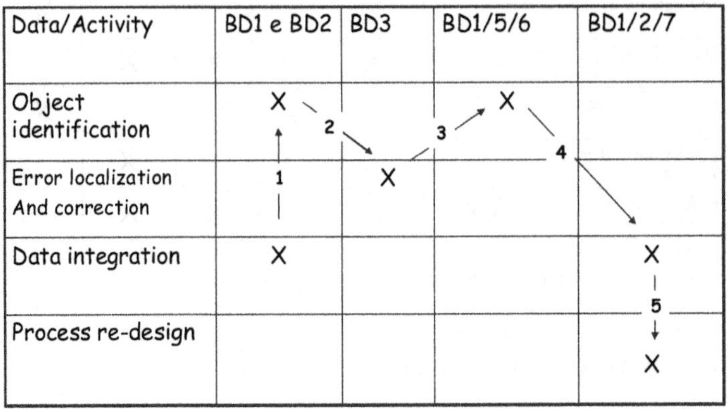

Data/Activity	BD1 e BD2	BD3	BD1/5/6	BD1/2/7
Object identification	X 2		3 X 4	
Error localization And correction	1	X		
Data integration	X			X 5
Process re-design				X

Fig. 7.21. An example of improvement process

7.4.10 Choose the Optimal Improvement Process

We are close to the solution; we now have to compare the candidate improvement processes from the point of view of the cost of the improvement program. For instance, anticipating a business process reengineering activity may lead to a more efficient object identification activity, and anticipating an object identification activity results in simpler error correction.

Items to be considered in cost evaluation include cost of equipment, cost of personnel, cost of licenses for tools and techniques, and cost of new custom software to be realized for ad hoc problems. Once the costs are evaluated and compared, we choose the most effective improvement process. At this point, it is important to compare again the costs of the selected improvement process with net savings (hopefully) resulting from the set new DQ levels step; the net final balance should be positive; otherwise, it is better to do nothing!

7.5 A Case Study in the e-Government Area

In this section we apply CDQM to a real-life case study, described in detail in [4], typical of Government-to-Business relationships in many countries. Businesses, in their life cycle have to interact with several agencies to request administrative services. The interactions are needed for several business events. Examples of such events and related services are

- starting a new business or closing down a business, which involves registering the business, e.g., with the chamber of commerce;

- evolving a business, which includes variations in legal status, board composition and senior management, number of employees, as well as the launching of a new location, and the filing for a patent;
- other services concern territorial marketing, i.e., providing thematic information on the territory in order to facilitate the creation of business networks and extend product markets; and
- security (e.g., issue of smart cards for service access, authentication, and authorization) and general enquiry services used by businesses.

In their interaction with businesses, agencies manage both agency-specific information, such as employee social insurance taxes, tax reports, balance sheets, and information common to all the businesses, typically including the following:

- attributes that characterize the business, including one or more identifiers, headquarters and branch addresses, legal structure, main economic activity, number of employees and contractors, and information about the owners or partners;
- milestone dates, including date of business start-up and date of cessation.

Each agency usually makes different use of pieces of the common information. As a consequence, each agency enforces different types of quality control, that are deemed adequate for local use of the information. Since every business reports independently to each agency, the copies have different levels of data accuracy and currency. As a consequence, similar information about one business is likely to appear in multiple databases, each autonomously managed by different agencies that historically have never been able to share their data about the businesses. The problem is aggravated by the many errors contained in databases, that cause mismatches between the different records that refer to the same business. One major consequence of having multiple disconnected views for the same information is that businesses experience severe service degradation during their interaction with the agencies.

Because of the above complications mentioned, a project is launched that follows two main strategies, aimed at improving the state of existing business data and at maintaining correct record alignment for all future data:

1. Extensive record matching and data cleaning should be performed on existing business information, resulting in the reconciliation of a large amount of business registry entries.
2. A "one-stop shop" approach is followed to simplify the life of a business and to ensure the correct propagation of its data. In this approach, a single agency is selected as a front-end for all communication with the businesses. Once the information received by a business is certified, it is made available to other interested agencies through a publish/subscribe event-driven infrastructure.

Now we apply CDQM assuming for simplicity that we deal with three agencies, namely the Social Security agency, the Accident Insurance agency, and Chambers of commerce.

Reconstruct the State of Data

In Figures 7.22 and 7.23 we report the present situation of the databases managed by the three agencies, and data flows between agencies and businesses. Each agency has its own registry of businesses; no shared database exists. Concerning flows, each agency receives information from businesses for service requests, and sends back to businesses information related to service provision.

Database/ Organization	Social Security Registry of businesses	Accident Insurance Registry of businesses	Chambers of Commerce Registry of businesses
Social Security	Creates/Uses		
Accident Insurance		Creates/Uses	
Chambers of Commerce			Creates/Uses

Fig. 7.22. The database/organization matrix

Dataflow/ Organization	Dataflow 1: Information for service request	Dataflow 2: Information related to service provision
Social Security	Consumer	Provider
Accident Insurance	Consumer	Provider
Chambers of Commerce	Consumer	Provider
Businesses	Provider	Consumer

Fig. 7.23. The dataflow/organization matrix

Reconstruct Business Processes

We focus on interactions between businesses and agencies where businesses have to inform agencies of a large set of variations in their status according to existing administrative rules. This covers change of address of the registered office, headquarters, and branches, and updates to main economic activity. In Figure 7.24 we show three of these processes that have the common feature of involving (in distinct threads) all three agencies. As evident from the figure, coordination does not presently exists between agencies in the management of common information.

Process/ Organization	Update registered office info	Update branches info	Update main economic activity info
Social Security	X	X	X
Accident Insurance	X	X	X
Chambers of Commerce	X	X	X

Fig. 7.24. The process/organization matrix

Reconstruct Macroprocesses and Rules

We assume that every interaction between a business and an agency that informs the agency of a variation of status, is ordered by a law or as more frequent by organizational rules specific to each agency. Examples of these rules are

1. the business can be represented by an agent, but in this case the agent should have been accredited in advance by the agency;
2. when the update is made a specific form has to be used;
3. the agency has to be informed of the variation within 60 days after the corresponding event.

With regard to macroprocesses, as we stated we assume a very fragmented situation of administrative activities, in which interactions with businesses are completely independent of each other. In this case, macroprocesses consist of the chain of activities related to the update, which consists of (i) entering information into the database, (ii) if necessary, providing a receipt to the business or intermediary, (iii) and sending a message to the business if inconsistencies have occurred.

Other processes concern, for example, the payment of pensions or insurance contributions. In some countries, they are deducted from wages and paid directly by businesses. For these processes the macroprocess is much more complex. It includes transactional activities such as collection and registration of payments, correctness checks, and other related processes such as discovery of and contribution evasion recovery.

Check Problems with Users

We have now to interact with the internal and final users of the data and analyze their perception of the quality of data they use (internal users) or get from the agencies. We assume that the results of interviews can be summarized as follows.

1. Internal users are frustrated by the fact that businesses contacted frequently complain about multiple letters, messages, or telephone calls. This is a sign of the presence of duplicate objects in the databases.
2. Internal users involved in tax frauds do not succeed in matching businesses when they perform cross-queries on several databases. For example, taxes paid and energy consumption are not found among the three databases of agencies in cross-queries searching for tax evaders. This is an indication of loose matching of records in databases.
3. Final users (businesses) contacted by phone interviews are burdened by the fact that for a long time after the communication of variations, e.g., of the address ("several months" is typical), they do not receive letters or messages from agencies at the new address. Conversely internal users receive a huge amount of messages back from addresses that correspond to unknown businesses. This in an indication of the lengthy period it takes to perform updates in the database.
4. Final users are very unhappy about the long lines at counters, the time lost in providing variation information, and the long delays in administrative procedures.

From the results of interviews, and a qualitative analysis of processes described in step 2, we conclude that we have to focus on the following quality dimensions and metrics:

- presence of duplicate objects in single databases, classified in Chapter 2 as inaccuracy;
- presence of non-matching objects in the three databases, again classified as inaccuracy;
- delay in the registration of updates, a case of low currency.

Apart from accuracy and currency, other quality dimensions, e.g., completeness of databases, result in similarly relevant problems. Furthermore, we could consider also the quality resulting from item 4 of the previous list, i.e. the burden for the business resulting from long lines, corresponds to time lost in interaction with the agency, and the service time spent by the agency; these are not data quality dimensions, but, in any case, they are important qualities that need to be improved on in the project. In a data quality improvement project, a larger set of problems and improvement objectives have to be addressed, in addition to those about the quality of data. These aspects are related to the quality of processes and the quality of the services.

Measure Data Quality

In the previous step we identified the quality dimensions to focus on. Now we have to choose related metrics, and organize a process to measure the actual values. With reference to previous dimensions,

- accuracy can be measured with the percentage of duplicates and the percentage of non-matching objects;
- currency can be measured as the average delay between the time t_1, at which the information "enters" the agency, and the time t_2, at which it is registered in the system.

The measurement process for accuracy (and for completeness if considered) can be performed on a sample of the database. In the choice of samples, a set of tuples must be selected that are representative of the whole universe, and in which the overall size is manageable. Methodologies for choosing suitable samples are described in [68]. For time dimension measurements, we interview internal or final users, in order to get a better estimate of their rough perception of the delay. Otherwise, for the time spent by the agency in performing the administrative process, we make a more precise evaluation: starting from the same sample chosen for accuracy, we measure time spent as the time interval between process start and process end. This is made easy by the presence of a workflow tool that traces interaction events in input and output to and from the agency. At the end of the measurement process, we should be able to fill in the table shown in Figure 7.25.

Set New Target DQ Levels

New data quality levels have to be correlated with the desired benefits, in terms of cost savings and other measurable benefits. Cost savings estimation needs to evaluate actual costs and reduced costs due to the data quality improvement.

Two cost drivers that are a direct consequence of the misalignment can be chosen as more relevant: the heterogeneity and the poor accuracy of names and addresses at the agencies. First, we assume that agencies, conscious of the misalignment and inaccuracy of addresses, spend an estimated 10 million Euros a year to correct and reconcile records using clerical review, for example to manually trace businesses that cannot be correctly and unequivocally identified. Second, because most tax fraud prevention techniques rely on cross-referencing records over different agencies, misalignment results in

Quality dimension/ Database	Duplicate objects	Matching objects	Accuracy of names and addressed	Currency
SocialSecurityDB	5%	--	98%	3 months delay
Accident Insurance DB	8%	--	95%	5 months delay
Chambers of Commerce DB	1%	--	98%	10 days delay
The three databases together	--	80%	--	--

Fig. 7.25. Actual quality levels

undetected tax fraud; this phenomenon is made more critical by the practical impossibility of reaching businesses whose addresses are incorrect or not current. Tax fraud can be roughly estimated as a percentage, depending on the country, between 1 % and 10 % of the gross domestic product. A country with a gross domestic product equal to 200 billion Euros, assuming a (conservative) percentage of 1.5 %, has reduced revenues equal to at least 300 millions Euros.

In a broader sense, we investigate other costs involved with the low quality of processes and services. In the traditional, non-integrated setting, the burden of business transactions is shared between the businesses and the agencies. The costs to businesses, in terms of personnel involved and fees to intermediaries, can be estimated on the basis of the number of events per year. If, for example, we assume two millions events per year, and three person-hours spent for each event, we estimate a loss of 200 million Euros per year. On the agency side, the cost of handling a single transaction is about five Euros, equivalent to 20-25 person-minutes devoted to the internal bookkeeping associated with a single business event. Overall, the cost for a single agency to handle the inefficiency, considering its own events, is no less than 10 million Euros per year. Assuming that the records of each business appear in the databases of at least ten agencies, this brings the total cost per year to 100 million Euros or more.

We come to the conclusion that in order to make the use of the publish and subscribe infrastructure effective, and to reduce tax evasion with the consequence of increasing revenues, we need to set the following targets (see Figure 7.26):

1. 1% of duplicates in the different databases, except for the Chambers of commerce, where we start with good quality, and set a higher target, i.e., 0.3%.
2. 3% of businesses that do not match in the three databases;
3. 1% inaccuracy of addresses; and

4. an acceptable delay of 3-4 days in the update of information in the three databases.

These targets are a qualitative balance between the "100% quality" ideal (and unreachable) objective, and the present situation. The increased revenues can be estimated assuming that tax fraud decreases proportionally with the number of businesses that can be matched or reached. Other savings will be estimated after having a more precise view of the new ICT infrastructure, provided in the next section.

Quality dimension/ Database matrix	Duplicate objects	Matching objects	Accuracy of names and addressed	Currency
SocialSecurityRegistry	1%	--	99%	3-4 days delay
Accident Insurance Registry	1%	--	99%	3-4 days delay
Chambers of Commerce registry	0.3%	--	99%	2-3 days delay
The three registries together	--	97%	--	--

Fig. 7.26. New quality targets

Choose Improvement Activities

We distinguish between process-driven and data-driven activities. First, we consider process-driven activities. While the present interaction between agencies and businesses involves multiple transactions against the proprietary interfaces of the agencies, a strategic decision of the project is to enable agencies to offer the front office services with a common infrastructure. Such an interface provides a coherent view of the agencies and a single point of access to their business functions. A back-office infrastructure is introduced into the architecture to hide the heterogeneity of the proprietary interfaces as well as their distribution. The approach followed to improve the interaction between administrations is based typically on a *cooperative architecture* that, with some variants, follows the general structure shown in Figure 7.27.

We now provide some comments on the back-office layers. Besides the *connectivity infrastructure*, a *cooperation infrastructure* is shown, including application protocols, repositories, gateways, etc., in which the main goal is to allow each agency to specify and publish a set of cooperative interfaces that include data and application services made available to other agencies. On top of this layer, an *event notification infrastructure* is placed, in which the

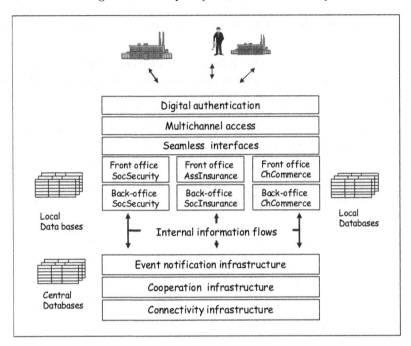

Fig. 7.27. New technological architecture for Government-to-Business interactions

goal is to guarantee synchronization between update events. This layer can be used by an agency when receiving an update from a business. It is published in the cooperative infrastructure; then the information can be subscribed to by all other agencies interested in the update. A number of administrative processes can be reengineered in order to take advantage of this architecture. Specific agencies can be selected as front-end entry points to businesses for specific types of information. In our example, the Chambers of commerce can be involved in updates related to administrative information, while Social Security can manage information related to the workforce, assuming that one of its missions is to collect insurance contributions.

With regard to data-driven activities, in order to make effective reengineered business processes, we need to restructure the data architecture. The two extreme possibilities are

- Create a central database in which all types of managed information on businesses are integrated from the three existing databases.
- Create a light central database in which the records result from the linkage of the identifiers of related business records managed by individual agencies. This new database, which we call *Identifiers database*, is needed to achieve object (business) identification between agencies, and allows for the re-addressing of information in the event notification infrastructure.

The first solution cannot be put into practice because of the autonomy of the agencies. Thus, we choose the second solution. The creation of the Identifiers database requires the object identification activity on the Social security, Accident insurance, and Chamber of commerce registries. At the end of the step, we draw the data/activity matrix (see Figure 7.28). In the databases and data flows we include the new Identifiers database and the new data-flows generated by the event notification infrastructure. We also include the process reengineering activity and the object identification activity discussed above.

Data/Activity	Type of activity	The three databases together	New flows between agencies	The new Identifiers database
Object identification	Data driven	X		
Process Reengineering on update processes	Process driven	X	X	X

Fig. 7.28. The data/activity matrix

We observe that the adoption of the new infrastructure leads to significant savings in costs of interactions. First, we deal with the costs handled by businesses. If businesses reduce interactions by a 3:1 ratio, we estimate that their costs decrease to 70 million Euros a year. With regard to the costs of agencies, in the original system configuration, three front office transactions were required for each business originated update (e.g., change of address), one for each of the three agencies involved in the project; given a cost of 5 Euros for each front office transaction, the total cost is 5 x 3 = 15 Euros. After reengineering, the new update process involves only one front office transaction, plus two new back office transactions to propagate the change. The cost of one back office transaction is 2 Euros, estimated as the sum of fixed costs amortized over the current life of the new system, plus variable costs, considering that initially only one-third of the business events may currently benefit from the new system. Hence, the total cost to the agency goes from 15 Euros to 9 Euros, and can further decrease to a limit cost of 6 Euros as more events are included in the system. Furthermore, if more agencies join the cooperative system, fixed costs will be distributed even further. Finally, provisions can be made to reduce the front office costs, by moving to an entirely paperless and certified submission process for the businesses, with improved up front validation of the input data. This brings the 5 Euros down significantly. Fixing the cost realistically to 6 Euros, we have a decrease in costs from 100 million Euros to 40 million Euros a year.

Choose Techniques for Data Activities

We now have to address the problem of choosing the best techniques for object identification, the main data activity to be performed. Several scenarios can be drawn.

First, we assume that in the past few years partial record linkage activities have been performed between two or all of the three agencies. This is reasonable in the case in which the agencies have a relevant amount of interaction. Consequently, we assume that in previous years they tried to remove, at least partially, errors and misalignments. In this case we have precious knowledge available, consisting of records previously matched and not matched. We take advantage of this knowledge, choosing a probabilistic technique, including a learning activity on frequencies of matching and mismatching.

A second scenario assumes that no previous activity has been performed; but we know that one of the three databases is more accurate than others in certain fields. For instance, one of the agencies is responsible, by law, to certify data related to the names and addresses of businesses. In this case we use the bridging file method.

A third scenario assumes that knowledge is available concerning the behavior of businesses interacting with agencies. For instance, we assume that from data mining tools it has been discovered that specific types of companies, e.g., small family companies, have different part-time activities, changing during different seasons. Consequently, they tend to declare different types of activities to the different agencies, choosing each time the most convenient solutions from an administrative point of view. Among them, certain patterns could be particularly frequent in pairs of records, e.g., <ice-cream vendor, doorkeeper>. In this case, it is worthwhile to adopt a knowledge-based technique with a rule based system that includes these types of patterns.

Find Improvement Processes

The analysis performed in previous steps simplifies the identification of improvement processes. We have a unique improvement process (see Figure 7.29) in which we perform the process reengineering activity in parallel, building the publish and subscribe infrastructure and the object identification on the stock. The two activities have to be synchronized at the moment at which the new system becomes operational. Other possibilities, such as data integration, have been excluded in step 8 (choose improvement activities). Note that we do not need a periodic object identification, since business process reengineering, once performed, aligns information hence in the three agencies.

Choose the Optimal Improvement Process

In this case, we have to consider only one improvement process. We have to check for this process to which extent benefits, especially cost savings, exceed the actual cost of quality plus the cost of the project. We apply a simple

Data/Activity	The three DataBases together	New flows between agencies	The new Identifiers DB
Object identification	Perform object identification on the stock and consequent deduplication on the three DBs		
Process Reengineering on update processes	Update first the Chambers ofCommerce DB	Use the P&S Infrastructure toUpdate SocSec DB and SocIns DB	Create the DB and use it in the new interagency update process

Fig. 7.29. An improvement process

methodology where we do not consider issues related to investment analysis and actualization of costs (see [68] and [123]). Concerning actual costs and future cost savings, we have to consider (see the classification provided in Chapter 4) the following major items: (i) costs due to poor data quality, in terms of clerical alignment costs and reduced revenues, and (ii) other costs to businesses and to agencies.

Concerning costs of the data quality improvement project, we have to consider costs related to (i) the object identification activity, in terms of software application and clerical costs (ii) the reengineering of the process, related to set up and maintenance of the publish and subscribe infrastructure.

Reasonable estimates are reported in Figure 7.30. We have estimated some items of the figure in previous sections. With regard to the cost of the improvement project, considering the different subitems, we conclude that the cost of the application architecture is 5 million Euros, and estimate 20% of maintenance costs a year. Object identification is estimated by analogy with previous projects. Finally, increased revenues are estimated on the basis of the percentage of irregular businesses that can be selected with the new target matching values.

In conclusion, if we consider a three-year period, the overall savings and increased revenues come to about 1.2 billion Euros, against a cost of the project that can be considered negligible. If we limit the balance to only data quality related costs and savings, we obtain a net balance of 600 million Euros; the data quality improvement project is extremely worthwhile.

7.6 Summary

Methodologies in general, and, therefore, also DQ methodologies, may be seen as providing common sense reasoning. Their role is to guide in the complex

Costs and benefits	Once for all	Yearly
Actual costs due to poor data quality		
Clerical alignement costs		10 MI
Reduced revenues (prudential)		300 MI
Other costs		
For businesses		200 MI
For agencies		100 MI
Costs of the improvement project		
Object identification - automatic	800,000	
Object identification - clerical	200,000	
Application architecture – set up	5MI	
Application architecture – maintenance		1MI
Future costs and savings due to improved data quality		
Increased revenues (prudential)		200MI
Clerical alignement costs		0
Other savings		
For businesses		130MI
For agencies		60MI

Fig. 7.30. Costs and savings of the data quality improvement process

decisions to be made, and to understand the knowledge that has to be acquired. At the same time, they have to be adapted to the application domain. A typical error made by designers is to interpret a methodology as an immutable and absolute set of guidelines that have to be applied as they are, without critical examination. The experience gained in working in different domains instructs on how to adapt general guidelines. Furthermore, it is more effective to see the guidelines, phases, tasks, activities, and techniques, which together form a methodology, as a toolbox, where single pieces are to be used in connection and/or in sequence, according to circumstances, and to specific characteristics of the application domain involved in the process.

Another critical issue in DQ methodologies concerns the knowledge available for performing the measurement and improvement defined by the methodology. Sometimes, acquiring the knowledge needed can be very costly, and even impossible. In these cases, the methodology has to be simplified and adapted to knowledge available; otherwise, it is refused by management and users, who are bothered by dozens of questions to which they are not able to reply, and whose purpose they do not understand. As a final point, in order to be effective, methodologies have to be used in connection with automatic tools. Tools and frameworks will be examined in the next chapter.

8

Tools for Data Quality

8.1 Introduction

In previous chapters we have seen that measuring and improving data quality is a complex process, with massive human resource involvement. Techniques discussed in Chapters 4, 5, and 6 are the starting point to automate the activities involved in data quality projects as far as possible. In order to achieve this goal, tools and frameworks have to be developed that encapsulate these techniques.

In this chapter we differentiate between tool, framework, and toolbox. A *tool* is a software procedure that, for one activity or a limited number of activities, e.g., object identification, implements one or a few techniques, e.g., the sorted neighborhood technique. A tool, compared to a technique, is fully automated, and is provided with an interface that allows for the selection of functionalities. A *framework* is a suite of tools that together provide a large amount of DQ functionality for different DQ activities. Thus, the boundary between tools and frameworks is mainly in the scope of the two. A *toolbox* is a tool conceived to compare a set of tools and corresponding techniques, usually for a single DQ activity, including performance and accuracy metrics.

We discuss tools, frameworks, and toolboxes proposed in the literature, limiting our overview to the research world, and not considering the large quantity of commercial tools available for DQ issues. This decision is consistent with the overall research-oriented focus of the book. Readers interested in commercial tools can find comparative reports in the literature providing technical specifications, and some comparisons (see [18] and [94]).

In Section 8.2 we examine tools typically conceived for information systems of a single organization. Initially, we discuss the tools comparatively; then, we detail each of them in a specific subsection. In Section 8.3 we shift our attention to frameworks devised for cooperative information systems. Finally, in Section 8.4 we examine toolboxes specifically conceived to compare tools.

8.2 Tools

Tools considered in this section are introduced comparatively in Figure 8.1; for each tool we quote the main reference, the name, the main activities addressed (according to the classification provided in Chapter 4), the main features, and the application domains in which experiences of use of the tool are reported.

The list of research tools reported in Figure 8.1 is not exhaustive, and provides a picture of the most recent proposals. For instance, the list does not include many government and academic tools for standardization and probabilistic record linkage techniques produced in the 1980s and 1990s, which are described and compared in several papers, e.g., [213] and [88].

Reference	Name	Activities	Features	Application domain
[Raman and Hellerstein 2001]	Potter's wheel	Standardization Object identification and deduplication Data integration – instance-level conflict resolution Profiling (Structure extraction)	Tightly integrates transformations and discrepancy/anomaly detection	Not mentioned
[Caruso et al. 2000]	Telcordia's tool	Standardization Object identification and deduplication	Record linkage tool parametric wrt to distance functions and matching functions	Addresses Tax-payers and their identifiers
[Galhardas et al. 2001]	Ajax	Object identification and deduplication Data integration – instance-level conflict resolution	Declarative language based on logical transformation operators Separates a logical plan and a physical plan	Bibliographic references
[Vassiliadis et al. 2001]	Artkos	Standardization Data integration – instance-level conflict resolution Error localization	Covers all aspects of ETL processes (architecture, activities, quality management) with a unique metamodel	ETL process of an enterprise DW for health appplications and pension data
[Buechi et al. 2003]	Choice Maker	Object identification and deduplication	Uses clues that allows rich expression of the semantics of data	People's names and addresses Business names and addresses Medical data Financial / credit card records
[Low et al. 2001]	Intelliclean	Object identification Choice of representative object	Uses two types of rules, for object identification and object merging	Not mentioned

Fig. 8.1. Names of tools, activities, main features, and application areas

Among the tools, only Telcordia's tool, Ajax [82] and Choice Maker [34] have been engineered into commercial products. The remaining tools are in the state of academic prototypes.

One of the tools, Intelliclean [124], has been described in Chapter 5 as a knowledge-based technique for object identification. In that chapter we described the research paradigms adopted by Intelliclean. Here, we simply compare the tool with the other ones, without further detailing it. With regard to the DQ activities implemented by the tools, the two activities most frequently addressed are (i) object identification, usually coupled with standardization, and (ii) data integration in the form of instance-level conflict resolution. This reflects the central role we have given to the two activities in this book. Notice that Potter's Wheel has a specific activity called *structure extraction*, which is part of the profiling activity mentioned in Chapter 4.

With regard to the main features, Potter's Wheel [166] stresses user friendliness and interactivity in object identification and conflict resolution, resulting in tight integration of transformations and discrepancy/anomaly detection. The main characteristic of Telcordia's tool [43] concerns the high level of flexibility and tailoring in performing record linkage, the tool being parametric with regard to distance and matching functions. The original issues of Ajax are twofold: (i) a declarative language for expressing transformations to be performed on tables for conflict resolution and (ii) the separation of a logical plan for decision for the DQ improvement process and a physical plan for optimizing the choice of techniques. The aim of Artkos [194] is to cover all aspects of the extract, transform, load (ETL) processes typical of data warehouses, namely, architecture, activity, and quality management. A unique descriptive metamodel for this goal is provided. Both Choice Maker and Intelliclean share rules as the main characteristic. We have seen in Chapter 5 that Intelliclean allows expressing domain-dependent rules of two types, (i) duplicate identification rules and (ii) merge/purge rules. Choice Maker provides a wider range of rules, all pertaining to the duplicate identification category, from simple rules such as swaps of groups of fields to complex clues that capture deep properties of the application domain.

With regard to application domains, the most investigated ones are the names and identifiers of individuals/businesses and addresses. Decision support data managed in data warehouses are also a natural area of application of tools, especially in standardization, data integration, instance-level conflict resolution, and error localization issues.

Before concluding the section, it is worth mentioning that there are several tools for profiling, a data activity introduced in Chapter 4, due to increasing interest in the business area. Among the research tools for profiling, we cite Bellman [51] as a good representative of the major profiling tasks, like analysis of the data source content and structure.

8.2.1 Potter's Wheel

Three main data cleaning activities are identified in Potter's Wheel: (i) measuring poor quality to find discrepancies, (ii) choosing transformations to fix the discrepancies, and (iii) applying the transformations on the data.

The major criticisms made by the designers of Potter's Wheel about other tools for data cleaning concern (i) the lack of interactivity and (ii) the significant need for user effort. With reference to the three previously identified data cleaning activities, transformations on data are typically performed with a batch process, operating on a table or the whole database, without any feedback. Furthermore, both discrepancy detection and transformations need significant user effort, making each step of the process difficult and error prone. In the following, we describe in detail how these aspects are addressed by the tool.

Potter's Wheel adopts a small set of transformations that support common transformations used in the DQ improvement process.

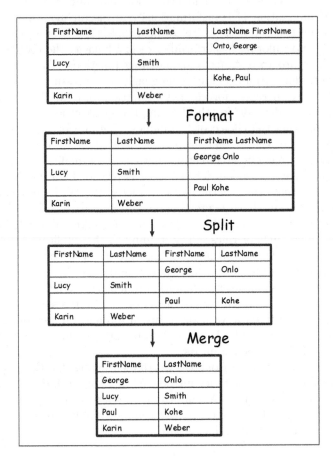

Fig. 8.2. Example of use of transformations in Potter's Wheel

Some of the supported transformations are

1. **Format**, which applies a function to every value in a column. An example of format function is shown in Figure 8.2, where in the last column each <Lastname, Firstname> string is transformed into a <Firstname, Lastname> one. Format functions can be built-in, or user defined.
2. **Split** (see again Figure 8.2) splits a column into two or more columns, and is used to parse a value into its parts.

3. **Merge** concatenates values in two columns to form a single new column. In Figure 8.2 we see the case of two pairs of columns of <Firstname, Lastname> merged into a single pair.

Other transformations help tackle schematic heterogeneities. For instance, **Fold** "flattens" tables by converting one row into multiple rows, merging a set of columns with similar values into one column. In order to reduce the user effort, user can specify the required transformation through examples; the tool produces the function that best matches the provided examples by using algorithms based on the identification of regular expressions. Transformations can be applied interactively, so that their effects can be immediately shown. Furthermore, Potter's Wheel allows the user to undo incorrect transformations. In order to avoid ambiguities, undos are performed logically, by removing the transformation involved from the sequence, and redoing the unchanged transformations.

8.2.2 Telcordia's Tool

Figure 8.3 shows an example of the specification of the record linkage process in Telcordia's tool. Three basic stages can be performed: source selection, standardization (called preprocessing in the tool), and record linkage (called match). Similarly to the activities described in the step "Define improvement process" of CDQM, the methodology described in Chapter 7, the tool allows a DQ administrator to specify complex data analysis flows in which the results of the match between two data sources are used as input to a new matching process with a third data source.

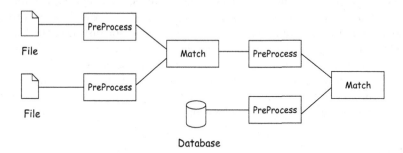

Fig. 8.3. Specification of stages in the Telcordia's Tool

The *source selection* stage enables the selection of the sources to be compared, corresponding to the icons *file* and *database* in Figure 8.3. At this stage, there is an option to select only a representative sample of the database of interest, instead of the entire database, in order to speed up the overall process.

The *preprocessing* stage performs standardization activities of the types described in Chapter 5. Specific examples for the tool include the elimination of special characters, replacement of name aliases, and removal of dashes in dates. Default rules can be specified for particular data types, such as addresses and names; this streamlines the effort involved in selecting rules for repetitive runs on similar data sets. The effects of the activity are shown to the user, who may iterate the activity until he or she is satisfied with the effect the rules have on the data.

The *matching* activity allows the user to select from a variety of matching functions. Examples of available functions include

- records that have an exact or approximate match in specified columns;
- records that match with one column and mismatch with another column; and
- mismatched records based on a measurement such as edit distance.

A claimed advantage of the tool is its ability to create new application specific matching functions that can assist in providing a useful characterization of the causes of data reconciliation problems. This is performed with the following process.

Under the assumption that a number of duplicates has already been detected by the owners of the database, a fraction of all record pairs are supposed to have been correctly labeled as duplicate. Those records can therefore be used as a training set. The strategy then is to determine a set of heuristic classification rules for the record pairs. For several groups of attributes, the frequency of record pairs for which the edit distance (or other comparison function) on such a group lies in a given range is calculated. Such a procedure may proceed with a hierarchical classification process. For instance, the frequency (and the corresponding sets) of record pairs for which the edit distance on the last name lies in a given range is initially calculated, for different ranges. Then, the distribution of members of these sets with respects to additional properties is computed. One can determine, for instance, the fraction of pairs, among those that mismatch slightly on last name, for which the first name disagrees. The resulting taxonomy of groups of pairs can then be used to infer classification rules that are tested and tuned on the training set, and finally applied to the whole set. Note that rules are not generated using the training set; hence, potential problems of overfitting rules are mostly avoided.

8.2.3 Ajax

In this section, we describe the two principal features of Ajax: (i) the declarative language for expressing *transformations* to be performed on tables and (ii) the separation of a *logical plan* and a *physical plan* in the DQ improvement process.

Ajax provides five *transformation operators*. Their composition expresses the principal data transformations proposed in the literature for the object identification activity. The five operators are

1. *Mapping*, is used to split one table into several tables, in order to manage them separately in the DQ process.
2. *View*, which corresponds to a SQL query, augmented by integrity constraints over its result. It can express the same many-to-one mappings of SQL, where each tuple of the output relation results from some combination of tuples taken from the input relation. Different from SQL, integrity constraints can generate exceptions that correspond to specific events in the DQ process (e.g., a field has to be non null).
3. *Matching*, computes an approximate join between two relations where, instead of the equality operator of SQL, a distance function is used to decide which pairs of values are to be joined.
4. *Clustering*, takes a single input relation and returns a single output relation that groups the records of the input relation into a set of clusters. Clusters can be calculated (i) on the basis of the usual *group by* SQL operator or (ii) by means of a distance function.
5. *Merging*, partitions an input relation according to various grouping attributes, and collapses each partition into a single tuple using an arbitrary aggregation function. User-defined aggregation functions can be expressed and used.

A large number of different matching algorithms can be used for implementing the matching operator, the most important of the five operators, depending on the distance function and the approximation adopted. These algorithms adopt techniques such as those described in Chapter 5. Different solutions are provided for the remaining four operators.

The separation of a logical plan and a physical plan corresponds to the typical separation in the design of computer artifacts (such as programs, database schemas, and queries) between a logical phase and a physical phase. We have adopted a similar distinction in CDQM, described in Chapter 7, where we introduced a sequence of decisions for (i) the choice of activities to be performed, (ii) the techniques to be adopted, and (iii) the sequences of the different steps in the process to be followed.

The DQ dimension mainly addressed in Ajax is *accuracy*. The first phase of the DQ improvement, called *logical plan*, concerns the design of the graph of data transformations that are to be applied to the input dirty data. These transformations are conceived in this step without worrying about the specific techniques to be adopted. The focus here is to define *quality heuristics* that can achieve the best accuracy of the results. The second phase, the physical plan, concerns the design of *performance heuristics* that can improve the execution of data transformations without affecting accuracy.

We explain this process of two phases using an example that is inspired by the one discussed in [82] (see Figure 8.4).

Let us suppose we want to perform a deduplication activity (see Figure 8.4a) for a table that represents Companies, with attributes CompanyId, Name, and TypeofActivity, and Owners of companies, with attributes SSN,

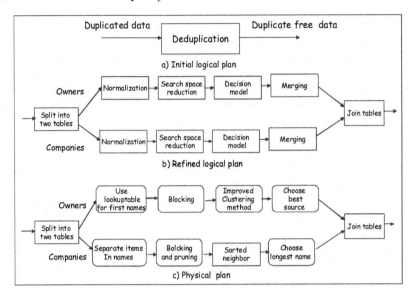

Fig. 8.4. Example of logical plan and physical plan in Ajax

`FirstName, LastName, DateofBirth`. Due to the different nature of the two
types of data, initially (Figure 8.4b) the table can be split into two tables,
representing `Owners` and `Companies`. At this point, the typical object identification activities can be performed as described in Chapter 5.

Considering the physical plan (Figure 8.4c), for each of the two flows and
for each activity, the most efficient technique can be chosen; for the normalization activity, we can perform for the `FirstName` attribute of `Owners` a
comparison with a lookup table; for `Companies`, in which `Name` values are less
uniform, we may simply separate items with specific meanings (e.g., Inc.) into
different fields. As another example, for the decision step, we may choose an
algorithm for `Owners` that customizes and improves a clustering method. For
`Companies`, we may choose a sorted neighborhood technique, with window
size optimized with respect to the distribution of company names.

8.2.4 Artkos

The main contributions of Artkos, the tool presented in [194], is the presentation of a uniform model covering all the aspects of a data warehouse
extract, transform, and load (ETL) process, and of a platform capable of supporting practical ETL scenarios with particular focus on issues of complexity,
usability, and maintainability. The most relevant tasks performed in the ETL
process include

- identification of relevant information sources;
- extraction of information;

- customization and integration of information coming from sources in a common format;
- cleaning of the resulting tables, on the basis of business rules; and
- propagation of data to the data warehouse.

The designers of Artkos claim that commercial tools are characterized by problems of complexity, usability, and price. To overcome such problems, they ground the architecture of Artkos on a uniform metamodel for ETL processes, covering the principal aspects of data warehouse architecture, activity modeling, and quality management. Artkos includes a metadata repository that has a set of basic assumptions

1. A clear distinction between different layers of instantiation. Therefore, there is (i) a *generic metamodel layer*, which deals abstractly with entities applicable to any data warehouse; (ii) a *metadata layer* dealing with the schemas of a specific data warehouse under examination; and (iii) an *instance layer* representing the real world (as an instance of the previous layers).
2. A clear distinction between perspectives, relying on the separation of (i) the *conceptual perspective*, which represents the world with a model close to the one of the final user; (ii) the *physical perspective*, which covers the data warehouse environment in terms of computer-oriented components; and (iii) the *logical perspective*, which acts as an intermediary between the conceptual and physical layers, though independent of implementation details.

In Figure 8.5 we see the most relevant entities involved in the Artkos metamodel. The generic entities represent three different models, i.e., the process model, the architecture model, and the quality model.

The *process model* describes all the different flows of activities that the designers of the data warehouse decide to perform to implement the ETL process. An *activity* is an atomic unit of work in the chain of data processing. Activities regard components of the architecture model that correspond to input and output tables of one or more databases. An *SQL statement* provides the declarative description of the work performed by each activity. A *scenario* is a set of activities to be executed together. Since data are likely to be affected by quality problems, a large part of the activities of a scenario is dedicated to the elimination of these problems, e.g., the violation of constraints.

Each activity is characterized by an error type and a policy. The *error type* identifies the kind of problem the activity is concerned with. The *policy* expresses how low quality data are to be treated. Several *quality factors* can be defined for each activity, corresponding to dimensions and metrics described in Chapter 2.

Finally, possible error types are listed in Figure 8.5. They give rise to the usual cleaning checks dealt with in the data wharehouse process in the case of

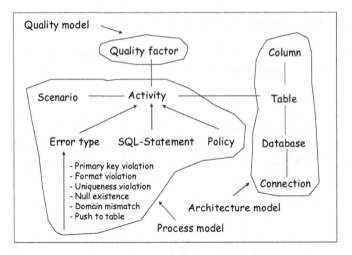

Fig. 8.5. The metamodel of Artkos

relational tables. Such error types can be customized by the user, graphically or declaratively, thus achieving better usability.

8.2.5 Choice Maker

Choice Maker [34] is based on rules, called *clues*. Clues are domain-independent or domain-dependent relevant properties of data. They are used in two phases: offline, the tool determines on a training set the relative importance of the various clues in an attempt to produce for as many examples as possible a decision that is consistent with the human marking, resulting in weight assignments to clues; and at runtime, the trained model is applied to the clues to compute a match probability, that is compared with a given threshold. Several types of clues can be defined in Choice Maker, such as:

1. *swaps of groups of fields*, e.g., swaps of first and last names, such as Ann Sidney with Sidney Ann;
2. *multi-clues*, i.e., groups of clues that differ only by a parameter. For example, one may want to create clues that fire if the first names of records representing persons match and belong to one of five name frequency categories; category 1 contains the very common names (such as "Jim" and "Mike" in the US) and category 5 contains very rare names;
3. *stacked data* describe data that store multiple values for certain fields. For example, current and old addresses may be stored in a relation so that a person can also be located when searching an old address;
4. *complex clues*, that capture a wider set of properties of the application domain.

Complex clues are original types in Choice Maker. They are domain dependent. For an example of a complex clue, assume we have a database of US citizens, a small portion of which is represented in Figure 8.6, and we want to eliminate duplicates from the relation. We can use a decision procedure based on attributes FirstName, LastName, and State. In this case, we probably decide that the pairs of tuples <1,4>, <5,8> are unmatched, since values of attributes FirstName and LastName are distant, due probably to several typos. Let us assume that rich senior citizens usually live for one period of the year (around summer) in northern states and for another period (around winter) in southern states. Such a clue can be expressed in Choice Maker as a complex rule, and leads to matched pairs of previously unmatched tuples <1,4>, <5,8>.

Record #	First Name	Last Name	State	Area	Age	Salary
1	Ann	Albright	Arizona	SW	65	70.000
2	Ann	Allbrit	Florida	SE	25	15.000
3	Ann	Alson	Louisiana	SE	72	70.000
4	Annie	Olbrght	Washington	NW	65	70.000
5	Georg	Allison	Vermont	NE	71	66.000
6	Annie	Albight	Vermont	NE	25	15.000
7	Annie	Allson	Florida	SE	72	70.000
8	George	Alson	Florida	SE	71	66.000

Fig. 8.6. A small portion of the registry of US citizens

The decision procedure can be overridden in special cases. For example, if we trust an identifier such as a social security number, we could use a rule that forces a non-match decision if the two records have different identifier values.

A basic choice for expressing clues is to define a new language, called Clue Maker. This is due to several reasons:

- productivity, because the set of clues written in Clue Maker, is shorter than the same set of clues written in a programming language such as Java;
- usability, because clues are more easily understood by customers;
- correctness, because since the language contains many constructs specific to record matching, it is less error prone than code in Java;
- efficiency, because the language allows for code optimizations that cannot be applied to Java programs due to side effects.

Choice Maker has been used in several projects, with results reported in terms of effort. For instance, a clue set with 200 clues for a complex schema consisting of 60 attributes in ten relations takes two to three person weeks, which is a relatively small amount of time.

8.3 Frameworks for Cooperative Information Systems

We recall the definition of cooperative information system as stated in Chapter 1. A *cooperative information system* (CIS) is a large scale information system that interconnects various systems of different and autonomous organizations, geographically distributed while sharing common objectives. Among the different resources that are shared by organizations, data is fundamental; in real world scenarios, an organization A may not request data from an organization B if it does not "trust" B's data, i.e., if A does not know that the quality of the data that B can provide is high. As an example, in an e-Government scenario, in which public administrations cooperate in order to fulfill service requests from citizens and enterprises [21], administrations usually prefer to ask citizens to provide personal data, rather than asking other administrations that own the same data, because the data quality is not known. Therefore, lack of cooperation may occur due to the lack of quality certification. Uncertified quality can also cause a deterioration of the data quality inside organizations.

On the other hand, CISs are characterized by high data replication, i.e., different copies of the same data are stored by different organizations. From a data quality perspective, this is a great opportunity: improvement actions can be carried out on the basis of comparisons between different copies, either to select the most appropriate one or to reconcile available copies, thus producing a new improved version to be sent to all organizations involved.

In this section we consider two frameworks that at the same time address the issues of supporting cooperation and quality improvement in CISs. The two frameworks are introduced in Figure 8.7. With regard to activities addressed, DaQuinCIS [175] covers a large set of issues, in the areas of assessment, object identification, and data integration, and others. The main focus of Fusionplex [135] is the provision of quality-based query processing services that incorporate instance-level conflict resolution. In the rest of the section we discuss two frameworks separately. Other recent frameworks worth to be mentioned for quality based query processing and instance level conflict resolution are iFuice [165] and HumMer [27].

8.3.1 DaQuinCIS Framework

In order to conceive a framework for DQ management in a CIS, the definition of CIS provided in the previous section has to be elaborated, resulting in the following: a *cooperative information system* is formed by a set of organizations { Org_1, ..., Org_n } which cooperate through a communication software infrastructure, which provides software services to organizations as well as reliable connectivity. Each organization Org_i is connected to the infrastructure through a gateway G_i, where services offered by Org_i to other organizations are deployed.

This new definition is the basis for the *DaQuinCIS architecture* (see Figure 8.8). The two main components of the architecture are a model for the

Name of Framework	Main references	Activities	Functionalites
DaQuinCIS	[Scannapieco 2004]	Assessment Data correction Object identification Source trustworthiness Data integration: - quality driven query processing - instance conflict resolution	Data quality broker Quality notification Quality factory Rating of sources
Fusionplex	[Motro 2004]	Data integration: - quality driven query processing - instance conflict resolution	Query parser and translator View retriever Fragment factory Query processor Inconsistency detection and resolution Query processor

Fig. 8.7. Comparison between frameworks

organizations to exchange data and quality data, and a set of services that realize data quality functions. The model for data quality proposed is the *data and data quality (D^2Q) model*, described in Chapter 3.

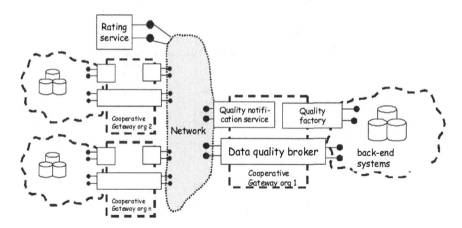

Fig. 8.8. The DaQuinCIS architecture

In the following we focus on services provided by the architecture. The *data quality broker* is the core of the architecture. On behalf of a requesting organization, a query is issued to all organizations, specifying a set of quality requirements on requested data (*quality brokering function*). Different copies of the same data received as responses to the request are reconciled and a best-quality value is selected and proposed to organizations, that can choose to replace their data with higher quality ones (*quality improvement function*). Essentially, the data quality broker is a data integration system [116] which poses quality-enhanced queries over a global schema and selects data satisfying

these requirements. The quality-driven query answering process performed by
the data quality broker is described in Chapter 6, Section 6.3.2.

The *quality notification service* is a publish/subscribe engine used as a general message bus between architectural components of the different cooperating organizations [174]. It allows quality-based subscriptions for organizations
to be notified on changes of the quality of data. For example, an organization
may want to be notified if the quality of data it uses degrades below a certain
acceptable threshold, or when high quality data are available.

The *quality factory* is responsible for evaluating the quality of internal
data of each organization [42]. Its functional modules are shown in Figure 8.9.
The quality factory operates as follows. Requests from external users (or the
organization information system), are processed by the *quality analyzer*, that
performs a static analysis of the values of the data quality dimensions associated with the requested data, and compares them with benchmark quality
parameters contained in the *quality repository*.

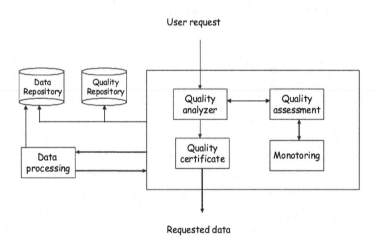

Fig. 8.9. The quality factory

If data values do not satisfy quality requirements, they have to be sent to
the *quality assessment* module. This improves the level of data quality, which
allows the complete or partial fulfilment of quality requirements. If new values
of quality are satisfactory, a quality certificate is associated with the data and
is sent to the *data processing* module. This module cooperates with other
software applications that are responsible for the final response to the user.
A *monitoring* module in charge of monitoring data quality is also included; it
executes monitoring operations on the data repository.

The *rating service* associates trust values with each data source in the CIS.
They are used to determine the reliability of the quality evaluations made by
organizations, which corresponds to its *trustworthiness*. The rating service

is a centralized service, to be performed by a third-party organization. The trustworthiness of a source is calculated with reference to a specific data type; therefore, in a cooperative system made up of public administrations, an agency can be more trusted with respect to addresses provided and less trusted with respect to names of citizens. The trustworthiness criterion is computed as a function of several parameters (see [59]), including the number of *complaints* made by other organizations and the number of requests made to each source unit. It may happen that an organization sends a large number of complaints in order to discredit another organization on the same data it owns. In order to prevent such malicious behavior, an adjusting term is introduced into the definition of the trustworthiness criterion.

8.3.2 FusionPlex Framework

The procedures provided by FusionPlex related to quality-driven query processing and instance-level conflict resolution have been described in detail in Chapter 6, Section 6.3.3. Here, we focus on the architecture and functionalities, as shown in Figure 8.10.

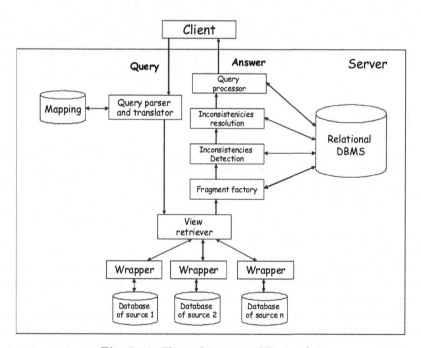

Fig. 8.10. The architecture of Fusionplex

FusionPlex adopts a client-server architecture. The server contains the functionalities that execute the procedure described in Chapter 6:

1. the *query parser and translator* parses the user's query, and determines the source contributions that are relevant to the query;
2. the *view retriever* retrieves the relevant views from the schema mapping;
3. the *fragment factory* constructs the *query fragments*;
4. the *inconsistencies detection module* initially assembles a polyinstance of the answer;
5. the *inconsistencies resolution module* resolves data conflicts in each polytuple according to the appropriate resolution policies;
6. the *query processor* processes the union of all resolved tuples, applies residual aggregations and specified ordering to the query, and returns the query result.

The query parser uses information on the virtual database to be queried, in terms of the global schema, the source schemas, and the mappings among them. Other source characteristics can be added, that quantify a variety of performance parameters of individual sources. Such information is stored at startup time in the *mapping* database, and modified subsequently using a management functionality. Finally, the *relational DBMS* is used to create and manipulate temporary tables.

FusionPlex also provides for powerful and flexible user control over the quality-driven query processing and conflict resolution processes. One user might emphasize the importance of updated information, corresponding to the *timestamp* feature; for another user, *cost* might be most important. User profiles specifying user preferences on the features are managed by the system.

8.4 Toolboxes to Compare Tools

Toolboxes proposed to compare tools focus on the object identification problem. [145] adopts a theoretical approach, while [65] describes a practical tool based on experiments, called Tailor. The two toolboxes are described in the following subsections.

8.4.1 Theoretical Approach

Neiling et al. [145] presents a theoretical framework for comparing techniques. Two aspects are addressed: the complexity of object identification problems and the quality of object identification techniques.

With regard to the first aspect, a reference indicator called *hardness* is introduced. It characterizes the difficulty of an object identification problem; for example, it is intuitive that it is more complex to perform record linkage over two files with low accuracy than over two correct files. As remarked in Chapter 5, the different techniques adopt very specific decision models, characterized in terms of inputs, outputs, and objectives. Therefore, each of the techniques can be more suitable for one class of problems and less suitable for another class of problems. The *hardness* measures how good a technique is for a specific class of problems. The hardness depends on several factors, such as (i) a set of semantic constraints valid in the domain of interest, (ii) the number of pairs to be identified, and (iii) the selectivity of the attribute set that contains identifying information used in the object identification problem.

The second issue addressed in [145] concerns a test framework for the comparison of techniques. The framework consists of a test database, its characteristics (e.g., the existence of semantic keys), several quality criteria for the evaluation of the quality of a solution, and a test specification. The *quality criteria*, inspired by database benchmarks (see [85]), are of two types, respectively *quantitative criteria* and *qualitative criteria*. Quantitative criteria are:

1. *correctness*, the estimation of misclassification rates for test runs;
2. *scalability* with respect to the size of the input;
3. *performance* in terms of computational effort;
4. *cost*, i.e., expenses for the running operations, e.g., hardware and software licenses.

The most important among the above criteria is correctness, which is measured by false negative percentage and false positive percentage, as defined in Chapter 5, Section 5.9.1.

Qualitative criteria include *usability, integrability, reliability, completeness, robustness, transparency, adaptability* and *flexibility*. From these we define three: *usability* is defined as the need for specialized experts and the possibility of automated or incremental updates; *integrability* is considered in the light of existing software architecture functionalities, such as interfaces, data/object exchange, remote control; *transparency* concerns understandability and non-proprietariness of algorithms and results. For definitions of the remaining criteria, see [145].

Similar to the benchmarks available for database management systems, the above set of qualities provides the general criteria for comparing object identification techniques.

8.4.2 Tailor

Tailor [65] is a toolbox for comparing object identification techniques and tools through experiments. The corresponding benchmarking process can be built by tuning a few parameters and plugging in tools that have been developed in-house or are publicly available.

Tailor has four main functionalities (see Figure 8.11), called *layers* in [65], corresponding to (i) the three main record linkage steps discussed in Chapter 5, i.e., *searching method, comparison function, decision model,* and (ii) *measurement*. Figure 8.11 shows the information flow between the four functionalities, and how the record linkage process operates. The flow is coherent with

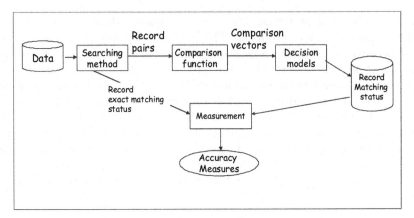

Fig. 8.11. Architecture of Tailor

the general procedure discussed in Chapter 5. At a final stage, a measurement step is performed, to estimate the performance of the decision model.

Layer	Techniques, models and metrics implemented in Taylor

Searching method	Blocking
	  Sorting
	  Hashing
	Sorted Neighborhood

Comparison function	Hamming distance Edit distance Jaro's algorithm n-grams Soundex code

Decision model	Probabilistic models
	  Fellegy & Sunter familiy
	  Cost based
	Clustering model
	Hybrid model

Fig. 8.12. Tailor list of implemented techniques

Figure 8.12 provides a complete list of the various techniques, models and metrics implemented in each of the three record linkage steps. All searching methods and comparison functions mentioned in the figure have been introduced and discussed in Chapter 5. For decision models, the reader may refer to [65] for the clustering model and the hybrid model.

8.5 Summary

Tools and frameworks are crucial for making the techniques and methodologies effective. A comparative analysis of commercial tools is out of the scope of this book. In this chapter we have discussed a specific group of tools and frameworks that closely implement research results. These tools cover various functionalities related to data quality activities, while commercial tools are more focused on specific issues.

In the area of data quality, as in many other areas, there is a temporal gap between research results and their implementation in tools. Furthermore, research groups tend to develop prototypes, characterized by uncertain compatibility and scarce documentation, due to the high investment needed for engineering and selling products. A researcher who aims at using tools in his/her research activity has three choices: (i) use commercial tools, trying to obtain academic licenses, (ii) use public domain tools, extending them with new functionalities, or (iii) develop own tools. The third choice has to be encouraged every time a new technique is conceived in order to experiment and compare results. A theoretical or even qualitative comparison, especially in the data quality area, is seldom possible also when similar paradigms are adopted; only the richness of experimental results can provide evidence of the superiority of a tool with respect to other. Another challenging issue is the production of highly specialized, integrated tools, as an evolution of present tools.

With regard to frameworks, the development process is at an early stage, despite the need for many DQ functionalities in distributed and cooperative information systems. Finally, we notice that the tool is not the solution. In the spirit of this book, this means that the measurement and improvement DQ process has to be carefully planned, using the methodologies discussed in Chapter 7, and the choice of tools has to be addressed only when the relationships between organizations, processes, databases, data flows, external sources, dimensions, and activities to be performed have been deeply understood.

9

Open Problems

In previous chapters we examined all the relevant issues of data quality, from dimensions, to models, activities, techniques, methodologies, tools and frameworks. Among techniques, we have focused mainly on object identification and data integration. We have also emphasized several times the relative immaturity of results and solutions provided in the literature and implemented in tools. In this final chapter we discuss open problems, referring to the more investigated and problematic issues among those addressed above. In Section 9.1 we deal with dimensions and metrics, while in Section 9.2 object identification issues are discussed. Section 9.3 describes data integration, both in trust-aware and in cost-driven query processing. Finally, Section 9.4 considers extensions recently proposed for methodologies. In all sections recent advances are first discussed, followed by an analysis of most relevant open problems.

9.1 Dimensions and Metrics

In Chapter 2, we discussed some data quality dimensions and metrics, showing their meaning and usage by means of examples. However, the problem of defining a reference set of data quality dimensions and metrics is still open. There are several issues to be considered for the purpose:

- Subjective vs. objective assessment. There is no doubt that a database can be of *high quality* for a given application, while being of *low quality* for a different one. Hence the common definition of data quality as "fitness for use". However, such consideration often leads to the wrong assumption that it is not possible to have an objective assessment of quality of data. We claim that for most data quality dimensions (including accuracy, completeness and consistency at least) it makes sense to have objective measures on the basis of which the perceived quality can be evaluated in relation to given user application requirements.

- Domain dependance. For the majority of application domains, a detailed characterization of data quality should take into account the peculiarities of the specific domain. For instance, a set of metrics for evaluating syntactic accuracy must take into account domain dictionaries where available, domain-specific structures (e.g., accuracy of a DNA sequence), etc. This intuition justifies the proposal of domain-specific standards for data quality dimensions and metrics (see Section 2.6). However, in several fields domain specific data quality is being characterized only recently by the scientific community (see e.g. [126] for the biological domain).

Therefore, the following research issues still need investigation. First, a comprehensive set of metrics allowing an objective assessment of the quality of a database should be defined. Metrics should be related to a given data model or format (e.g., relational, XML, or spreadsheets), to a given dimension (typically a single one), and to different degrees of data granularity. Second, appropriate measurement methods are still missing. These methods should allow the clear definition of the sources to measure, e.g., by sampling procedures, the measurement tools, and the measurement precision and errors. Third, there is the need to characterize quality of data in the context of information services. This characterization is required, for instance, as an extension of languages that permit the specification of the quality of service of semantic services (e.g., [219]) or in the definition of service level contracts (e.g., [158]). Fourth, as also highlighted in Chapter 2, data quality dimensions are not orthogonal, instead, we often need to manage tradeoffs among them. Possible tradeoffs within the set of dimensions characterizing quality of data are still worth investigating.

9.2 Object Identification

As described in Chapter 5, traditional record linkage techniques need to be integrated with techniques for matching more complex data structures. We recall that the denomination *object identification* has been used in this book in order to highlight the migration from records to objects, which can be parts of XML documents or pieces of structured information, even stored in different formats, like in *personal information management* (PIM). In Chapter 5 we described the problem of object identification for XML documents; therefore, in Section 9.2.1 we focus on the description of the principal research challenges characterizing XML object identification, not providing further details on the problem specification. In Section 9.2.2 we describe both the problem and the research issues of object identification of information in the PIM context. Finally, in Section 9.2.3 we describe the relationships between record linkage and privacy, which are gaining increasing importance in networked information systems [1].

9.2.1 XML Object Identification

Performing object identification on XML data has two principal peculiarities, when compared to traditional record linkage techniques, namely:

- Identification of the objects to compare. In the relational case, objects coincide with the tuples of a relational table. Conversely, in the XML case, there is the need to identify the XML elements to compare. The delimitation of the boundaries of such elements in the XML document is an issue to be considered. Specifically, the linkage process should be able to identify which portion of the subtree rooted in the elements to compare can be used for performing object identification. Indeed, for deep or wide XML trees, a solution considering the whole subtree can be rather expensive. In Figure 9.1, the problem of identifying which portions of two distinct XML trees referring to a real-world entity "Julia Roberts" is depicted.

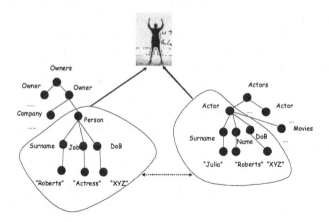

Fig. 9.1. Identifying objects to compare in XML documents

- Exploitation of the flexibility of the XML data model. As a semistructured data model, XML permits the definition of an element in multiple ways, and allows the definition of optional attributes. Such features need to be taken into account in the object identification process in order to make the process as effective as possible. For instance, let us suppose we have two XML documents storing persons. The first document has a schema defining persons, according to a DTD syntax, as follows:

---

[1] Notice that in this last case we use the term record linkage as we refer again to traditional data structures, like records of a file.

$$<!ELEMENTperson1(name, surname)|(surname, DoB) >$$

The second document has a different definition for persons, namely:

$$<!ELEMENTperson2(name, surname, DoB) >$$

The matching process should take into account both representations of person1. Specifically, instances conforming to the representations of person1 can be matched with instances conforming to the representation of person2, by performing the matching on name and surname or alternatively on surname and DoB.

As described in Chapter 5, the above problems have only started to be addressed by recent techniques [207], and therefore there is room for further research investigation.

9.2.2 Object Identification of Personal Information

Personal information management (PIM) has the goal of providing a unified view of information stored on one's desktop. To this end, there is the need to build an integration layer that provides the user with the possibility to store any object of interest according to its semantics, i.e. to relate it to the concepts of a personal ontology, where an object may be a mail, a document, a picture, or any other type of data. In the big picture, such an integration layer could be used for unifying all personal information, even stored on portable devices like PDAs or mobile phones. Focusing on the desktop-level integration, the idea is to enable the user to query the personal ontology, whereas the system carries out the task of suitably processing the query, accessing the different pieces of information involved in the query, and assembling the data into the final answer [108]. This vision can be realized if an object identification activity is performed across a variety of sources including mails, files, pictures, contacts and spreadsheets.

As an example, let us suppose that the same person, e.g., Julia Roberts, is stored as an email contact, as an interviewed person, and as the subject of a picture (see Figure 9.2). In order to build the global object related to Julia Roberts, an object identification activity must be performed, with the purpose of identifying that the three represented objects are actually the same real-world entity.

The described problem gives rise to some open issues, related to the peculiarities of object identification in PIM. First, as remarked in [62], in PIM a small amount of information is used to represent an entity, like for instance a person; indeed, a person representation extracted from an email has only the email address attribute. Conversely, object identification techniques need to rely on several attributes for performing the matching. Second, in a personal information space, information needs to be modeled in a flexible way; hence object identification techniques have problems which are similar to those described for XML object identification.

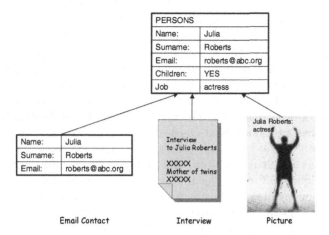

Fig. 9.2. Object identification in PIM

9.2.3 Record Linkage and Privacy

When considering networked information systems, the relationship between record linkage and privacy can be characterized in two ways:

1. Record linkage *prevention* in data publishing. A node can publish its own data so that they are available to the whole networked system. If privacy constraints must be enforced on published data, the node must ensure that no record linkage could be done on published data with the purpose of identifying identities of published individuals and entities.
2. Record linkage *promotion* in data exchanges. Nodes joining a networked system are willing to share information with other nodes. If such information need be privacy protected, record linkage should be enabled while preserving privacy.

In data publishing, a major problem is to assess the risk of privacy violation, once properly disclosed data are published. Typically, anonimyzation does not guarantee zero privacy risk. Indeed, suppose that personal data like DateOfBirth, City and MaritalStatus are published, whereas identifiers like SSN, Name and Surname are removed for the purpose of privacy preservation. By performing record linkage of such data with a public available list, such as an electoral list, it can be easy to identify the individuals with whom the publish data are referenced. Therefore, more sophisticated techniques need to be applied for more properly dealing with privacy assurance.

Among the techniques proposed in the literature, two major classes can be distinguished, namely: perturbation-based techniques and suppression-based techniques. *Perturbation-based techniques* are based on data transformation that include some *noise* for the purpose of privacy preservation; an example of a data perturbation technique consists of swapping data to be published. Data perturbation techniques have been deeply investigated, in the context of statistical databases [2] and privacy-preserving data mining [196]. Some recent proposals for *suppression-based techniques* are briefly described in the following. K-anonymity [171] is a technique that, given a relation T, ensures that each record of T can be indistinctly matched to at least k individuals. It is enforced by considering a subset of T's attributes, called *quasi-identifiers*, and forcing the values that T's records have on quasi-identifiers to appear with at least k-occurrences. In the example above, `DateOfBirth`, `City`, and `MaritalStatus` are examples of quasi-identifiers; for instance, if k=2, in the published data set at least two records must have the same `DateOfBirth`, `City`, and `MaritalStatus` values, and thus are made indistinguishable. A recent technique [112] considers the quantitative evaluation of the privacy risk in case anonymized data are released. In such a work, a database is modeled as a sequence of transactions, and the frequency of an item x in the database is the fraction of transactions that contain that item. A hypothetical attacker can have access to similar data and use them in order to breach the privacy of disclosed data. The knowledge of the attacker is modeled as a belief function that represents the guess that the attacker can make on the actual frequencies of items in the database. In [129], the authors provide an analysis of the *query-view security problem*. Given n views, in such a problem we check if the views disclose any information about a given secret query. The query-view security problem is characterized by means of the notion of *critical tuple* for a query Q that considers a tuple t critical for Q if there are some instances of the database for which dropping t makes a difference. In [129], the authors demonstrate that a query Q is insecure w.r.t. a set of views if and only if they share some common critical tuples. However, so far the problem of characterizing the risk of privacy violation when publishing elementary data in the general case is still open.

In data exchanges, few methods for private record linkage have been proposed. Private record linkage has the purpose of performing record linkage between two sources, say A and B, such that at the end of the process A will know only a set $A \cap B$, consisting of records in A that match with records in B. Similarly B will know only the set $A \cap B$. Of particular importance is the aim that no information will be revealed to A and B concerning records that do not match each other. Figure 9.3 depicts a private record linkage scenario, in which the information that each of the two sources wants to keep secret is represented within a padlock.

Some initial approaches are motivated by the strict privacy requirements of e-health applications [164, 48], or by efficiency issues [5]. Some work that can be related to the problem of private record linkage has also been done in the security area, and involves secure set intersection and secure string comparison. Secure set intersection methods (see [110] for a survey) deal with exact matching and are too expensive to be applied to large databases due to their reliance on cryptography. Furthermore, these protocols deal with the intersection of sets of simple elements, and are not designed for exploiting the semantics behind database records. The problem of securely comparing

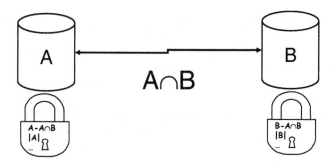

Fig. 9.3. Private record linkage across the two sources A and B

strings has been addressed by homomorphic encryption schemes, characterized by the property that $E(a) * E(b) = E(a + b)$. For example Atallah et al. [10] have proposed an algorithm for comparing sequences based on such schemes. While such an algorithm works for sequence similarity, like DNA sequence comparison, the communication cost of this algorithm, proportional to the product of the sequence lengths, is prohibitive for databases.

9.3 Data Integration

Several data quality problems arise when data integration must be performed. As also remarked in Chapter 6, there are still interesting research issues concerning query processing in data integration systems when assuming that conflicts may arise across sources. Specifically, conflicts can be revealed when tuples from different databases are brought together into an integrated database. From the perspective of the data integration system's semantics, there is no general way to restore consistency, and several possible repairs can be applied. Consistent query answering techniques have been proposed for the purpose of performing such repairs and removing incorrect tuples from the query result. In Chapter 6, we have described some research results and open problems regarding conflict resolution and quality-driven query processing in centralized data integration systems. In Section 9.3.1 we sketch some interesting problems that arise when moving to peer-to-peer (P2P) systems. In Section 9.3.2 we focus instead on the open issues related to query processing in data integration systems when economic models and cost aspects are taken into account.

9.3.1 Trust-Aware Query Processing in P2P Contexts

Peer data management systems (PDMSs) have been proposed as an architecture for decentralized data sharing [188]. Differently from a centralized data integration system, PDMSs do not provide a *mediated schema* on which user queries have to be posed, but data are stored at each peer and only local schemes are used for query answering. P2P systems are characterized by their openness, i.e. a peer can dynamically join or leave the system. When joining a PDMS, a peer has to identify the peers with which to perform data exchanges, and in this respect trust plays an important role. The evaluation of the trust (or confidence) of the data provided by a single peer is crucial because each source can in principle influence the final, integrated result. While several trust and reputation systems have been proposed in the literature (see [106] for a survey), there is still the need to characterize the trust of a peer with respect to provided data and use such information in the query processing step.

More specifically, some open issues involved in trust characterization and evaluation in PDMS include:

- How to model and measure the trust of data provided by a given source. A common distinction is between the reputation of a source, which refers to the source as a whole, and the trust of provided data, e.g., the trust of the mapping that the source establishes with the other sources in a PDMS. Methods for evaluating trust and reputation are needed, with the specific aim of supporting decisions to be taken on result selection.
- Algorithms to compute trust-aware query results. In all the cases a user query can yield a set of different results, such algorithms should allow the selection of the most trustable answer(s). As a secondary effect, whereas a big amount of data is returned as a query result, the trust characterization can provide an "ordering" for processing such results, whereas other priority criteria are not available.

9.3.2 Cost-Driven Query Processing

Information has a cost, which is determined in part by its quality. So, when querying a set of data sources, we have to plan a reasonable cost-quality trade-off. Recently, advances in the technology for large-scale deployment of information services, e.g. over service-oriented software infrastructures, have enabled cost-effective data exchange across organizations. In business terms, this means that it is becoming increasingly feasible for organizations to (i) purchase or otherwise acquire data from other peers, and (ii) exploit their own information assets for marketing purposes. Several studies have analyzed the economic relevance of the potential information market. Public agencies have been found to be the greatest producers of information by far, and the information they create and disseminate is often relevant for both the private and public processes, products and services. In [162] an analysis of the commercial exploitation of *public sector information* is presented both for the USA and the European Union. With the final goal to improve this kind of market in the European Union, rules for managing the reuse of information owned by public sector bodies of the member states have since been issued [71].

The problem of matching information demand to information offer under quality constraints, minimizing on the cost, has been addressed so far in a few papers. The model considered for data sources is a data integration system, as discussed in Chapter 6. A local schema may contain source queries that represent a partial answer to the global query; furthermore, the same source queries may be offered by different suppliers, with different quality levels and costs. In order to satisfy the entire demand, it is necessary to collect source queries from multiple local schemes, possibly selecting among equivalent queries with different quality and cost, in such a way that the quality requirements on the resulting whole are satisfied.

In the approach described in [13], the optimal choice is performed in two steps. First, a query decomposition algorithm selects feasible source queries from the local relations, given a global query. Then, an *integer linear programming* optimization problem is formulated that uses the selected queries and produces a cost-optimal bag of queries that satisfy the entire demand. The composition of qualities of queries is made on the basis of simple composition functions such as, e.g., average.

In the approach of [8], in order to obtain the required data, customers must buy multiple data sets from different providers and then clean and merge them. In this case (see Figure 9.4), a broker architecture intermediates between users and syndicated data providers. On the basis of data quality and cost requirements, the broker builds the most suitable data set by integrating data fragments from different providers. In the selection phase, the broker uses optimization and negotiation mechanisms in order to satisfy requirements. The broker is modeled according to the local-as-view (LAV) perspective, where the data of a provider are represented as views of a global schema, called *broker schema*. The broker is in charge of managing the relationship with providers, and it is also supposed to receive from providers the average value of quality of each data set. Providers have the responsibility to evaluate data quality, along the accuracy, completeness, and timeliness dimensions.

On the basis of data quality and cost requirements, the broker builds the most suitable data set by integrating data from different providers. The optimization approach is based on the tabu search algorithm [83]. A negotiation is started between the broker, behaving on behalf of its user, and the providers, when a solution is infeasible from the point of view of data quality constraints, while still satisfying the constraint referred to price. The aim of the negotiation process is to generate a new set of data fragments that is used in a new exploration; the exploration in performed in an area neighboring to the unfeasible solution, to find the best result for the user query.

Open issues in the area originate from its interdisciplinary background, which includes both technical and economic perspectives. They concern the following aspects:

1. Modeling providers as offering *bundles*, which are indivisible units of data, each one with a single associated price and quality level. Both the cost

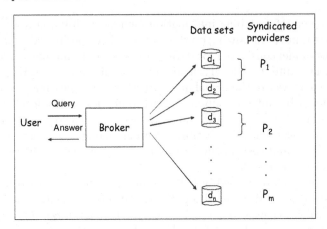

Fig. 9.4. Users, broker, and syndicated data providers

structure behind the production and the selling of digital information goods, and the need to implement anti-competitive strategies can induce more and more data providers to offer indivisible units of different types of data (see for example [191], [14], and [138]).

2. Adopting cost models in which (i) discounts to consumers who acquire two or more (complementary) information goods are provided, or (ii) the cost is a function of the offered quality.

3. Extending economic models to support a *coordinated spot market*, where multiple consumers simultaneously require portions of data with specified quality levels, and multiple suppliers submit their offers and associated quantity-quality matrices to a central public supplier mediator. For instance, the mediator might be in charge of selling data owned by multiple local public agencies to individuals, businesses and other public agencies. In such a case, in order to exploit the quantity/quality discounts as much as possible, the purchasing process could be coordinated by collecting and then matching the overall demand and offer.

4. Considering the case where the improvement in quality of information input to a process has an impact on the quality of information output from the process, resulting in a progressive improvement of the information assets for each participating organization.

9.4 Methodologies

Methodologies for data quality measurement and improvement are evolving in several directions: (i) relating more closely data quality issues and business process issues, and (ii) considering new types of information systems, specifically web information systems.

The relationship between data quality and process quality is a wide area of investigation, due to the relevance and diversity of characteristics of business processes in organizations. We have analyzed the influence of data quality on costs of processes in Chapter 4. Here we broaden the perspective. The different impacts of data quality at the three typical organizational levels, namely operations, the tactical level and the strategic level, are analyzed in [168] reporting interviews and the outcomes of several proprietary studies. Data quality and its relationship with the quality of services, products, business operations, consumer behaviors is investigated in very general terms in [179] and [178], where generic propositions such as "information quality of a firm is positively related to the firm's performance" are stated. The symmetric problem of investigating how improving information production processes positively influences data and information quality is analyzed in [67].

A few papers address more specific issues, and, consequently, present more concrete results. [195] examines the issue of electronic data interchange (EDI), which concerns the exchange of data among organizations using standard formats, and its influence on the efficiency and effectiveness of business processes. EDI may be seen as a DQ technology enabler, since it potentially reduces paper handling related activities, data-entry errors, and data-entry functions. The conclusions of the paper were unforseen. When using EDI technology, the quality of the communication context, namely the degree to which the contexts of the communicating parties are aligned, becomes crucial for the effectiveness of the process. Cases are reported that show a positive effect of EDI on processing time, while poor context DQ resulted in a negative effect. The errors occurring in the EDI process do not occur in the non-EDI one, since in this last case the two parties talk to each other on the phone.

The influence of data quality on extreme conditions in processes, such as disasters, is investigated in [78]. Flaws in accuracy, completeness, consistency, and timeliness are considered in decision making, for example for the 1986 NASA space shuttle Challenger accident, that killed seven people, and the US Navy cruiser Vincennes firing at an Iranian Airbus, that brought 290 people to their death.

The role of information in supply chains is considered in [60], where the *quality robustness* of an information chain is proposed as the ability of the information productive process, of its internal organization in terms of activities and flows among activities, to construct the final information product also in the presence of threats that cause information distortion, transformation variabilities and information failures. A methodological framework called *process quality robustness design* is proposed as a framework for diagnosing, prescribing, and building quality into information chains.

Open problems in the area concern the identification of more precise statistical, probabilistic or functional correlations among data quality and process quality, in the issues related to:

1. more extensive research and empirical validation of the models presented;

2. extension of the analysis to a wider set of dimensions and to specific types of business processes and business areas.

Concerning web information systems, methodologies address several areas: (i) general approaches to web data quality measurement and improvement processes, (ii) more complex data than structured data, namely unstructured data and in particular documents, (iii) new types of dimensions, such as accessibility, considered under different perspectives.

The information quality measurement (IQM) methodology, described in [69] provides general guidelines for measuring and, to a limited extent, improving the quality of information on the web. Considered dimensions are in principle a wide number, ranging from accessibility to consistency, timeliness, currency, comprehensiveness; some of them are evaluated in a narrow sense, e.g., consistency is measured as the number of pages with style guide deviation. IQM consists of two major elements: an action plan on how to conduct the measurement, and an information quality framework that defines which criteria are worth measuring. It is made up of the following phases:

1. measurement planning, made up of: (i) identification of relevant information quality criteria through interviews with stakeholders, (ii) analysis and definition of trade-offs and interdependencies between criteria, (iii) definition of qualitative and quantitative indicators, and (iv) selection of measurement tools for the required indicators;
2. measurement configuration, through weighting of the indicators according to strategic priorities and definition of alert and target values for every indicator;
3. measurement, in terms of (i) data gathering (e.g., monitoring or surveys), (ii) data analysis and presentation;
4. follow-up activities such as corrective measures based on alert indicators, controlling of activities (e.g., assigning responsibilities, and adjustment of measurement according to implementation experiences).

The role played in the process by several tools, such as performance monitoring, site analyzers, traffic analyzers, and web mining is discussed.

Pernici and Scannapieco in [159] propose a model to associate and improve quality information to web data, namely to each item in a web page, a page, and groups of pages, and a methodology for data quality design and management of web information systems. They suggest to enrich methodologies for web information systems design (such as [128] and [102]) with additional steps specifically devoted to data quality design (see Figure 9.5). Several dimensions such as volatility, completability, and semantic and syntactic accuracy as defined in Chapter 2 are covered.

The issue of quality of documents in the web is of increasing relevance, since the number of documents that are managed in web format is constantly

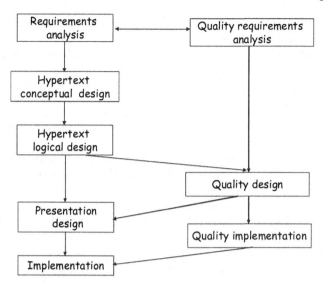

Fig. 9.5. A web information system design methodology (left side) enriched with activities for data quality design (right side)

growing. Several studies have shown that 40% of the material on the net disappears within one year, while a further 40% is altered, leaving only 20% in its original form. Other studies indicate that the average lifetime of a web page is 44 days (see [125]), and the overall web changes completely about four times in a year. As a consequence, the preservation of web data becomes more and more crucial; the term preservation indicates the ability to prevent the losses of information in the web, by storing all significant versions of web documents.

In [41] a methodology to support the preservation process over the entire life cycle of information, from creation, to acquisition, cataloguing, storage, and access is proposed. Main phases are summarized in the following.

1. Each time a new page is published, a procedure named the *static preservation model* has to be executed. At creation time, data are associated with metadata, describing their quality, in terms of accuracy, completeness, consistency, currency and volatility as defined in Chapter 2. Metadata also include properties of the document, such as the author and the document type.

2. Before the acquisition phase is executed, the user specifies acceptable values for all quality dimensions. If new data satisfy quality requirements, they are physically or virtually incorporated into an archive. After acquisition, the web page is cataluoged. If evaluation results do not meet quality requirements, data are returned to their owner with a warning and are not catalogued until their quality is satisfactory. Different suggestions

are provided for data formats to be used in the preservation stage, e.g., translating HTML pages into XML pages.

3. In the publishing stage, when a new page is published by replacing an old web page, the volatility of old data has to be evaluated. If evaluation results indicate that old data are still valid, data are not deleted, but they are associated with a new URL.

A second model called *dynamic preservation model* allows periodic evaluation of the volatility dimension.

Assessment methodologies for evaluating specific qualities of web sites are proposed in [12], [128] and [80]. [12] is specifically focused on *accessibility* as defined in Chapter 2. Accessibility is evaluated on the basis of a mixed quantitative/qualitative assessment. The quantitative assessment activity checks the guidelines mentioned in Chapter 2, provided by the World Wide Web Consortium in [198]. The qualitative assessment is based on experiments performed with disabled users. [80] focuses on the *usability* of the site and proposes an approach based on the adoption of *conceptual logs*, which are web usage logs enriched with meta-data deriving from the application of conceptual specifications expressed by the conceptual schema of the web site. The novelty of the approach is that traditional measures of several qualities of web sites are performed in terms of indicators based on the hypertext representation of the information, e.g., the number of accesses to the different pages, while in this approach new indicators are proposed based on the conceptual representation of the content of the site.

Open problems in the area of methodologies concern:

1. the validation of methodologies. Usually (see references above) a methodology is proposed without any specific experimentation, and with scarce availability of supporting tools. Research on experiments to validate the approaches and on the development of tools to make them feasible is worthwhile;

2. the extension of methodological guidelines to (i) a wider set of dimensions, such as performance, availability, security, accessibility, and to (ii) dependencies among dimensions. For example, a dependency among currency and accuracy is the rule "in 70% of data if an item is not current it is also inaccurate". Knowledge on dependencies, acquired with data mining techniques, can greatly improve the efficiency and effectiveness of the improvement process;

3. in web information systems and in data warehouses, data are managed at different aggregation levels; *quality composition*, as discussed in Chapter 4, should be investigated to derive quality information in aggregate web data from quality information associated with elementary data;

4. the development of more effective assessment methodologies in which, as we have seen in Chapter 7 and in this section when we have discussed [12], both qualitative elements and quantitative indicators are considered.

9.5 Conclusions

In this last chapter we outlined the future development of the data quality research area. In addition to what was presented in this book, in the next ten years there will probably be a widespread increase in contributions in the area, with new paradigms and approaches. Indeed, information is a "plastic" concept and resource, that can hardly be encapsulated into fixed models and techniques. We use textual information to write poetry, facial information to express emotions, musical information to compose or listen to operas. What does it mean that a note in a symphony is executed wrong? It is not easy to formalize this concept, and, probably, it is not useful, since a huge number of phenomena, luckily for us, have to be perceived, and will continue to be perceived, on the basis of our feelings and emotions.

References

1. ABITEBOUL, S., BUNEMAN, P., AND SUCIU, D. *Data on the Web: From Relations to Semistructured Data and XML*. Morgan Kaufmann Publishers, 2000.
2. ADAM, N. R., AND WORTMANN, J. C. Security Control Methods for Statistical Databases: A Comparative Study. *ACM Computing Surveys 21*, 4 (1989), 515–556.
3. AGRAWAL, R., GUPTA, A., AND SARAWAGI, S. Modeling Multidimensional Databases. In *Proc. ICDE 2000* (Birmingham, UK, 1997).
4. AIMETTI, P., MISSIER, P., SCANNAPIECO, M., BERTOLETTI, M., AND BATINI, C. Improving Government-to-Business Relationships through Data Reconciliation and Process Re-engineering. In *Advances in Management Information Systems - Information Quality (AMIS-IQ) Monograph*, R. Y. Wang, E. M. Pierce, S. E. Madnick, and C. W. Fisher, Eds. Sharpe, M.E., April 2005.
5. AL-LAWATI, A., LEE, D., AND MCDANIEL, P. Blocking-aware Private Record Linkage. In *Proc. IQIS 2005 (SIGMOD Workshop)* (Baltimore, MC, 2005).
6. AMAT, G., AND LABOISSE, B. Une Gestion Operationnelle de la Qualite Donnees. In *Proc. 1st Data and Knowledge Quality Workshop (in conjunction with ECG)* (18th January 2005, Paris, France).
7. ANANTHAKRISHNA, R., CHAUDHURI, S., AND GANTI, V. Eliminating Fuzzy Duplicates in Data Warehouses. In *Proc. VLDB 2002* (Hong Kong, China, 2002).
8. ARDAGNA, D., CAPPIELLO, C., COMUZZI, M., FRANCALANCI, C., AND PERNICI, B. A Broker for Selecting and Provisioning High Quality Syndicated Data. In *Proc. 10th International Conference on Information Quality (IQ 2005)*.
9. ARENAS, M., BERTOSSI, L. E., AND CHOMICKI, J. Consistent Query Answers in Inconsistent Databases. In *Proc. PODS'99*.
10. ATALLAH, M. J., KERSCHBAUM, F., AND DU, W. Secure and Private Sequence Comparisons. In *Proc. ACM Workshop on Privacy in the Electronic Society (WPES 2003)* (Washington, Washington DC, 2003).
11. ATZENI, P., AND DE ANTONELLIS, V. *Relational Database Theory*. The Benjamin/Cummings Publishing Company, 1993.
12. ATZENI, P., MERIALDO, P., AND SINDONI, G. Web Site Evaluation: Methodology and Case Study. In *Proc. International Workshop on Data Semantics in Web Information Systems (DASWIS 2001)* (Yokohama, Japan, 2001).

13. AVENALI, A., BERTOLAZZI, P., BATINI, C., AND MISSIER, P. A Formulation of the Data Quality Optimization Problem in Cooperative Information Systems. In *Proc. CAISE International Workshop on Data and Information Quality* (Riga, Latvia, 2004).

14. AYRES, I., AND NALEBUFF, B. Going Soft on Microsoft? The EU's Antitrust Case and Remedy. The Economists' Voice.

15. BALLOU, D. P., AND PAZER, H. L. Modeling Completeness versus Consistency Tradeoffs in Information Decision Contexts. *IEEE Transactions on Knowledge Data Engineering 15*, 1 (2003), 240–243.

16. BALLOU, D. P., AND TAYI, G. K. Enhancing Data Quality in Data Warehouse Environments. *Communications of the ACM 42*, 1 (1999).

17. BALLOU, D. P., WANG, R. Y., PAZER, H., AND TAYI, G. K. Modeling Information Manufacturing Systems to Determine Information Product Quality. *Management Science 44*, 4 (1998).

18. BARATEIRO, J., AND GALHARDAS, H. A Survey of Data Quality Tools. *Datenbank Spectrum 14* (2005), 15–21.

19. BASEL COMMITTEE ON BANKING SUPERVISION. http://www.ots.treas.gov.

20. BATINI, C., CERI, S., AND NAVATHE, S. B. *Conceptual Data Base Design: An Entity Relationship Approach.* Benjamin and Cummings, 1992.

21. BATINI, C., AND MECELLA, M. Enabling Italian e-Government Through a Cooperative Architecture. *IEEE Computer 34*, 2 (2001).

22. BATINI, C., NARDELLI, E., AND TAMASSIA, R. A Layout Algorithm for Data Flow Diagrams. *IEEE Transactions on Software Engineering* (April 1986).

23. BELIN, T. R., AND RUBIN, D. B. A Method for Calibrating False Matches Rates in Record Linkage. *Journal of American Statistical Association 90* (1995), 694–707.

24. BERTI-ÉQUILLE, L. Quality-Adaptive Query Processing over Distributed Sources. In *Proc. 9th Internation Conference on Information Quality (IQ 2004)*.

25. BERTI-ÉQUILLE, L. Integration of Biological Data and Quality-driven Source Negotiation. In *Proc. ER 2001* (Yokohama, Japan, 2001).

26. BERTOLAZZI, P., DE SANTIS, L., AND SCANNAPIECO, M. Automatic Record Matching in Cooperative Information Systems. In *Proc. DQCIS 2003 (ICDT Workshop)* (Siena, Italy, 2003).

27. BILKE, A., BLEIHOLDER, J., BÖHM, C., DRABA, K., NAUMANN, F., AND WEIS, M. Automatic Data Fusion with HumMer. In *Proc. VLDB 2005 Demonstration Program* (Trondheim, Norway, 2005).

28. BITTON, D., AND DEWITT, D. J. Duplicate Record Elimination in Large Data Files. *ACM Transactions on Databases Systems 8*, 2 (1983).

29. BOAG, A., CHAMBERLIN, D., FERNANDEZ, M. F., FLORESCU, D., ROBIE, J., AND SIMÉON, J. XQuery 1.0: An XML Query Language. W3C Working Draft. Available from http:///www.w3.org/TR/xquery, November 2003.

30. BOUZEGHOUB, M., AND PERALTA, V. A Framework for Analysis of Data Freshness. In *Proc. IQIS 2004 (SIGMOD Workshop)* (Paris, France, 2004).

31. BOVEE, M., SRIVASTAVA, R. P., AND MAK, B. R. A Conceptual Framework and Belief-Function Approach to Assessing Overall Information Quality. In *Proc. 6th International Conference on Information Quality (IQ 2001)*.

32. BRAVO, L., AND BERTOSSI, L. E. Logic Programming for Consistently Querying Data Integration Systems. In *Proc. IJCAI 2003*.

33. BRUNI, R., AND SASSANO, A. Errors Detection and Correction in Large Scale Data Collecting. In *Proc. 4th International Conference on Advances in Intelligent Data Analysis* (Cascais, Portugal, 2001).

34. BUECHI, M., BORTHWICK, A., WINKEL, A., AND GOLDBERG, A. ClueMaker: a Language for Approximate Record Matching. In *Proc. 8th International Conference on Information Quality (IQ 2003)*.

35. BUNEMAN, P. Semistructured Data. In *Proc. PODS 1997*.

36. BUNEMAN, P., KHANNA, S., AND TAN, W. C. Why and Where: A Characterization of Data Provenance. In *Proc. International Conference on Database Theory (ICDT 2001)* (London, UK, 2001).

37. CALI, A., CALVANESE, D., DE GIACOMO, G., AND LENZERINI, M. On the Role of Integrity Constraints in Data Integration. *IEEE Data Eng. Bull. 25*, 3 (2002), 39–45.

38. CALÌ, A., LEMBO, D., AND ROSATI, R. On the Decidability and Complexity of Query Answering over Inconsistent and Incomplete Databases. In *Proc. PODS 2003*.

39. CALÌ, A., LEMBO, D., AND ROSATI, R. Query Rewriting and Answering under Constraints in Data Integration Systems. In *Proc. IJCAI 2003*.

40. CALVANESE, D., DE GIACOMO, G., AND LENZERINI, M. Modeling and Querying Semi-Structured Data. *Networking and Information Systems Journal 2*, 2 (1999), 253–273.

41. CAPPIELLO, C., FRANCALANCI, C., AND PERNICI, B. Preserving Web Sites: a Data Quality Approach. In *Proc. 8th International Conference on Information Quality (IQ 2003)*.

42. CAPPIELLO, C., FRANCALANCI, C., PERNICI, B., PLEBANI, P., AND SCANNAPIECO, M. Data Quality Assurance in Cooperative Information Systems: a Multi-dimension Certificate. In *Proc. DQCIS 2003 (ICDT Workshop)* (Siena, Italy, 2003).

43. CARUSO, F., COCHINWALA, M., GANAPATHY, U., LALK, G., AND MISSIER, P. Telcordia's Database Reconciliation and Data Quality Analysis Tool. In *Demonstration at VLDB 2000*.

44. CHARNES, A., COOPER, W. W., AND RHODES, E. Measuring the Efficiency of Decision Making Units. *European Journal of Operational Research 2* (1978).

45. CHAUDHURI, S., GANTI, V., AND MOTWANI, R. Robust Identification of Fuzzy Duplicates. In *Proc. ICDE 2005*.

46. CHEN, Z., KALASHNIKOV, D. V., AND MEHROTRA, S. Exploiting Relationships for Object Consolidation. In *Proc. IQIS 2005 (SIGMOD Workshop)*.

47. CHITICARIU, L., TAN, W., AND VIJAYVARGIYA, G. An Annnotation Management System for Relational Databases. In *Proc. VLDB 2004* (Toronto, Canada, 2004).

48. CHURCHES, T., AND CHRISTEN, P. Some Methods for Blindfolded Record Linkage. *BMC Medical Informatics and Decision Making 4*, 9 (2004).

49. CUI, Y., WIDOM, J., AND WIENER, J. L. Tracing the Lineage of View Data in a Warehousing Environment. *ACM Transactions on Database Systems 25*, 2 (2000), 179–227.

50. DASU, T., AND JOHNSON, T. *Exploratory Data Mining and Data Cleaning*. J. Wiley Series in Probability and Statistics, 2003.

51. DASU, T., JOHNSON, T., MUTHUKRISHNAN, S., AND SHKAPENYUK, V. Mining Database Structure or, How to Build a Data Quality Browser. In *Proc. SIGMOD 2002* (Madison, WI, 2002).

52. DATA WAREHOUSING INSTITUTE. Data Quality and the Bottom Line: Achieving Business Success through a Commitment to High Quality Data. http://www.dw-institute.com/.

53. DAVIS, G. B., AND OLSON, M. H. *Management Information Systems: Conceptual Foundations, Structure, and Development (2nd ed.)*. McGraw-Hill, 1984.

54. DAVIS, R., STROBE, H., AND SZOLOVITS, P. What is Knowledge Representation. *AI Magazine 14*, 1 (1993), 17–33.

55. DAYAL, U. Query Processing in a Multidatabase System. In *Query Processing in Database Systems*. Springer, 1985, pp. 81–108.

56. DE AMICIS, F., AND BATINI, C. A Methodology for Data Quality Assessment on Financial Data. *Studies in Communication Sciences* (2004).

57. DE GIACOMO, G., LEMBO, D., LENZERINI, M., AND ROSATI, R. Tackling Inconsitencies in Data Integration though Source Preferences. In *Proc. IQIS 2004 (SIGMOD Workshop)* (Paris, France, 2004).

58. DE MICHELIS, G., DUBOIS, E., JARKE, M., MATTHES, F., MYLOPOULOS, J., PAPAZOGLOU, M. P., , SCHMIDT, J., WOO, C., AND YU, E. Cooperative Information Systems: A Manifesto. In *Cooperative Information Systems: Trends & Directions*, M. Papazoglou and G. Schlageter, Eds. Accademic-Press, 1997.

59. DE SANTIS, L., SCANNAPIECO, M., AND CATARCI, T. Trusting Data Quality in Cooperative Information Systems. In *Proc. 11th International Conference on Cooperative Information Systems (CoopIS 2003)* (Catania, Italy, 2003).

60. DEDEKE, A. Building Quality into Information Supply Chain. In *Advances in Management Information Systems - Information Quality (AMIS-IQ) Monograph*, R. Y. Wang, E. M. Pierce, S. E. Madnick, and C. W. Fisher, Eds. Sharpe, M.E., April 2005.

61. DEMPSTER, A., LAIRD, N., AND RUBIN, D. Maximum Likelihood from Incomplete Data via the EM Algorithm. *Journal of the Royal Statistical Society Series B 39*, 1 (1977).

62. DONG, X., HALEVY, A. Y., AND MADHAVAN, J. Reference Reconciliation in Complex Information Spaces. In *Proc. SIGMOD 2005*.

63. DUBLIN CORE. http://dublincore.org/.

64. DUNN, H. L. Record Linkage. *American Journal of Public Health 36* (1946), 1412–1416.

65. ELFEKY, M. G., VERYKIOS, V. S., AND ELMAGARMID, A. K. Tailor: A Record Linkage Toolbox. In *Proc. 18th International Conference on Data Engineering* (San Jose, CA, 2002).

66. ELMASRI, R., AND NAVATHE, S. *Foundamentals of Database Systems (5th ed.)*. Addison-Wesley Publishing Company, 1994.

67. ENGLISH, L. Process Management and Information Quality: How Improving Information Production Processes Improves Information (Product) Quality. In *Proc. 7th International Conference on Information Quality (IQ 2002)*.

68. ENGLISH, L. P. *Improving Data Warehouse and Business Information Quality*. Wiley & Sons, 1999.

69. EPPLER, M., AND MUENZENMAIER, P. Measuring Information Quality in the Web Context: A Survey of State-of-the-Art Instruments and an Application Methodology. In *Proc. 7th International Conference on Information Quality (IQ 2002)*.

70. EPPLER, M. J., AND HELFERT, M. A Classification and Analysis of Data Quality Costs. In *Proc. 9th International Conference on Information Quality (IQ 2004)*.

71. EUROPEAN PARLIAMENT. Directive 2003/98/EC of the European Parliament and of the Council of 17 November 2003 on the Re-use of Public Sector Information. Official Journal of the European Union, 2003.

72. EUROSTAT. http://epp.eurostat.cec.eu.int/pls/portal/.

73. FALORSI, P. D., PALLARA, S., PAVONE, A., ALESSANDRONI, A., MASSELLA, E., AND SCANNAPIECO, M. Improving the Quality of Toponymic Data in the Italian Public Administration. In *Proc. DQCIS 2003 (ICDT Workshop)* (Siena, Italy, 2003).

74. FALORSI, P. D., AND SCANNAPIECO, M., Eds. *Principi Guida per la Qualità dei Dati Toponomastici nella Pubblica Amministrazione (in Italian).* ISTAT, serie Contributi, vol. 12. Available at: http://www.istat.it/dati/pubbsci/contributi/Contr_anno2005.htm, 2006.

75. FAN, W., LU, H., MADNICK, S., AND CHEUNGD, D. Discovering and Reconciling Value Conflicts for Numerical Data Integration. *Information Systems 26*, 8 (2001).

76. FELLEGI, I. P., AND HOLT, D. A Systematic Approach to Automatic Edit and Imputation. *Journal of the American Statistical Association 71*, 353 (1976), 17–35.

77. FELLEGI, I. P., AND SUNTER, A. B. A Theory for Record Linkage. *Journal of the American Statistical Association 64* (1969).

78. FISHER, C. W., AND KINGMA, B. R. Criticality of Data Quality as Exemplified in Two Disasters. *Information Management 39* (2001).

79. FOWLER, M. *UML Distilled: A Brief Guide to the Standard Object Modeling Language.* Pearson Education, 2004.

80. FRATERNALI, P., LANZI, P. L., MATERA, M., AND MAURINO, A. Model-Driven Web Usage Analysis for the Evaluation of Web Application Quality. *Journal of Web Engineering 3*, 2 (2004), 124–152.

81. FUXMAN, A., FAZLI, E., AND MILLER, R. J. ConQuer: Efficient Management of Inconsistent Databases. In *Proc. SIGMOD 2005* (Baltimore, MA, 2005).

82. GALHARDAS, H., FLORESCU, D., SHASHA, D., SIMON, E., AND SAITA, C. A. Declarative Data Cleaning: Language, Model, and Algorithms. In *Proc. VLDB 2001* (Rome, Italy, 2001).

83. GLOVER, F., AND LAGUNA, M. *Tabu Search.* Kluver Academic Publishers, 1997.

84. GOERK, M. SAP AG Data Quality@SAP: An Enterprise Wide Approach to Data Quality Goals. In *CAiSE Workshop on Data and Infomation Quality (DIQ 2004)* (Riga, Latvia, 2004).

85. GRAY, J. *The Benchmark Handbook for Database and Transaction Systems.* Morgan Kaufmann, 1993.

86. GRECO, G., GRECO, S., AND ZUMPANO, E. A Logical Framework for Querying and Repairing Inconsistent Databases. *Transactions on Knowledge and Data Engineering 15*, 6 (2003), 1389–1408.

87. GRECO, G., AND LEMBO, D. Data Integration with Preferences Among Sources. In *Proc. ER 2004* (Shangai, China, 2004).

88. GU, L., BAXTER, R., VICKERS, D., AND RAINSFORD, C. P. Record Linkage: Current Practice and Future Directions. Technical Report 03/83, CMIS 03/83, Camberra, Australia.

89. GUPTIL, C., AND MORRISON, J. *Elements of Spatial Data Quality.* Elsevier Science Ltd, Oxford, UK, 1995.

90. HALL, P. A., AND DOWLING, G. Approximate String Comparison. *ACM Computing Surveys 12*, 4 (1980), 381–402.

91. HAMMER, M., AND CHAMPY, J. *Rengineering the Corporation: a Manifesto for Business Revolution.* 2001.

92. HAN, J., AND KAMBER, M. *Data Mining: Concepts and Techniques.* Morgan Kaufmann Publishers, 2000.

93. HERNANDEZ, M. A., AND STOLFO, S. J. Real-world Data is Dirty: Data Cleansing and The Merge/Purge Problem. *Journal of Data Mining and Knowledge Discovery 1*, 2 (1998).

94. INFOIMPACT. http://www.infoimpact.com/iqproducts.cfm.

95. INTERNATIONAL CONFERENCE ON INFORMATION QUALITY (IQ/ICIQ). http://www.iqconference.org/.

96. INTERNATIONAL MONETARY FUND. http://dsbb.imf.org/.

97. INTERNATIONAL ORGANIZATION FOR STANDARDIZATION. http://www.iso.org.

98. INTERNATIONAL WORKSHOP ON DATA AND INFORMATION QUALITY (DIQ). http://www.computing.dcu.ie/research/dataquality/diq/.

99. INTERNATIONAL WORKSHOP ON INFORMATION QUALITY IN INFORMATION SYSTEMS (IQIS). http://iqis.irisa.fr/.

100. INTERNATIONAL WORKSHOP ON QUALITY OF INFORMATION SYSTEMS (QoIS). http://deptinfo.cnam.fr/qois2006/.

101. INTERPARES PROJECT. http://www.interpares.org.

102. ISAKOWITZ, T., STOHR, E. A., AND BALASUBRAMANIAN, P. RMM: a Methodology for Structured Hypermedia Design. *Communication of the ACM 58*, 8 (1995).

103. JARKE, M., JEUSFELD, M. A., QUIX, C., AND VASSILIADIS, P. Architecture and Quality in Data Warehouses: an Extended Repository Approach. *Information Systems* (1999).

104. JARKE, M., LENZERINI, M., VASSILIOU, Y., AND VASSILIADIS, P., Eds. *Fundamentals of Data Warehouses.* Springer Verlag, 1995.

105. JARO, M. A. Advances in Record Linkage Methodologies as Applied to Matching the 1985 Cencus of Tampa, Florida. *Journal of American Statistical Society 84*, 406 (1985), 414–420.

106. JOSANG, A., ISMAIL, R., AND BOYD, C. A Survey of Trust and Reputation Systems for Online Service Provision. *Decision Support Systems* (2005).

107. KAHN, B. K., STRONG, D. M., AND WANG, R. Y. Information Quality Benchmarks: Product and Service Performance. *Communications of the ACM 45* (2002).

108. KATIFORI, V., POGGI, A., SCANNAPIECO, M., CATARCI, T., AND IOANNIDIS, Y. OntoPIM: how to rely on a Personal Ontology for Personal Information Management. In *Proc. Workshop on The Semantic Desktop 2005.*

109. KIM, W., AND SEO, J. Classifying Schematic and Data Heterogeneity in Multidatabase Systems. *IEEE Computer 24*, 12 (1991), 12–18.

110. KISSNER, L., AND SONG, D. Private and Threshold Set-Intersection. Tech. Rep. CMU-CS-05-113, Carnegie Mellon University, February 2005.

111. KRAWCZYK, H., AND WISZNIEWSKI, B. Visual GQM Approach to Quality-driven Development of Electronic Documents. In *Proc. 2nd International Workshop on Web Document Analysis (WDA2003)* (Edinburgh, UK, 2003).

112. LAKSHMANAN, L. V., NG, R. T., AND RAMESH, G. To Do or Not to Do: the Dilemma of Disclosing Anonymized Data. In *Proc. SIGMOD 2005.*

113. LARSEN, M. D., AND RUBIN, D. B. An Iterative Automated Record Matching using Mixture Models. *Journal of American Statistical Association 79* (1989), 32–41.

114. LEE, Y. W., STRONG, D. M., KAHN, B. K., AND WANG, R. Y. AIMQ: A Methodology for Information Quality Assessment. *Information and Management* (2001).

115. LEHTI, P., AND FANKHAUSER, P. Probabilistic Iterative Duplicate Detection. In *Proc. OTM Conferences 2005*.

116. LENZERINI, M. Data Integration: A Theoretical Perspective. In *Proc. PODS 2002* (Madison, WI, 2002).

117. LEVY, A. Y., MENDELZON, A. O., SAGIV, Y., AND SRIVASTAVA, D. Answering Queries Using Views. In *Proc. PODS 1995* (San Jose, CA, 1995).

118. LIM, E. P., AND CHIANG, R. H. A Global Object Model for Accommodating Instance Heterogeneities. In *Proc. ER'98* (Singapore, Singapore, 1998).

119. LIN, J., AND MENDELZON, A. O. Merging Databases Under Constraints. *International Journal of Cooperative Information Systems 7*, 1 (1998), 55–76.

120. LIU, L., AND CHI, L. Evolutionary Data Quality. In *Proc. 7th International Conference on Information Quality (IQ 2002)*.

121. LOHNINGEN, H. *Teach Me Data Analysis*. Springer-Verlag, 1999.

122. LONG, J. A., AND SEKO, C. E. A Cyclic-Hierarchical Method for Database Data-Quality Evaluation and Improvement. In *Advances in Management Information Systems - Information Quality (AMIS-IQ) Monograph*, R. Y. Wang, E. M. Pierce, S. E. Madnick, and C. W. Fisher, Eds. Sharpe, M.E., April 2005.

123. LOSHIN, D. *Enterprise Knowledge Management - The Data Quality Approach*. Morgan Kaufmann Series in Data Management Systems, 2004.

124. LOW, W., LEE, M., AND LING, T. A Knowledge-based Approach for Duplicate Elimination in Data Cleaning. *Information Systems 26*, 8 (2001).

125. LYMAN, P., AND VARIAN, H. R. How Much Information.

126. MARTINEZ, A., AND HAMMER, J. Making Quality Count in Biological Data Sources. In *Proc. IQIS 2005 (SIGMOD Workshop)*.

127. MCKEON, A. Barclays Bank Case Study: Using Artificial Intelligence to Benchmark Organizational Data Flow Quality. In *Proc. 8th International Conference on Information Quality (IQ 2003)*.

128. MECCA, G., MERIALDO, P., ATZENI, P., AND CRESCENZI, V. The (Short) ARAENEUS Guide to Web-Site Development. In *Proc. 2nd International Workshop on the Web and Databases (WebDB'99)* (1999).

129. MIKLAU, G., AND SUCIU, D. A Formal Analysis of Information Disclosure in Data Exchange. In *Proc. SIGMOD 2004*.

130. MISSIER, P., AND BATINI, C. A Multidimensional Model for Information Quality in Cooperative Information Systems. In *Proc. 8th International Conference on Information Quality (IQ 2003)*.

131. MISSIER, P., AND BATINI, C. A Model for Information Quality Management Framework for Cooperative Information Systems. In *Proc. 11th Italian Symposium on Advanced Database Systems (SEDB 2003)* (Cetraro, Italy, June 2003).

132. MISSIER, P., AND BATINI, C. An Information Quality Management Framework for Cooperative Information Systems. In *Proc. International Conference on Information Systems and Engineering (ISE 2003)* (Montreal, Canada, July 2003).

133. MISSIER, P., LACK, G., VERYKIOS, V., GRILLO, F., LORUSSO, T., AND AN-GELETTI, P. Improving Data Quality in Practice: a Case Study in the Italian Public Administration. *Parallel and Distributed Databases 13*, 2 (2003), 135–160.

134. MONGE, A., AND ELKAN, C. An Efficient Domain Independent Algorithm for Detecting Approximate Duplicate Database Records. In *Proc. SIGMOD Workshop on Research Issues on Data Mining and Knowledge Discovery (DMKD'97)* (Tucson, AZ, 1997).

135. MOTRO, A., AND ANOKHIN, P. Fusionplex: Resolution of Data Inconsistencies in the Data Integration of Heterogeneous Information Sources. *Information Fusion* (2005).

136. MOTRO, A., AND RAGOV, I. Estimating Quality of Databases. In *Proc. 3rd International Conference on Flexible Query Answering Systems (FQAS'98)* (Roskilde, Denmark, 1998).

137. MUTHU, S., WITHMAN, L., AND CHERAGHI, S. Business Process Re-engineering: a Consolidated Methodology. In *Proc. 4th Annual International Conference on Industrial Engineering Theory, Applications and Practice* (San Antonio, TX, 1999).

138. NALEBUFF, B. Competing Against bundles. P. Hammond and G. Myles, Eds., Oxford University Press.

139. NAUMANN, F. *Quality-Driven Query Answering for Integrated Information Systems*. Springer Verlag, LNCS 2261, 2002.

140. NAUMANN, F., FREYTAG, J. C., AND LESER, U. Completeness of Integrated Information Sources. *Information Systems 29*, 7 (2004), 583–615.

141. NAUMANN, F., AND HÄUSSLER, M. Declarative Data Merging with Conflict Resolution. In *Proc. 7th International Conference on Information Quality (IQ 2002)*.

142. NAUMANN, F., LESER, U., AND FREYTAG, J. C. Quality-driven Integration of Heterogenous Information Systems. In *Proc. VLDB'99* (Edinburgh, UK, 1999).

143. NAVARRO, G. A Guided Tour of Approximate String Matching. *ACM Computing Surveys 31* (2001), 31–88.

144. NEBEL, B., AND LAKEMEYER, G., Eds. *Foundations of Knowledge Representation and Reasoning*, lecture notes in artificial intelligence ed., vol. 810. Springer-Verlag, 1994.

145. NEILING, M., JURK, S., LENZ, H. J., AND NAUMANN, F. Object Identification Quality. In *Proc. DQCIS 2003 (ICDT Workshop)* (Siena, Italy, 2003).

146. NEWCOMBE, H. B., KENNEDY, J. M., AXFORD, S. J., AND JAMES, A. P. F. Automatic Linkage of Vital Records. *Science 130* (1959).

147. NIGAM, K., MCCALLUM, A., THRUN, S., AND MITCHELL, T. Text Classification from Labeled and Unlabeled Documents using EM. *Machine Learning 39* (2000), 103–134.

148. OBJECT MANAGEMENT GROUP (OMG). Unified Modeling Language Specification, Version 1.5. OMG Document formal/03-03-01, 2003.

149. OFFICE OF MANAGEMENT AND BUDGET. Information Quality Guidelines for Ensuring and Maximizing the Quality, Objectivity, Utility, and Integrity of Information Disseminated by Agencies. http://www.whitehouse.gov/omb/fedreg/reproducible.html.

150. OMG. Data Quality and the Bottom Line: Achieving Business Success through a Commitment to High Quality Data. http://www.uml.org/.

151. ORACLE. http://www.oracle.com/solutions/business-intelligence.
152. OSTMAN, A. The Specifications and Evaluation of Spatial Data Quality. In *Proc. 18th ICA/ACI International Conference* (Stockholm, Sweden, 1997).
153. OZSU, T., AND VALDURIEZ, P. *Principles of Distributed Database Systems.* Prentice Hall, 2000.
154. PAPAKONSTANTINOU, Y., ABITEBOUL, S., AND GARCIA-MOLINA, H. Object Fusion in Mediator Systems. In *Proc. VLDB 1996* (Bombay, India, 1996).
155. PARSSIAN, A., SARKAR, S., AND JACOB, V. Assessing Information Quality for the Composite Relational Operation Join. In *Proc. 7th International Conference on Information Quality (IQ 2002)*.
156. PARSSIAN, A., SARKAR, S., AND JACOB, V. Assessing Data Quality for Information Products: Impact of Selection, Projection, and Cartesian Product. *Management Science 50*, 7 (2004).
157. PARSSIAN, A., SARKAR, S., AND JACOB, V. Assessing Data Quality for Information Products. In *Proc. 20th International Conference on Information Systems (ICIS 99)* (Charlotte, NC, December 1999).
158. PASCHKE, A., DIETRICH, J., AND KULHA, K. A Logic Based SLA Management Framework. In *ICSW 2005 Workshop on Semantic Web and Policy Workshop (SWPW 2005)* (2005).
159. PERNICI, B., AND SCANNAPIECO, M. Data Quality in Web Information Systems. *Journal of Data Semantics* (2003).
160. PIERCE, E. M. Extending IP-MAPS: Incorporating the Event-Driven Process Chain Methodology. In *Proc. 7th International Conference on Information Quality (IQ 2002)*.
161. PIPINO, L. L., LEE, Y. W., AND WANG, R. Y. Data Quality Assessment. *Communications of the ACM 45*, 4 (2002).
162. PIRA INTERNATIONAL. Commercial Exploitation of Europe's Public Sector Information, Final Report for the European Commission, Directorate General for the Information Society, October 2000.
163. POIRIER, C. A Functional Evaluation of Edit and Imputation Tools. In *UN/ECE Work Statistical Data Editing* (Rome, Italy, 2-4 June 1999).
164. QUANTIN, C., BOUZELAT, H., ALLAERT, F., BENHAMICHE, A., FAIVRE, J., AND DUSSERRE, L. How to Ensure Data Security of an Epidemiological Follow-up: Quality Assessment of an Anonymous Record Linkage Procedure. *International Journal of Medical Informatics 49*, 1 (1998).
165. RAHM, E., THOR, A., AUMUELLER, D., DO, H. H., GOLOVIN, N., AND KIRSTEN, T. iFuice - Information Fusion Utilizing Instance Correspondences and Peer Mappings. In *Proc. 8th International Workshop on the Web and Databases (WebDB 2005)* (2005).
166. RAMAN, V., AND HELLERSTEIN, J. M. Potter's Wheel: An Interactive Data Cleaning System. In *Proc. VLDB 2001* (Rome, Italy, 2001).
167. REDMAN, T. C. *Data Quality for the Information Age.* Artech House, 1996.
168. REDMAN, T. C. The Impact of Poor Data Quality on the Typical Enterprise. *Communications of the ACM* (1998).
169. REDMAN, T. C. *Data Quality The Field Guide.* The Digital Press, 2001.
170. SAATY, T. L. *The Analytic Hierarchy Process.* McGraw-Hill, 1980.
171. SAMARATI, P. Protecting Respondents' Identities in Microdata Release. *IEEE Transactions on Knowledge and Data Engineering 13*, 6 (2001), 1010–1027.
172. SARAWAGI, S., AND BHAMIDIPATY, A., Eds. *Interactive Deduplication Using Active Learning* (Edmonton, Alberta, Canada, 2002).

173. SCANNAPIECO, M., AND BATINI, C. Completeness in the Relational Model: A Comprehensive Framework. In *Proc. 9th International Conference on Information Quality (IQ 2004)*.

174. SCANNAPIECO, M., PERNICI, B., AND PIERCE, E. M. IP-UML: A Methodology for Quality Improvement based on IP-MAP and UML. In *Advances in Management Information Systems - Information Quality (AMIS-IQ) Monograph*, R. Y. Wang, E. M. Pierce, S. E. Madnick, and C. W. Fisher, Eds. Sharpe, M.E., April 2005.

175. SCANNAPIECO, M., VIRGILLITO, A., MARCHETTI, C., MECELLA, M., AND BALDONI, R. The DaQuinCIS Architecture: a Platform for Exchanging and Improving Data Quality in Cooperative Information Systems. *Information Systems 29*, 7 (2004), 551–582.

176. SCHALLEHN, E., SATTLER, K. U., AND SAAKE, G. Extensible and Similarity-Based Grouping for Data Integration. In *Proc. of the ICDE 2002* (San Jose, CA, 2002).

177. SHANKARANARAYAN, G., WANG, R. Y., AND ZIAD, M. Modeling the Manufacture of an Information Product with IP-MAP. In *Proc. 5th International Conference on Information Quality (IQ 2000)*.

178. SHENG, Y. H. Exploring the Mediating and Moderating Effects of Information Quality on Firms? Endeavor on Information Systems. In *Proc. 8th Internationa Conference on Information Quality (IQ 2003)*.

179. SHENG, Y. H., AND MYKYTYN JR., P. P. Information Technology Investment and Firm Performance: A Perspective of Data Quality. In *Proc. 7th Internationa Conference on Information Quality (IQ 2002)*.

180. SMITH, T. F., AND WATERMAN, M. S. Identification of Common Molecular Subsequences. *Molecular Biology 147* (1981), 195–197.

181. STOICA, M., CHAWAT, N., AND SHIN, N. An Investigation of the Methodologies of Business Process Reengineering. In *Proc. of Information Systems Education Conference* (2003).

182. STOLFO, S. J., AND HERNANDEZ, M. A. The Merge/Purge Problem for Large Databases. In *Proc. SIGMOD 1995* (San Jose, CA, 1995).

183. STOREY, V., AND WANG, R. Y. Extending the ER Model to Represent Data Quality Requirements. In *Data Quality*, R. Wang, M. Ziad, and W. Lee, Eds. Kluver Academic Publishers, 2001.

184. STOREY, V. C., AND WANG, R. Y. An Analysis of Quality Requirements in Database Design. In *Proc. 4th International Conference on Information Quality (IQ 1998)*.

185. SU, Y., AND JIN, Z. A Methodology for Information Quality Assessment in the Designing and Manufacturing Processes in Mechanical Products. In *Proc. 9th International Conference on Information Quality (ICIQ 2004)*.

186. TAMASSIA, R., BATINI, C., AND DI BATTISTA, G. Automatic Graph Drawing and Readability of Diagrams. *IEEE Transactions on Systems, Men and Cybernetics* (1987).

187. TARJAN, R. E. Efficiency of A Good But Not Linear Set Union Algorithm. *Journal of the ACM 22*, 2 (1975), 215–225.

188. TATARINOV, I., AND HALEVY, A. Y. Efficient Query Reformulation in Peer-Data Management Systems. In *Proc. SIGMOD 2004*.

189. TEJADA, S., KNOBLOCK, C. A., AND MINTON, S. Learning Object Identication Rules for Information Integration. *Information Systems 26*, 8 (2001).

190. ULLMAN, J. D. *Principles of Database and Knowledge-Base Systems.* Computer Science Press, 1988.

191. ULUSOY, G., AND KARABULUT, K. Determination of the Bundle Price for Digital Information Goods. University of Sabanci, Istanbul, 2003.

192. U.S. NATIONAL INSTITUTE OF HEALTH (NIH). http://www.pubmedcentral.nih.gov/.

193. VAN DER AALST, W., AND TER HOFSTEDE, A. YAWL: Yet Another Workflow Language. *Information Systems 30*, 4 (2005), 245–275.

194. VASSILIADIS, P., VAGENA, Z., SKIADOPOULOS, S., KARAYANNIDIS, N., AND SELLIS, T. ARTKOS: Toward the Modeling, Design, Control and Execution of ETL Processes. *Information Systems 26* (2001), 537–561.

195. VERMEER, B. H. P. J. How Important is Data Quality for Evaluating the Impact of EDI on Global Supply Chains ? In *Proc. HICSS 2000.*

196. VERYKIOS, V. S., ELMAGARMID, A. K., BERTINO, E., SAYGIN, Y., AND DASSENI, E. Association Rule Hiding. *IEEE Transaction on Knowledge and Data Engineering 16*, 4 (2004).

197. VERYKIOS, V. S., MOUSTAKIDES, G. V., AND ELFEKY, M. G. A Bayesian Decision Model for Cost Otimal Record Matching. *The VLDB Journal 12* (2003), 28–40.

198. W3C. http://www.w3.org/WAI/.

199. WAND, Y., AND WANG, R. Y. Anchoring Data Quality Dimensions in Ontological Foundations. *Communications of the ACM 39*, 11 (1996).

200. WANG, R. Y., CHETTAYAR, K., DRAVIS, F., FUNK, J., KATZ-HAAS, R., LEE, C., LEE, Y., XIAN, X., AND S., B. Exemplifying Business Oppurtunities for Improving Data Quality from Corporate Household Research. In *Advances in Management Information Systems - Information Quality (AMIS-IQ) Monograph*, R. Y. Wang, E. M. Pierce, S. E. Madnick, and C. W. Fisher, Eds. Sharpe, M.E., April 2005.

201. WANG, R. Y., LEE, Y. L., PIPINO, L., AND STRONG, D. M. Manage Your Information as a Product. *Sloan Management Review 39*, 4 (1998), 95–105.

202. WANG, R. Y., AND MADNICK, S. E. A Polygen Model for Heterogeneous Database Systems: The Source Tagging Perspective. In *Proc. VLDB'90* (Brisbane, Queensland, Australia, 1990), pp. 519–538.

203. WANG, R. Y., PIERCE, E., MADNICK, S., AND FISHER, C. *Information Quality, Advances in Management Information Systems.* M.E. Sharpe, Vladimir Zwass Series, 2005.

204. WANG, R. Y., STOREY, V. C., AND FIRTH, C. P. A Framework for Analysis of Data Quality Research. *IEEE Transaction on Knowledge and Data Engineering 7*, 4 (1995).

205. WANG, R. Y., AND STRONG, D. M. Beyond Accuracy: What Data Quality Means to Data Consumers. *Journal of Management Information Systems 12*, 4 (1996).

206. WANG, R. Y., ZIAD, M., AND LEE, Y. W. *Data Quality.* Kluwer Academic Publisher, 2001.

207. WEIS, M., AND NAUMANN, F. DogmatiX Tracks down Duplicates in XML. In *Proc. SIGMOD 2005.*

208. WHITE, C. Data Integration: Using ETL, EAI, and EII Tools to Create an Integrated Enterprise. http://ibm.ascential.com, 2005.

209. WIEDERHOLD, G. Mediators in the Architecture of Future Information Systems. *IEEE Computer 25*, 3 (1992).

210. WINKLER, W. Improved Decision Rules in the Fellegi-Sunter Model of Record Linkage. In *Proc. of the Section on Survey Research Methods, American Statistical Association* (1993).
211. WINKLER, W. E. Using the EM Algorithm for Weight Computation in the Fellegi and Sunter Modelo of Record Linkage. In *Proc. of the Section on Survey Research Methods, American Statistical Association* (1988).
212. WINKLER, W. E. Matching and Record Linkage. In *Business Survey Methods*. Wiley & Sons, 1995.
213. WINKLER, W. E. Matching and Record Linkage. In *Business Survey Methods*. Wiley & Sons, 1995.
214. WINKLER, W. E. Machine Learning, Information Retrieval and Record Linkage. In *Proc. of the Section on Survey Research Methods, American Statistical Association* (2000).
215. WINKLER, W. E. Methods for Evaluating and Creating Data Quality. *Information Systems 29*, 7 (2004).
216. WINKLER, W. E. Quality of Very Large Databases. Technical Report RR-2001/04, U.S. Bureau of the Census, Statistical Research Division, Washington, Washington DC, 2001.
217. WISZNIEWSKI, B., AND KRAWCZYK, H. Digital Document Life Cycle Development. In *Proc. 1st International Symposium on Information and Communication Technologies (ISICT 2003)* (Dublin, Ireland, 2003).
218. YAN, L. L., AND OZSU, T. Conflict Tolerant Queries in AURORA. In *Proc. CoopIS'99* (Edinburgh, UK, 1999).
219. ZHOU, C., CHIA, L. T., AND LEE, B. S. QoS Measurement Issues with DAML-QoS Ontology. In *Proc. 2005 IEEE International Conference on e-Business Engineering (ICEBE'05)* (2005).

Index